D0891137

Lethal
Faith:

Missional Apologetics for Students, Families, and Local Churches

Michael Knight, DSL

DEDICATION

To Lillie, Ella, and Aidan, the loves of my life and the original reason for this book.

CONTENTS

Introduction

Author's Note: the more common use of the word *lethal* is "devastating; causing death." However, I am using the term *lethal* in the sense of "very potent or effective" in connection with faith. Believers need a potent, effective faith to help them stand the tests and trials of this life.

—Michael Knight

The lion facing me was an ancient one. Its colors were mesmerizing, although faded by time, their dull hues still called to me to come closer much like the fall leaves on the old oak tree I used to swing on as a child. At first, I did not realize what I was observing. In my subconscious, just another piece of antiquity that has been ignored by the masses as they passed on to something far more interesting, such as Alexander the Great's sarcophagus. My eyes glanced at the plaque, strategically placed in the corner. I had heard the story of Babylon in the Scriptures a hundred times. Such a name had become apocalyptic and reserved only for the future eschatological events in the Book of Revelation. Yet, this time, the word Babylon brought me backward, not forward. It was then I realized that I was standing in front of the ancient gates of Ishtar.

The Istanbul Natural History Museum of Turkey is a beautiful expression of historical truths. Nestled behind an iron gate which protected the wonders of the world, it brought to life thousands of objects all around me. The pottery from Galatia evoked my imagination as I observed the very pottery from which the people in the Book of Galatians had possibly dined. Archaeological treasures filled the room, reinforcing to me the trustworthiness of the historical narrative of our Holy Scriptures. My heart pounded, as I realized that the Scriptural stories were not only true but also confirmed by archaeology as being real people, from real cities, and actual cultures. I pondered the surreal experience of being able to touch the same Babylonian gate that Daniel had probably seen as he entered the Babylonian kingdom after having been imprisoned after the fall of Jerusalem. Later, he would have seen these very wall panels as he walked past them every day going to work serving the Babylonian kings like Nebuchadnezzar. It was here in the midst of the cradle of archaeology that I realized something deep within me—I was standing in front of lethal faith.

We live in a hostile world where faith is anything but lethal. Faith today, for many parents and families is one that is often platonic, apathetic, or spoken with a deep sense of shame, as if we in the Christian community had some need to feel ashamed about our own historical contributions to world history. It has been "our" community that often taught the world to read, established schools and hospitals, cleared out the mosquito-infested swamps of Europe, fought for the rights of women to vote, instituted child labor laws, and fought for the slave to be free, as we built the foundations to some of the world's greatest academic institutions. It was "our" community which has feed the poor, housed the orphans, engaged the sciences, and brought the wonder of art to the masses. There was a day in "our" community when we were considered the "thinkers" and "intellectuals"—the "creators of culture." It has been a lofty fall from the place of contextualizing our message into the culture we established to now being the subject of bigoted phrases, which implies that ignorance and Christianity are synonymous. As Israel lamented, "How can we sing the songs of the Lord while in a foreign land?" (Psalm 137:4 NIV). How do we live a Christian life in a post-Christian America or Western civilization? As Christian parents and leaders our thoughts are far from how we sing our songs in Babylon to more focused thoughts of simple survival. We find ourselves as Christians "circling the wagons" as we weep over the cultural loss of our own children. The words of the psalmist are most fitting here as we too ask, regarding our familial systems: Is a *lethal faith* possible today?

Today, lethal deaths, not lethal faith surround our families. How can we trust the Bible after it has been written and rewritten so many times by so many different people? Hasn't the science of archaeology made a fool of those who believe in a literal biblical message? German Higher Criticism buried any chance of the Bible ever being resurrected as a respectable piece of historical literature—ever! Our students' science teachers have all made it clear to them. The earth is not unique, and neither are they. They have all been randomly placed in the galaxy with no hint of divine destiny. Teachers constantly remind them of how they found "water" on Mars and the "possibility" of life on other planets. Earth is just one of billions and billions of planets, which is not unique in any special way. They dismiss design, purpose, beauty, and symmetry as unplanned evolutionary accidents. The Bible, they say, is not a scientifically accurate book. The masses demand that the Bible is antiscientific and that the two cannot coexist. All the universe is a result of a random chance. And in this universe, there is no right and wrong because there is no moral lawgiver to govern man's existence. Man, who exists in this unplanned universe is just another evolved animal with no purpose. Furthermore, except for language, we are really no different from any other animal, minus the hair (and we can thank artistic license for it). We evolved from primates, and because there is no Creator there is no purpose or moral law that clearly defines a "right" and a "wrong."

Also, according to these same teachers, there is no design or purpose behind the dolphin, sockeye salmon, or sea turtle. No real Creator engineering the great white whale. And besides, evolution is a scientific fact and only fools believe

11

that God created the world and all that is in it. They mock the words of Colossians 1:16-17:

> For in Him all things were created: things in heaven and on the earth, visible and invisible, whether thrones or powers or rulers or authorities: all things have been created through him and for him. He is before all things, and in him all things hold together.

These unbelievers mock as if the Bible were written by a god too stupid to understand atoms and hydrogen energy. Besides this, if there is a God who created the world, how could this good, benevolent God sit idly by and watch one of His people He created endure so much pain and suffering, yet not intervene? He is, after all, "sovereign" and "all powerful," right? Some "good God" you have. Have you seen this world lately?

As Christian families, we are bombarded by these and many other accusatory questions. Our students are being sent to the slaughterhouse, formally called academia. I am proeducation. The apostle Paul warned young Timothy that there would be people in the name of science or knowledge who would try to convince him that scientifically it is not rational to believe in God.

> Timothy, guard what has been entrusted to your care. Turn away from godless chatter and the opposing ideas of what is falsely called knowledge, which some have professed and in so doing have departed from the faith (1 Timothy 6:20).

Unfortunately, parents haven't the slightest idea how to respond intellectually to these questions. This is partly because too many parents place the academic advancement of their children above their personal faith. As if the two were ever meant to be separated. Too many parents spend no time on faith development of their own children.

Yet, they spend countless hours preparing for mathematics and other academic subjects, as well as soccer tournaments and a host of other extracurricular activities. The average Christian parent assumes that such faith development will somehow, through osmosis, be transmitted through luck by well-meaning Sunday school teachers, youth groups, or Sunday sermons once a month. The scientific data is reporting just the opposite.

Our children are not learning about faith through the supposed mystical osmosis of the church's teachings. What we have taught our children by leaving this "life and death" eternal decision to chance is that God has been tamed and neatly wrapped in a box. Kendra Dean at Princeton's Center for Faith, Religion, and Culture calls this dilemma, Moralistic Therapeutic Deism. Our absence has created for our children a God that is not only tame, but tamable, which will be glad to perform tricks for our enjoyment. He is safe, predictable, and benevolent. So safe, He has put our own children to sleep sitting on the front pew. There is absolutely nothing dangerous about Him. He has become more mystical than Santa Claus, more elusive than Sesame Street's Mister Snuffleupagus, and less dangerous than a pacifist negotiating atomic energy at a nuclear convention. How do we wake up our children and families in "our" community to live a lethal faith?

There is now a multitude of studies that speak to the retention of students in the church, to families that desire to give their faith a legacy, to churches that want to really make discipleship count. Christian Smith, with the National Youth and Religion Survey, alerted us to the importance of the faith of parents in adolescent faith. In other words, your children's faith will more than likely be a direct mirror of your own faith in Christ, whether hot or cold, or too often, lukewarm. At AIG, Fuller Theological Seminary, and Princeton Theological Seminary there have been great advances in the study regarding students and their faith, and the immense role that the church and the nuclear family play in retention as well. These studies remind us of the role that a passionate faith plays in retention. As Dean said in her book, *Almost Christian*, "hot faith...." They also remind us that we are not left on an island with no science, wisdom, or truths to guide our journey in firmly establishing a lethal faith. The Christian faith can be intellectual, rational, and logical. However, what this research brings to us is the unbelievable power of presenting our faith in the context of a historically accurate narrative. AIG, in its landmark research with the American Research Group, a well-respected research company, found that the greatest contributors to the "nones" (no religious preference) category on the U.S. census were those children raised in the mainline church. They predominantly were taught, "That the Bible is true...." Yet, they were, "Least likely to believe." When the data was properly analyzed, they discovered something very crucial to lethal faith. The problem was not "with" the teachers, youth leaders, or pastors, but the problem lies within "how" they "taught" the lesson. If they taught their lesson within the confines of confirming the historical narratives, the students embraced the Scriptures as truth. When Scripture is taught as a story, alluded to as being mystical or allegorical, the faith is rejected as nothing more than just another enchanted wonderland, complete with its own fictitious characters and happy endings in a far-off place in the merry old land of Oz.

We don't have to lose this war. It is a winnable one if we will educate not only ourselves but also our children to the historical and scientific truths found within the Scriptures. Then it can become a *lethal faith*. To help you do so, the Never Before Project has commissioned a three-volume training text which is to be used devotionally and professionally in a classroom, or church service, or more appropriately by sitting on your grandpa's lap at six o'clock and looking at all the pictures. When the church reassumes its call to educate our children, intellectually, rationally, and logically in the science of the Christian faith, then we can expect a heart change. Are you skeptical? Just ask Doubting Thomas what "proof" did for his faith? Then, you will understand just how *lethal* faith can be.

The Importance of Understanding Archaeology, Apologetics, and the Scriptures

"I tell you, if they were to keep silent, the stones would cry out." (Luke 19:40 HCSB).

To many Christians, it's just an "old rock" but to others, especially people of intellectual faith, it can become lethal faith. Why? What you may see as an "old rock" may have a name, a date, a place, cultures, or even a statement written thousands of years ago. Those rocks are actually connected to those boring "Benjamin begot so and so," verses that we all skip because we think they are not connected at all to our spirituality! These rocks contain inscriptions that can be used to confirm that the Bible is a trustworthy source of history. And if we can prove that the Bible is a trustworthy source of history, then we may be able to say in all probability that the Bible would then be more likely than not to be true in other matters of spirituality. If it can be factually proven to be wrong in its names, dates, places, cultures, or statements, outside of minor scribal errors, then the likelihood of trusting the book further in matters of spirituality are less than probable. Therefore, what the "rocks are saying" then becomes extremely important to those of us who trust in the Scriptures to point our way to spiritual truths. Therefore, building a lethal faith begins with taking a deep look at the historical claims, people, places, and cultures in the Bible. Are they real people, from real cities? And does the Scripture accurately describe their times, beliefs, and cultures? The science of archaeology—knowing what archaeology is and how it helps us to apologetically defend our faith—is vitally important!

The History of Archaeology

Archaeology is "the recovery of man's past by systematically discovering, recording, and studying material remains that he has left behind." It comes from two Greek words, *archaios* and *logos*, meaning "study of things." Archaeology is a relatively young discipline spanning only the last 150 years. Science can take us all the way back to 1550–1070 B.C. to the new kingdom of Egypt where the ancient pharaohs excavated an ancient Sphinx, originally built in the old kingdom in the fourth-century dynasty of Pharaoh Khafre. He built the second largest Egyptian pyramid at Giza and the sphinx.

It is believed by many that Herodotus was the first systematic scholar to study archaeological artifacts followed by the Song Dynasty of Imperial China in 960–1279. It was however the fifteenth- and sixteenth-century antiquarians from Renaissance Europe that led to the science of archaeology. Antiquarians were usually wealthy benefactors who traveled the world and collected artifacts for their curio cabinets. Such were their collections that they developed their own motto: "We speak from facts, not theory." These cabinet collections gave way to the original contributions which birthed our national museums.

William Harvey and Gilbert North, Inigo Jones, and the Duke of Buckingham all pioneered this field by excavating Stonehenge in the late seventeenth century. William Stukeley in the eighteenth century is still considered today as "probably...the most important of the early forerunners of the discipline of archaeology."[1] Archaeologists followed Stonehenge by the excavations of Pompeii and Herculaneum. Thomas Jefferson in 1784 led an excavation of a Native American burial mound, Napoleon's army defined archaeology overseas as it explored Egyptian antiquities. However, it was Jean-Francois Champollion who discovered the Rosetta stone that unlocked the meaning to Egyptian hieroglyphics. Yet, it was William Cunnington (1754–1810) who is considered the father of archaeological excavation. Each of these early pioneers contributed something unique to the developing science of archaeology. So how did the Bible unfold in its importance to archaeology?

Biblical archaeology is often called *paleethnology*, but its sphere of influence is now much broader than the land of Palestine itself. Biblical archaeology is a science that specifically concerns itself with the history of the Bible. Just like the early pioneers of archaeology itself, biblical archaeology also had its pioneers.

Adriaan Reland, from the University of Harderwijk, was a teacher of Hebrew antiquities in 1713. He published the first modern work of biblical archaeology in a

---

[1] Ronald Hutton, *Blood and Mistletoe: The History of the Druids in Britain* (New Haven: Yale University Press, 2009), 86.

book titled, *Palaestina ex monumentis veteribus illustrate.*[2] Johann Jahn, Edward Robinson, each added to this developing field of Biblical archaeology. The American School of Oriental Research began in 1900, as well as the British School of Archaeology in 1919, each adding to the academic study of archaeology on a professional scale. Yet, in the field of biblical archaeology, there was a man who not only defined this field, but also became the teacher to some of the most respected biblical archaeologists; his name was William F. Albright.

William F. Albright became one of the leading pioneers in biblical archaeology during the early 1900s. This is important for several reasons. One, archaeology was just developing as a respected scientific field of study. Two, with the rise of Social Darwinism, the lingering effects of the French Enlightenment, a field of study called German Higher Criticism had firmly taken hold of many clergy and theologians' religious consciousness. They believed and German Higher Criticism taught that many of the stories in the Bible were not only embellished, but were nothing more than allegorical stories, regarding myths and legends of their day. In other words, the people of the Bible were not intended to be "real" people form "real" places. Scholars such as Hermann Gunkel, Albrecht Alt, and Martin Noth believed otherwise. They believed that the books of the Bible rested on oral traditions and reflected accurate historical narratives.

William F. Albright wrote thousands of books and articles. He went on to teach and train some of the most respected archaeologists of his time—pioneers such as Nelson Glueck, G. Ernest Wright, Cyrus Gordon, and E.A. Speiser. All these pioneers helped to build a consensus that the biblical passages were historically accurate. In speaking to

---

[2] WayBack Machine, "Adriaan Reland (1676–1718)," The Wayback Machine, accessed November 16, 2017, *http://www.web.archive.org.*

the Old Testament, Albright said, "Discovery after discovery has established the accuracy of innumerable details of the Bible as a source of history."[3] This is a very important lesson to learn as we begin our search for a lethal faith.

Much of the older criticism formed against Scriptures did not have the vital testimony of archaeological evidence nor did they have the knowledge we do today. So many times, those who have rejected God and the Bible have done so on the premise of relying only upon the knowledge that they had available to them at the time of their decisions. To Darwin it was the understanding of the cell as a simple life form, yet we now know that the cell is a very elaborate, complex issue. Hume, Nietzsche, G. Stanley Hall, Charles Templeton, all made decisions to leave a belief in God based only upon the science available to them during the time they lived. They abandoned faith and assumed that their present understanding of science had sealed the issue shut. In reality, the Bible has proven itself over and over again to be accurate. This could include the fact that the Bible has always said that earth had a definite beginning, while almost every scientist in the 1920s refuted such a ludicrous claim. The famed scientist, Stephen W. Hawking later refuted such a claim in a lecture by announcing that the earth did indeed have a definite point of genesis. The same could be said about archaeology and trusting the Bible when the *New York Times* argued that the Hittites mentioned in the Bible were fictitious (At the time, the Bible was the only source that mentioned their existence.), and never signed a treaty with the Egyptians (1 Samuel 26:6; 1 Chronicles 11:41). Later, this treaty which is often referred to as the Treaty of Kadesh was proven to be true and archaeological

---

[3] William F. Albright, *The Archaeology of Palestine* (Middlesex: Harmondsworth, 1960), 127–128.

excavations proved the reality of the Hittite people. Yet, between hundreds of years, the "experts" consistently said that Hittites were nothing more than an allegorical, highly embellished story found within the Bible, a book of fiction. Therefore, the next time you find a "tension" between science and the Bible, wait. Because in every previous instance, the Bible was later exonerated such as the indictment from German Higher Criticism. William F. Albright wrote, "The form-critical school founded by M. Dibelius and R. Bultman a generation before the discovery of the Dead Sea scrolls has continued to flourish without the slightest regard for the Dead Sea scrolls. In other words, all radical school in New Testament criticism which have existed in the past or which exist today are prearchaeological, and are, therefore, since they were built in *der Luft* ("in the air"), quite antiquated today.[4] Such revelations actually changed the mind of several students of German Higher Criticism. One such person was a leading pioneer in the archaeological development of the New Testament.

Sir William Ramsay, began his historical and academic journey based on the German (Tubingen) liberal/critical school that insisted that the Bible could not be a historically reliable book, written in the first century. He began to study the Book of Acts with the sole intentions of discrediting the book as reliable history. He spent years researching, as one of the most prominent archaeologists in the world, the Book of Acts. Later he would write in *St. Paul the Traveler*, "Our hypothesis is that Acts was written by a great historian, a writer who set himself to record the facts as they occurred, a strong partisan indeed, but raised above partiality by his perfect confidence that he had only to describe the facts as they occurred, in order to make the

---

[4] Josh McDowell, "The Historical Reliability of the New Testament," *Bible and Spade* 27.2 (Spring 2014), 46.

truth of Christianity and the honor of Paul apparent."[5] Most archaeologists do not set out to prove or disprove the Bible. "However, biblical archaeology has generally provided more relevant information that can be correlated with the narratives of the Hebrew Bible."[6] Ramsay would later become the leading scholar in the study of the New Testament and highly acclaimed both academically and professionally. While it is debatable as to whether he ever came to faith, it is not debatable that he changed his mind about the authenticity of the Book of Acts being historically correct. He was a leading pioneer in the historical reliability of Scriptures.

The history of archaeology is a long one with many contributors, some of faith, some of no faith, and some who never notes their faith. Yet, this science can help us to understand the cultural and historical settings of biblical events. It gives us knowledge of the people, and it can confirm to us whether they were real or imaginary individuals. Archaeology can confirm places like the cities of Sodom and Gomorra or Capernaum. It can bring us insight into the tools, and things that a past civilization used, like the armor of a Roman legion. It can confirm or disconfirm events like the Treaty of Kardish or the edicts of Pontius Pilate. Archaeology can help us as believers in our hermeneutical and exegesis journeys into biblical passages, bringing greater clarity to biblical events. It can confirm the events of Scripture as historical facts. Many archaeologists, however, clearly separate themselves as historians, not theologians. Therefore, Evangelicals should recognize that the greatest value of

---

[5] Sir William Ramsay, *St. Paul the Traveler and Roman Citizen* (Grand Rapids, Michigan: Hodder and Stoughton/Reproductions: Baker Books, 1960), 402.

[6] Eric H. Cline, *Biblical Archaeology: Very Short Introduction* (New York: Oxford, 2009), 3.

biblical archaeology is its ability to increase understanding of the cultural and material settings within which the truths of God were given."[7] Therefore, it is important to realize what archaeology is and what it is not.

What Archaeology Is and Is Not

What is archaeology? According to Robert J. Braidwood, "Archaeology is that science or art—it can be maintained that it is both—which is concerned with the material remains of man's past. There are two aspects to the archaeologist's concern. The first of these is the discovery and reclamation of ancient remains; this usually involves field excavation or at least surface collecting. The second concern is the analysis interpretation and publication of the findings."[8] The word "archaeology" comes from two Greek words, *acrhaios* (ancient) and *logos* (discourse), or the "study of things." "The ancient Greeks used the word archaeology to describe their discussion of ancient legends or traditions. Its first known appearance in English was in 1607, where it was used to refer to the "knowledge" of ancient Israel from literary sources such as the Bible."[9]

What archaeology is not is an infallible source or a definitive answer as to the truth of Scriptures. We must understand seven things about the role of archaeology and the Bible:

---

[7] Alfred J. Hoerth, *Archaeology and the Old Testament* (Grand Rapids, Michigan: Baker Academics, 1998), 21.

[8] Ibid., 14.

[9] Randall Price, *The Stones Cry Out: What Archaeology Reveals About the Truth of the Bible* (Eugene, Oregon: Harvest House, 1997), 25.

1. Archaeology is unable to address the theological conclusions of the Bible.

2. Archaeology is limited because it is confined to the realm of the material.

3. Archaeology can confirm the historical events of the Bible, but it cannot prove the Bible is God's Word.

4. Archaeology does not "prove" the Bible. Such proof is beyond history. It can, however, confirm, bring confidence, clarify, and complement the historical reliability and trustworthiness of our Holy Scriptures.

5. Archaeology can provide clarity to the Scripture.

6. Archaeology can bring a certain dimension of reality and concreteness to a biblical passage.

7. Archaeology can refute criticism from those who question the historical narrative of the Bible. It is the finest example of an archeological document.

Many archaeologists believe their findings contradict a biblical passage, such as the walls of Jericho falling. "The skeptic would be wrong. In archaeology any theory, no matter how well established, can be turned on its head by the next shovel of dirt at the next dig."[10] Subjects such as the existence of King David and his palace were once hotly debated. Today, few would intellectually argue with the recent findings, which are proving the extensiveness of his kingdom. Biblical personalities such as King Nebuchadnezzar, Pontius Pilate, Jeroboam, and others have now corrected the archaeological record. Although archaeology cannot scientifically prove the Bible, it can prove the historical presence

---

[10] Phillip Climer, "Archaeology and the Bible," accessed November 16, 2017, *http://www.answersingenesis.org.*

and existence of real people, places, and things which are found in the Bible. And if the Bible is true historically, then archaeology would more likely than not prove many of these stories, people, places, and things that it mentions, and often alludes to, as true events. And to that, we as Christians should be infinitely grateful to those archaeologists who work, not to prove the Bible, but examine history.

What Is Apologetics and Why Should It Be Important to Me as a Christian?

The word "apologetics" comes from the Greek word *apologia* and means "a verbal defense." The word is used seven times in the Holy Scriptures: Acts 22:1; 25:16;1 Corinthians 9:3; 2 Corinthians 10:5-6; Philippians 1:7; 2 Timothy 4:16; and 1 Peter 3:15. It is this last verse that is most commonly used as a citation for Christian apologetics.

"But sanctify Christ as Lord in your hearts, always being ready to make a defense to everyone who asks you to give an account for the hope that is in you, yet with gentleness and reverence" (NASB).

Therefore, Christian apologetics is that branch of Christianity that deals with answering any and all critics who oppose or question the revelation of God in Christ and the Bible. It can include studying such subjects as biblical manuscript transmissions, philosophy, biology, mathematics, evolution, and logic. Apologetics is the work of convincing people to change their views. The Christian Apologetics and Research Ministry (CARM), defines apologetics as "The branch of Christian theology which attempts to give a rational defense for the Christian faith."[11]

---

[11] Ryan Turner, "What Is Apologetics?" An outline, accessed November 16, 2017, *http://www.carm.org*.

Apologetics should be important to every believer; furthermore, apologetics is not optional in a postmodern and post-Christian world. There are ten reasons why we need apologetics today.

1. The Scriptures admonish us to be able to "defend" our faith (1 Peter 3:15).

2. Christians are human, and humans use reason to form beliefs, thus helping us master the fundamentals of doctrine. Therefore, we need to give a reason for the faith that is in us (Isaiah 1:18; Colossians 3:10; Hebrews 5:14; Jude 10).

3. Apologetics creates an environment where humans wrestle with their belief systems, which in turn has an amazing possibility—the maturity of their faith. This maturity is aided by learning to think critically through the philosophies of opposing worldviews.

4. Evangelism in a postmodern world demands answers as they search for faith or prove to reject such faith. It therefore provides objections leveled against the Christian faith.

5. Apologetics is required today if we are to thwart the possibility of apostasy.

6. Apologetics can help us expose unbelief in the human heart.

7. Apologetics are needed in the lives of our children, students, and families since many secular universities are often outright hostile and bigoted toward the Christian faith. Richard Rorty, a late, prominent atheist professor said, "We are to arrange things so that students who enter as bigoted, homophobic, or religious fundamentalists will leave college with views more like our

own...we do our best to convince these students of the benefits of secularization...So we are going to go right on trying to discredit you in the eyes of your children, trying to strip your fundamentalist religious community of dignity, trying to make your views seem silly rather than discussable."[12]

8. It helps us to explain Christianity to our current culture.

9. It provides help to those in a crisis of faith.

10. It confirms a biblical worldview and aggregates the faith of our children.

Apologetics are required for every Christian family that wants to assimilate the faith to their children. It is required of every local church that wants to mature each believer with a solid Christian worldview. It is required of every leader who intends to champion the banner of Jesus Christ to a lost and dying world.

Why Is the Bible Such a Big Deal?

In the movie, "The Da Vinci Code," they said, "The Bible is a product of man, my dear, not of God...Man created it as a historical record...History has never had a definitive version of the book...The Bible, as we know it today, was collected by the pagan Roman Emperor Constantine the Great...More than eighty gospels were considered part of the New Testament, and yet only a few were chosen for

---

[12] Jeff Shafer, "We Hate You. Now Give Us Your Kids So That We Can Turn Them Against You," March 22, 2011, accessed April 9, 2018, *http://www.blogs.christianpost.com/liberty/we-hate-you-now-give-us-your-kids-so-that-we-can-turn-them-against-you-5301/.*

inclusion."[13] While, Dan Brown might make interesting movies he is absolutely a poor historian. Therefore, we need to look at the truth.

What Is the Bible?

So many people are confused as to what exactly the Bible is anyway? Let me make it simple for you. Robert McAfee Brown answers the question in the best possible way: *It is the record of man's search for God and God's search for man.*[14] Therefore, the Bible is a compilation of books about the greatest love story and chase scene of all times. God has been chasing man, looking for man, trying everything to bring man back to God since the beginning in the Garden of Eden. The Bible recounts this journey. As you begin your journey, have you ever stopped and realized how the Bible is the story of what extent God would go to find you?

Why Do We Call the Bible a Covenant?

The book you call the Bible is, in reality, two covenants in one book. The Bible, since the end of the second century A.D., has been divided into "two covenants." The old and new covenants are the same thing as the Old and New Testaments. "The Latin term *testamentum* was used to translate the Greek and Hebrew words for covenant. The English word was derived from the Latin. Hence, the old and new covenants became the Old and New Testaments."[15] The word "covenant" is used to describe a contract of the

---

[13] Norman L. Geisler and Ronald M. Brooks, *When Skeptics Ask: A Handbook on Christian Evidences: Revised and Updated* (Grand Rapids, Michigan: Baker Books, 2013).

[14] Robert McAffee Brown, *The Bible Speaks to You* (Philadelphia: Westminister Press, n.d.), 15.

[15] Don Stewart, "Covenant," Blue Letter Bible, accessed April 20, 2018, *http://www.blueletterbible.org/faq/don_stewart/don_stewart_271.cfm.*

will between God and man. So, the Old Testament is a contract based on receiving salvation by the shedding of blood from bulls and goats (Hebrews 9:18-20). A covenant is an agreement between two people. In this case, the covenant would be between God and man or God's contract with you.

The Bible Is a Compilation of Sixty-Six Books.

The Bible is one book with sixty-six books bound inside its pages. The Bible has two main sections—the Old and the New Testaments. Both the Old and New are divided into a specific organized subdivision.

The Old Testament

The Old Testament contains thirty-nine books which are divided into five main sections.

1) **The Law:** Genesis, Exodus, Leviticus, Numbers, and Deuteronomy
2) **History:** Joshua, Judges, Ruth, 1 and 2 Samuel, 1 and 2 Kings, 1 and 2 Chronicles, Ezra, Nehemiah, and Esther
3) **Poetry/Wisdom:** Job, Psalms, Proverbs, Ecclesiastes, and Song of Solomon
4) **Major Prophets:** Isaiah, Jeremiah, Lamentations, Ezekiel, and Daniel
5) **Minor Prophets:** Hosea, Joel, Amos, Obadiah, Jonah, Micah, Nahum, Habakkuk, Zephaniah, Haggai, Zechariah, and Malachi

The New Testament

The New Testament contains twenty-seven books.

1) **The Gospels:** Matthew, Mark, Luke, and John
2) **Historical:** The Acts of the Apostles (Acts)
3) **Church Epistles:** Romans, 1 and 2 Corinthians, Galatians, Ephesians, Philippians, Colossians, 1 and

2 Thessalonians, 1 and 2 Timothy, Titus, Philemon, Hebrews, James, 1 and 2 Peter, 1, 2, and 3 John, and Jude

4) **Prophetic:** Revelation

What Words Do We Use to Describe the Bible?

- **First, we use the word Bible.** This word comes from a Greek word, *biblos*, which means "book." The Bible is "the Book."
- **Second, The Old and New Testaments** are English words that came from the Latin word, "covenant."
- **Third,** "Scripture" comes from the Greek word, *graphe*, meaning "writing."
- **Fourth,** "Sacred Writing" is how Paul refers to them in 2 Timothy 3:15.

The Spectacular Achievement of the Bible

It is the most unique book ever printed; therefore, it has arisen to spectacular achievements in which no other written book has even come close to it. When we look at the facts and figures of the Bible, something pretty amazing takes place.

1. **It is spectacular in printing and translations.** According to the Wycliffe Bible translators,

   - Today, more than 1,500 languages have access to the New Testament and some portion of the Scripture in their language.
   - More than 650 languages have the complete translated Bible
   - About 7,000 languages are known to be in use today.
   - At least 1.5 billion people do not have the full Bible in their first language. More than 10 million

do not have a single verse of Scripture.

- More than 2,500 languages across 170 countries have active translations and linguistic development work happening right now.

- Approximately 1,600 languages still need a Bible translation project to begin (The Wycliffe Bible Translator, 2018, p. 15).

- It is soon to become the first universally translated book in the world.

2. It is spectacular in its global printing.

If I were to ask you what is the bestselling book of all time? You might say, *A Christmas Carol by Charles Dickens, Lord of the Rings, or The Hobbit* by J.R.R. Tolkein, *The Lion, the Witch, and the Wardrobe,* by C.S. Lewis! Not even *Harry Potter*'s combined figures have come close to achieving the top spot. The bestselling book of ALL TIME, every year, is the Bible.

The *Guinness Book of World Records* estimates that between 1815 and 1975 more than 2.5 BILLION Bibles were printed, sold, or distributed. Today, they estimate that figure to be greater than five billion. Over 80 percent of all American households own a Bible (Steven and Jackie Green, 2017, p. 62). Now keep in mind that *Harry Potter and the Philosopher's Stone* has sold only 100 million copies! There are 168,000 Bibles sold in the United States every day.[16] The Gideons distributed 59,460,000 Bibles in 2016 alone![17] The YouVersion Bible has more than 100 million total downloads.[18] The annual sales figures for the Bible

---

[16] Brandon Gaille, "29 Good Bible Sales Statistics," accessed April 23, 2018, *http://www.brondongaille.com/27-good-bible-sales-statistics/*.

[17] Ibid.

[18] Ibid.

are very high, averaging between 425m and 650m, repeatedly, year after year...*The Economist* estimates more than 100m new Bibles are printed every year, making a staggering total of more than 6 billion in print."[19]

Do you know the country that prints the MOST Bibles? This is a shocker, but its China! They are now the largest Bible printers in the world.

Something must be going on with this book to make it the bestselling book of all time.

Or else why would so many people continue to purchase it? Why do so many people purchase a Bible? Why all the fuss about an old book?

3. It is spectacular in its compilation!

It took over 1,500 years to write the Bible. It was copied by hand for most of those 1,500 years by professional scribes. These scribes were highly prized and highly trained. They would stand if they were taking brief notes and sit on a bench if they were copying a manuscript.

To write, they used a reed for a pen and soot for their ink. Later, a metallic ink and various colors were used. They used a stylus, a ruler, a sponge, and a penknife with a piece of pumice. Using these tools, they would draw a colorless line over the parchment and write within its borders in a specific room called a Scriptorium. What is so fascinating is, they would do this listening to someone read aloud from the text.

---

[19] "Think About It, Why the Bible Is the True Bestseller," accessed April 23, 2018, *http://www.nowthinkgaboutit.com/2012/06/why-the-bible-is-the-true-best-seller/.*

It has more than *40 different authors*—such personalities as military generals, political leaders, rabbis, prime ministers, peasants, kings, physicians, and fishermen. All these different personalities and worldviews had a part in writing the bestselling book on earth, while all delivering a single solitary message of hope.

These personalities also wrote in different environments. They wrote in a multitude of environments like a dungeon, prison, wilderness, in exile or a hillside, giving us books with a multiple set of tenses and moods.

These environments represented three distinct continents—*Asia, Africa, and Europe.* These continents gave us the three languages in which the Bible was originally written—Hebrew, Greek and Aramaic.

Hebrew: The Hebrew language is the language of Canaan or Judah (Isaiah 19:18). It is the language of the Jewish people. The original founders of Colonial America called it "the mother of all languages." They called it that because the Hebrew language comes from a large family of languages called "Semitic" and is akin to such languages as Aramaic, Syriac, Akkadian (Assyrian-Babylonian), and Arabic."[20] In 1974, 70,000 tablets were dug up in the country of Syria in a city called Ebla. These tablets dated back to 2400 B.C. and many believe that these tablets contain many Hebrew names, and biblical places, linking them to around the time of Moses.

The language is unique because it is written from right to left. Furthermore, it contains no vowels. The Hebrew language concentrates on observation more

---

[20] Neil R. Lightfoot, *How We Got the Bible, Third Edition* (Grand Rapids, Michigan: Baker Books, 2003), 26.

than reflection. It is an amazingly concise and direct language. The Hebrew language, while direct and concise, is a language that operates much like a picture. Have you ever heard that "a picture is worth a thousand words?" Pictures can tell powerful stories. The English language requires more words than the Hebrew language to say the same thing. The Hebrew language is a poetic use of figures of speech. The easiest way to understand how the Hebrew Bible affects the reading of the Old Testament is to realize that a Hebrew word is always a pictorial representation of some person, place, or thing.

Greek: When Alexander the Great conquered the known world, he instituted and left the Greek language behind. It didn't take long until the Greek language was being spoken all over the world. This language had fully infiltrated most cultures by the time of Christ. That is why the logical, best language in which to write the Scriptures would be Greek. More people spoke *Koine* Greek (a common man's Greek), than most any other language. What is so special about the Greek language? It is a rich and beautiful language with deep, strong harmony. It is used to express vigorous thoughts. It was the "universal" language of its day.

Aramaic: Both the Old and New Testament have portions written in Aramaic. Aramaic was the language that Jesus spoke. The Aramaic language is akin to Hebrew and the common language of the people of Palestine. This large vocabulary language helped to provide a more superior speech with its exact expressions.

I Thought There Were No Alphabetical Languages During the Time of Moses.

The skeptics of the church have for years exclaimed that there were no known languages during the time of Moses. Therefore, he could have never written the first five books of the Bible. However, history has once again proven that was not the case at all. As Neil R. Lightfoot writes:

> Such information as this has important implications for the origins of the Bible, for skeptical Bible critics formerly held that writing was unknown in the days of Moses (He wrote the first five books of the Bible), and therefore that Moses could not have been the author of the first five books of the Bible. We know now that writing was practiced many centuries before Moses and that an alphabetic script was in use in the vicinity of Sinai. Indeed, at least five different systems of writing are known to have existed in the general area of Syria-Palestine when Moses lived."[21]

It was written down on seven types of material—stone, clay, wood and wax, metal, ostraca, papyrus, leather and parchment and then eventually compiled into a "Codex." A codex is what we would refer to as being a bound book. They used chisels, metal styli, pens, and even ink to write upon the items previously mentioned, etching in stone prophetic words.

4. It is spectacular in that one-quarter of the Bible contains prophetic speech.

The Bible represents over four hundred complete pages of predictive prophecies found within its pages. Twenty-seven percent of the Bible is prophetic. "The Bible contains approximately 2,500 predictions about events that were future when the words were recorded or spoken. Two thousand of these predictions have been fulfilled in every detail. That means five hundred predictions made in the Bible have yet to be fulfilled."[22]

---

[21] Ibid., 12.

[22] Douglas Connelly, *The Ultimate Guide to Bible Prophecy and End Times* (New York: Guidepost, 2013), 3.

5. **It is spectacular in how it was used to establish our world today.**

   Every pillar and segment of civilization owes much of its advancements to the publication of the Bible—science, education, art and architecture, justice, government, labor and economics, music, literature, sexual morality, the sanctity of human life, women, liberty, and slavery.

6. **It is spectacular in that it takes sixty-six books and tells the single solitary story of the personhood of Jesus Christ.**

   The Bible details His life 400 to 1,500 years before He was even born as a baby in a manager. The Bible specifically names the town where the Messiah would be born—the smallest known city in the world at that time, Bethlehem Ephrathah (Micah 5:2).

   The Bible has been attacked, burned, banned, spit on, torn apart by both skeptics and people of faith more than any other book in the world. It has even withstood more scrutiny than any other book ever written. It is spectacular in its printing and translations, reach, compilation, prophetic ability, and as a guidebook to establish what we know today as civilization. And one reason for this is that it claims to be the very Word of God.

The Bible Claims Divine Inspiration.

In claiming to be the very Word of God it makes many bold claims:

- In Jude 3, the Bible tells us that it is a record of "faith which was once for all delivered to the saints" (NKJV).

- In 2 Timothy 3:16, it says, "All Scripture is given by inspiration of God, and is profitable for doctrine, for reproof, for correction, for instruction in righteousness" (NKJV).

- In John 7:17 it claims, "Anyone who chooses to do the will of God will find out whether my teaching comes from God or whether I speak on my own" (NIV).

- Second Peter 1:20 says, "First of all, you should know this: No prophecy of Scripture comes from one's own interpretation, because no prophecy ever came by the will of man; instead, men spoke from God as they were moved by the Holy Spirit" (HCSB).

- Paul said in 1 Thessalonians 4:8, "Anyone who rejects this instruction does not reject a human being but God . . . who gives you his Holy Spirit" (NIV).

The Bible makes the very bold claim that God inspired every word in its pages. Just how trustworthy are the stories written upon those pages?

The Historical Accuracy of Scriptures

I am sure you have heard that "The Bible cannot be trusted. It has been written and rewritten many times." Or maybe you have heard, "The Bible cannot be trusted as a good source of history. The science of archaeology has disproven the historical record." Well, none of these is true. Actually, archaeological science confirms the Bible's trustworthiness as a historical source.

Here is what no one is telling you! Do you realize that there are more than 100,000 archaeological artifacts just from the Palestinian (Jerusalem) area that relates directly to the Bible's stories of events, characters, and places? Furthermore, do you know there are more than 25,000 archaeological sites that confirm the Bible as accurate history? While archaeology cannot prove that the Bible is God's Word, it can aid in our trust of its historical record. It does so with such amazing truth that even the legends of archaeology attest to its historical accuracy.

The American Schools of Oriental Research says, "Finally, it is perfectly true to say that biblical archaeology has done a great deal to correct the impression that was abroad at the close of the last century and in the early part of this century, that biblical history was of doubtful trustworthiness in many places."[23] The renowned Jewish archaeologist Nelson Glueck, known as one of the most famous and highly respected archaeologists said: "As a matter of fact, however, it may be stated categorically that no archaeological discovery has ever controverted a biblical reference."[24] W.F. Albright, the teacher of Nelson Glueck says: "All radical schools in the New Testament criticism which have existed in the past or which exist today are prearchaeological, and are therefore, since they were built in *Der Luft* (in the air), are quite antiquated today."[25] Millar Burrows, Yale University, says: "Archaeology has in many cases refuted the views of modern critics. This is a real contribution (to the Bible), and not to be minimized.... On the whole, however, archaeology work has unquestionably strengthened confidence in the reliabilityof the scriptural record."[26]

In considering the Old Testament, archaeology has vindicated the biblical record time and again. *The New International Dictionary of Biblical Archaeology*, written by a score of experts in various fields, repeatedly shows that biblical history is vindicated. To illustrate, the editor's preface remarks are:

---

[23] J. A. Thompson, *The Bible and Archaeology* (Grand Rapids, Michigan: Eerdmans, 1975), 5.

[24] Nelson Glueck, *Rivers in the Desert* (New York: Grove Press, 1959), 31–32.

[25] W. F. Albright, *The Teacher's Yoke*, ed. E. J. Vardaman (Waco: Baylor Press, 1969), 29.

[26] Millar Burrows, *What Mean These Stones?* (New York: Meridian Books, 1956), 1.

Near Eastern archaeology has demonstrated the historical and geographical reliability of the Bible in many important areas. By clarifying the objectivity and factual accuracy of biblical authors, archaeology also helps correct the view that the Bible is avowedly partisan and subjective. It is now known, for instance, that, along with the Hittites, Hebrew scribes were the *best historians in the entire ancient Near East*, despite contrary propaganda that emerged from Assyria, Egypt, and elsewhere.[27]

You may be thinking: *Well, ok so it can be trusted to tell the truth about history. But how did we get the Bible? Who decided what was in it and how did they make those decisions?*

How Do We Know the Process of Canonization?

So how did we get our Bible? In *Lethal Faith, Volume Two*, we will go into greater detail about "How we got our Bible. However, for now, answering a few basic questions is all that is needed. So, how did they choose which books to include in the Bible? This question has a technical name—it's called the process of canonization.

The name "canon" comes from a leaf on a perennial herbaceous plant found in tropical marshes called papyrus plants. This papyrus (reed) plant has large reeds and grows in Egypt. Egyptians and other cultures used this "reed" to measure their belongings. The word "canon" is borrowed from Greek, in which *kanon* means "a rule as standard of measurement." So when we call the Bible a "canon," we are suggesting that it is the "measuring rod of righteousness."[28] The word *canon* means "the rule of standard by which something is judged." This is why the Bible is considered to be the "rule of faith" for Christians.

---

[27] Zondervan, *Resource Reference Library* (Grand Rapids, Michigan: Zondervan, 1983), vii–viii.

[28] F.F. Bruce et al., *The Origin of the Bible*, ed. Philip Wesley Comfort (Carol Stream, Illinois: Tyndale House, 2003), 51.

Furthermore, the biblical languages added to our understanding of the word "canon." In Hebrew, the word *canon* means a "reed" or a "rod." In Greek, it could also mean "a series" or a "list." In English, it means a "cane." The word "Bible" comes from a Greek word called *Biblos* and refers to the papyrus plant which was used to make "a book." The ancients used papyrus to make paper.

The process of canonization describes how we got our Bible. It is "the historical process by which the Spirit of God led the church to recognize those writings that were genuinely inspired. This historical process produced the canon we have today."[29]

So, the canonization of the Bible is a very important subject, especially when asked, "How did you get your Bible?" Needless to say, someone will eventually ask you about how the Church decided which books were of God in this process of canonization. There is a simple answer to this as well!

Didn't I See a History Channel Special About "Lost Books of the Bible?"

Usually when someone mentions a book that was found but was not included in the Bible, they make the faulty assumption that somehow, "it was accidently left out," and "I found it!" That is not the case at all. Apocrypha books or "Lost Books" of the Bible are easily understood.

The Apocrypha is a term that refers to the group of books related to the Old Testament stories which were judged by the early church not be inspired and thus rejected as canon. There are fifteen books in the Apocrypha— 1 and 2 Esdras, Tobit, Judith, additions to Esther, Wisdom

---

[29] William Combs, "How We Got Our Bible," Community Bible Church, April 1, 2018, *http://www.bctrenton.com/how-we-got-our-bible/*. This is an excellent source in understanding the process of our English Bible.

of Solomon, Ecclesiasticus/Sirach, Baruch, Letter of Jeremiah, Prayer of Azariah and Song of the Three Young Men, Susanna, Bel and the Dragon, Prayer of Manasseh, and 1 and 2 Maccabees.

The Catholic Church in 1546 declared all these books "canon" except 1 and 2 Esdras, and The Prayer of Manasseh. Why were all of these books rejected and not placed in the Protestant Bible? Here are eight reasons why these books were rejected as "canon."

1) The New Testament writers never refer to them in their writings as being inspired.

2) They were not written by the "Prophets of God."

3) There were no church councils in the earliest days of Christianity that saw them as inspired.

4) They were not confirmed as inspired by supernatural acts.

5) Many of these books suggest doctrines that are not found in the Protestant Bible.

6) The apostles did not quote them.

7) They are not historically trustworthy.

8) Early Hebrews did not use them as part of their Old Testament.

9) The Apocrypha is missing from all early lists during the canonization process. Melito of Sardis, one of the first investigators of biblical sites, did not list them in his list of Scriptures in 170 A.D. He writes in 170 A.D.

When I came to the east and reached the place where these things were preached and done, and learned accurately the books of the Old Testament, I set down the facts and sent them to you. These are their names: the five books of Moses, Genesis, Exodus, Leviticus, Numbers,

Deuteronomy, Joshua the son of Nun, Judges, Ruth, four
books of the Kingdom, two books of Chronicles, the Psalms
of David, the Proverbs of Solomon and his wisdom, Ecclesiastes, the Song of Songs, Job, the prophets Isaiah, Jeremiah, The Twelve in a single book, Daniel, Ezekiel, Ezra.
Furthermore, the Apocrypha was not on any list until the
fifth century.[30]

Melito of Sardis, the Bishop of Sardis, made this list
of "Holy Scriptures" and included all the Old Testament
books, except the Book of Esther. Most people believe that
any other discrepancies in the list is a matter of ancient
semantics. However, the Apocrypha is not mentioned.

What are the "lost books of the Bible?"

I realize that you are subject to the biblical theology
of the History Channel, Discovery Channel, etc. I too am
actually a big fan on most every subject except their shows
regarding the Bible. They usually use liberal theologians
who have an agenda and who furthermore adhere to the
proven failure of German Higher Criticism. With that being said, we will proceed. There are many books which are
often called "the lost gospels" or the "lost scriptures." Their
titles do not often represent the truth.

While, I will write much more about this in *Lethal
Faith, Volume 2*, as it relates to "Lost books," there are only
about two dozen books which fall under this title, and none
of them were written in the first 100 years of Christianity.
As a matter of fact, one of our earliest church leaders (fathers) who took the realm of leadership of the Church after
the Twelve died was called Irenaeus, he wrote in a book
called, *Against Heresies*. In it he writes regarding these
"lost books":

---

[30] Eusebius, *Ecclesiastical History*, IV.

Indeed, they have arrived at such a pitch of audacity, as to entitle their comparatively recent writings 'the Gospel of Truth, though it agrees in nothing with the Gospels of the Apostles, so that they have really no Gospel, which is not full of blasphemy....But that these Gospels [of the Apostles] alone are true and reliable, and admit neither an increase nor diminution of the aforesaid number [four], I have proved by so many such arguments.[31]

They were rejected for the same reason that the Apocrypha books were rejected as stated above. However, many of these "lost gospels" were written by the first cults of Christianity such as Gnosticism, which believes that matter is evil; Pantheism, which believes that God is in every innate object of nature; or even Docetism, which pronounced that Jesus was not human. These are just to name a few.

They really are not "lost books" at all. We have always known about them, and we have clearly known as the Church why we rejected each of them for canonization.

In conclusion, The Bible did not just "happen." It was developed over a process of 1,600 years. Furthermore, it did not just "fall out of the sky." And it most certainly did not survive by mere chance. So, you are holding in your hand exactly what Steven and Jackie Green called, *A Dangerous Book*. It's dangerous because it's true.

---

[31] Irenaeus, *Against Heresies*, 3.11.9.

Chapter 2

Archeology of the Old Testament

Is the Bible true? Can the Bible be trusted to give insights into the true history of civilization? Can people know if the stories in the Old Testament are true? The one answer to all these questions is yes! Through the science of archaeology, one can simply prove or disprove the assumption that the Bible is a reliable source for ancient history. So where should this investigation begin? A good starting place is with real, actual people in the Old Testament!

Fifty Real People in the Bible Confirmed by Secondary Sources

Dr. Lawrence Mykytiuk, associate professor of Library Science and historical librarian from Purdue University, wrote an article in the *Biblical Archaeological Review* in 2014 that caught the attention of the scholastic world. His article is titled, "Archaeology Confirms Fifty Real People in the Bible," in the March/April edition. His challenge was intriguing to me, so I thought: *What if I found the actual pictures of these fifty secondary sources used to prove the existence of these people?* I started a journey to find the actual sources Dr. Lawrence Mykytiuk used; therefore, I took a plane to London. I visited the British Museum, considered one of the best in the world, where I spent two days snapping pictures of many of Dr. Mykytiuk's sources. I eventually traveled to many other museums around the world, including the Pergamon Museum in Berlin, Germany. To my joy, many times I found not just "one secondary source" in antiquities which proved a person's existence, but multiple sources. I encourage you to read not only the original article, but also the updated edition in the *Biblical Archaeological Review* found in the April 12, 2017, issue. Dr. Lawrence Mykytiuk has done a wonderful job proving the historical reliability of Scriptures. He is a specialist in history and Jewish studies. The rest of this chapter will be a study in Dr. Mykytiuk's research notes. A close examination will reveal fifty people clearly mentioned in the Bible as real human beings. This will be accomplished by going to another resource *outside* the Bible to prove their existence as real human beings. This potential proof will come through the eyes of geographical regions within Bible times.

The Land of Egypt

The Greek historian, Hecataeus of Miletus, called Egypt "the gift of the Nile." "Egyptian civilization was initially derived from the many regional cultures of the Nile Valley."[1] These 387,000 miles of sunny landscape are constrained by a tubular-shaped geographical land that has brought the world an immense amount of creative brilliance and communicative ingenuity. However, the Egyptian land of the Bible was sealed off from much outside contact. "Many Egyptologists believe that these secure borders contributed to an essentially optimistic Egyptian worldview."[2] This world powerhouse found at the helm of civilization is mentioned in

---

[1] Brian M. Fagan, *The Oxford Companion to Archaeology* (New York: Oxford University Press, 1996), 194.

[2] Hoerth, *Archaeology and the Old*, 127.

the Bible more than 750 times. The word *Pharaoh* is mentioned more than 200 times. Egypt is so old that it is one of 70 original nations mentioned in the Table of Nations in Genesis chapter 10 under the name *Misrayim.* Think about how accurate the Bible is by mentioning the land of Egypt as one of the oldest civilizations in the world sometime between 2000 and 1600 B.C.

Egyptian leaders were like many of us today—they hated to tell the truth about their own destructions, setbacks, and losses. So, they didn't. That should be kept in mind as we explore these ancient artifacts of the Egyptian cultural. Additional reference materials for these fifty people can be found in the appendix.

1. Shishak

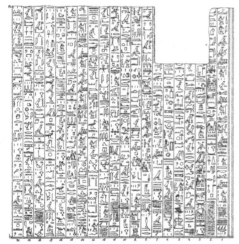

Shishak, who was also known as Shoshenq I, was the Egyptian Pharaoh in the 22nd Dynasty of Egypt who sacked the city of Jerusalem. Shishak received the fugitive Jeroboam. He left a record on the walls of the great temple El-Karnak. He is also mentioned in a victory stele discovered at Megiddo.

He is directly mentioned in I Kings 11:40 and 14:25.

2. "So," King of Egypt

So ruled around 700 B.C. during the 24th Dynasty of Egypt. He is also known by the name Osorkonviv IV.

So was the Pharoah of Egypt mentioned directly in the Bible in 2 Kings 17:4.

3. Tirhakah:

Tirhakah, also known as Taharqa, can be found in many Egyptian and Assyrian inscriptions, as well as the Babylonian Chronicle. He ruled between the years of 690 and 664 B.C. during the 25th Dynasty.

He is directly mentioned in 2 Kings 19:9

4. Necho II

Necho, also known as Neco, was part of the 26th Dynasty of Egypt. He ruled between 610 and 595 B.C. He was an influential player for the kingdoms of Assyria, Babylon, and Judah. He is probably the most mentioned Pharaoh in the Bible. He ruled during the time of Josiah, King of Judah. He is mentioned in the inscriptions of the Assyrian King, Asturbanipal and with the Esarhaddon Chronicle.

He is directly mentioned in the Bible in 2 Kings 23:29; 2 Chronicles 35:20, 22; 36:4.

5. Hophra

Hophra, was also known as Apries, Wahirbe in the 26th Dynasty of Egypt around the nineteenth century B.C. during the approximate years of 589–570, B.C. He is mentioned in an Egyptian inscription and by Nebuchadnezzar himself when he defeated Hophra in war around 572 B.C.

Hophra is referred to in Jeremiah 44:30.

The Kingdom of the Moabites

Moab was the son of Lot from an incestuous relationship Lot had with his eldest daughter. The country of Moab is now known as the Kingdom of Jordan, but specifically, the exact spot today is called Kerak, which is east of the Dead Sea. Pharoah Ramses II mentions this country. The Moabites ruled during the ninth century. Ruth was a Moabite who immigrated to Israel. Later, David hid in Moab with their king when Saul was hunting for him (1 Samuel 22:3-4). The Moabites worshiped the god Chemosh.

6. Mesha

Mesha was a king who ruled during the mid-ninth century. He was the King of Moab and ruled during the reign of Jehoshaphat, King of Judea and Joram, King of Israel. He is mentioned in the Mesha inscription known as the Moabite Stone.

He is mentioned directly in 2 Kings 3:4-27.

The Aram-Damascus Area

This was an ancient Aramaean state around the city of Damascus in the country of Syria. This kingdom flourished from the 12th century to 732 B.C. Second Samuel 10:6-19 mentions this location which is north of Israel and named after the son of Shem—Aram.

7. Hadadezer

Hadadezer ruled during the nineteenth century B.C. The Ammorites asked his army to help them fight King David who ruled Israel during this time. He is mentioned in the Assyrian inscriptions of Shalmaneser III, the Melqart stele, on the statue of Shalmanesar III at Assur, and the Black Obelisk.

He is mentioned in 1 Kings 22:3, 31; 2 Kings 5–6:8-23, as the "King of Aram."

8. Ben-hadad, Son of Hadadezer

Ben-hadad II, ruled during the biblical times of Ahab and the Judean King Jehoshaphat. Ben-hadad is actually a title much like Pharoah was a title to an Egyptian king. Ben-hadad is the title used by ancient Syrian kings. *Ben-hadad* means, "son of the god, Hadad. Hadad was the deity (god) of both storms and thunder (2 Kings 5:18). Ben Hadad II is referred to in the Melqart stele.

His biblical reference can be found in 2 Kings 6:24; 8:7-15.

9. Hazael

Hazael was the king of Damascus, which is the oldest continuous inhabited city today. Hazael ruled from 844 to 842 B.C. He was the man sent to the prophet Elisha to inquire about healing. He lived during the times of Elisha, Jehu, Jehoram, king of Israel, and Ahaziah, king of Judah. He is referred to in multiple ancient inscriptions, four of which follow: (1) The Kurbail stele, which is an ancient inscription of Shalmaneser III; (2) The Zakkur stele; (3) The Bridle stele; and (4) inscriptions referenced on pieces of ivory found on the form frames of possibly his own ancient bed.

Hazael is referred to in 1 Kings 19:15.

10. Ben-hadad Son of Hazael

Ben-hadad III, son of Hazael, lived during the early nineteenth century B.C. He lived during the time of Jehoash around 840 B.C. He was not related to Ben-hadad II, but appropriated his name for dynastic reasons, much like the Great Ramses I did in Egypt. He was often referred to in antiquities as "Mari," a title for a king like Ben-hadad or Pharoah. This title was used to refer to the King of Aram. He is referenced in the Zakkur stele found near Aleppo, an inscription from the reign of Adadnirari III.

He is biblically referred to in 2 Kings 13:3, 24-25.

11. Rezin

Rezin was the king of Damascus and was also known as Rahianu. He ruled during the middle of the eighteenth century to 732 B.C. He ruled during the time of Jotham and Ahaz of Judea. He united with the King of Israel, Pekah, to invade Judah in 742 B.C. He is mentioned in the inscriptions of Tiglath-pileser III, king of Assyria.

His biblical reference can be found in 2 Kings 15:37. He was the last of the kings of Syria to reign in Damascus.

The Northern Kingdom of Israel

After King Solomon died as king over a united Israel, his son Rehoboam reigned. Rehoboam was approached by Jeroboam, son of Nebat, for a lighter tax on its kingdom's families (1 Kings 12:16). Rehoboam rejected Jeroboam's pleas for a lighter tax. Jeroboam split the kingdom over taxation. The northern kingdom was called Israel and the southern kingdom was called Judea. The capital of the northern kingdom was Samaria and in the south, Jerusalem.

The northern kingdom consisted of ten tribes, excluding Judea and Benjamin. This division lasted nearly 210 years before the kingdom was destroyed by the Assyrians. This northern kingdom had nine dynasties throughout its lifetime with a total of nineteen kings. Eight of these kings died violent deaths, predominantly at the hands of their enemies. The northern kingdom is a story of mostly evil kings who rebelled against the God of Israel.

12. Omri, King of Israel

Omri ruled Israel from 884 to 873 B.C. and did not worship the God of Israel, but continued the worship of a golden calf. He arose to power after a series of assassination plots against a preceding king. He is mentioned in the Mesha inscriptions where he, in the Israelite territory, is referred to as "the House of Omri."

His biblical reference is found in 1 Kings 16:16.

13. Ahab, king of Israel

Ahab lived from 871 to 852 B.C. and ruled Israel for 22 years. He was the seventh king of Israel and the son of Omri. He married Jezebel who pressured him to build pagan temples of worship in Israel to the god Baal. Ahab was considered to be the most evil of all Israel's kings who forsook God (1 Kings 16:30). Archaeologists have found ivory plaques from his Samaritan palace. This confirms another biblical reference found in 1 Kings 22:39 that states he lived in an ivory palace.

Ahab was rebuked by both Elijah and Micaiah the prophets. Elijah rebuked him for the temple of Baal and prophesied a drought upon the land if he did not remove it. Ahab and his priests were the ones who confronted Elijah on Mount Carmel in a battle to call down fire from heaven and consume the sacrifices. Elijah won when God miraculously intervened (1 Kings 18:18-39). Ahab is referred to by name in the ancient inscription upon two stelae called Kurkh Monoliths written by his enemy, Shalmaneser III of Assyria. Shalmaneser simply calls him, "Ahab the Israelite."

Ahab is biblically referred to in 1 Kings 16:28.

14. Jehu, King of Israel

Jehu, the son of Jehoshaphat, commander of the chariots was the tenth king which ruled during the ninth century B.C. He lived between 842 and 815 B.C. during the time of Elisha, the prophet who replaced Elijah. Jehu led a revolt against the throne. Jehu was told by Elisha the prophet to exterminate the entire house of Omri. Jehu had Jezebel killed and her son. He purged the land of Israel from Baal worship, restoring worship to the one true God. Jehu is referred to in the ancient inscriptions of Shalmaneser III, as well as multiple other pieces of antiquities, one of which is the Kurba'il Statue.

He is biblically referred to in 1 Kings 19:16.

15. Joash, King of Israel—the Northern Kingdom

Joash, the son of King Jehoahaz reigned for 16 years as the twelfth king of Israel. He lived during the time of Elisha, the prophet. Joash loved Elisha, but he did not always follow his instructions carefully. Joash tolerated the worship of golden calves. He broke down the walls of Jerusalem, carrying off the treasures from the Temple. He is referred to in the Tell al-Rimah inscriptions and in a stela of Adad-Nirari III.

He is biblically referred to in 2 Kings 13:9.

16. Jeroboam II, King of Israel

Jeroboam II was the thirteenth king of Israel and reigned for 41 years. He was the son of Joash and lived between 790 and 749 B.C. Jeroboam II ruled during the time of the prophets Isaiah, Jonah, Hosea, Joel, and Amos. Jeroboam II also ruled during the time of King Uzziah (2 Kings 15:1). Jeroboam II did evil in the sight of the one true God by allowing the people of Israel to worship the golden calf as a source of controlling the people. Although he restored a great deal of lost territory, he was another king who failed God—in spite of the fact that God sent many prophets to warn the people of Israel during his leadership. He is referred to in history by the seal of his royal servant Shema. The seal was discovered at Megiddo.

He is biblically referenced in 2 Kings 13:13.

17. Menahem, King of Israel

Menahem, was the sixteenth king of Israel and ruled during the eighth century. He founded the dynasty of "House of Gad." Menahem was previously a general in the army of Israel. His leadership as king tolerated not only idol worship but also was marked by immense cruelty, such as cutting open pregnant women. He ruled during the times of Azariah, king of Judah. He is referenced in the Calah Annals of Tiglath-pileser III and in a stele of Tiglath-pileser III.

He is biblically referenced in 2 Kings 15:14-22.

18. Pekah, King of Israel

Pekah, was the son of Remaliah and the former captain of the armies of Pekahiah, king of Israel. Pekah came into power via the route of planning the assassination of king Pekahiah (752 B.C.). Pekah reigned for 22 years and continued to do evil in God's eyes by allowing pagan practices among the Israelite people. Pekah, had grown tired of paying a yearly taxation to the king of Syria and fought for his freedom. He was eventually overthrown by the same way he had overthrown the previous king—assassination. He is referenced in history by the inscriptions of Tiglath-pileser III.

He is biblically referred to in 2 Kings 15:25.

19. Hoshea, King of Israel

Hoshea was the nineteenth and final king of the northern kingdom of Israel. He was son of Elah and reigned nine years. He led the assassination against the former king Pekah. Hoshea stopped paying the taxation demanded by the Assyrians and asked So, king of Egypt, for help in fighting off the Assyrian forces. Hoshea relied on Egypt, not the God of Israel. Hoshea was one of the least evil kings of Israel. In the end, Assyria won the war and carried off the golden calf of Israel (2 Kings 17:6). Hoshea is mentioned in Tiglath-Pileser's Summary Inscription.

He is biblically referred to in 2 Kings 15:30.

20. Sanballat "I," Governor of Samaria

Sanballat ruled as the governor of Samaria during the middle of the fifth century B.C. He was often referred to as the "Horonite." He was the chief opponent of Nehemiah who was trying to rebuild the walls of Jerusalem under the direct assignment of Artaxerxes, the Persian king. Sanballat's son married the daughter of the high priest, a son of Joiada. Sanballat is directly referred to in the Jewish community of Elephantine in Egypt on a piece of papyri. He is also referred to in the Wadi Daliyeh bulla.

He is biblically referred to in Nehemiah 2:10.

The Southern Kingdom of Judah

Please see notes above regarding the northern kingdom of Israel. The southern kingdom was known as Judea and consisted of only two tribes—Judah and Benjamin. Its borders were the Jordan River and the Mediterranean Sea. Almost immediately after the split of the two kingdoms (north and south), Shishak, the Pharoah of Egypt, attacked Judea, pillaging and plundering its Temple and royal palace (2 Chronicles 12:1-12). Judah never recovered from this sudden loss of its national wealth. Rehoboam, son of Solomon, was rebuked by the prophet Shemaiah (1 Kings 12:24). Rehoboam and Judah spent nearly the first sixty years trying to forcefully cause the unification of the northern and southern kingdom of Israel.

Out of nearly 28 kings, eight of them served the God of Israel, while 20 led the country in wicked adultery. There was only one dynasty in Judah, the kingdom of David. It is important to remember that much of ancient archaeology has seen the grandeur of the kingdom of David as a strictly embellished story used to intimidate their enemies. It was long thought that the size of David's kingdom was small and rather insignificance. Today, however, this thought is being dismantled as the archaeological digs in Tel-Dang have probably uncovered the kingdom of David; thus, confirming the biblical narrative as a powerful kingdom in the Southern Judea kingdom.

21. King David

He ruled around 1000 B.C. and reigned as king for forty-years. He reigned in Hebron for seven and a half years and for 33 years in Jerusalem. He led the people of Israel in what is referred to as the "Golden Age" of Israel. New archaeological finds in 2018 are confirming the sophistication of the Davidic Kingdom, correcting prior thoughts that it was only a small insignificant kingdom.

Until the last decade, there was no archaeological proof that David was a real human being. This is no longer the truth due to the discovery of three specific pieces of antiquities: (1) He is noted on the victory stele in Aramaic known as the "House of David," discovered at Tel Dan; (2) The Mesha Inscription

57

mentions the "House of David"; and (3) An Egyptian inscription in the region of Negev called "the heights of David."

He is biblically referenced in 1 Samuel 16:13.

22. King Uzziah

King Uzziah started his reign at the age of 16 and ruled for 52 years. His father was King Amaziah. His son, King Jotham, became the king later. He lived around 790 to 739 B.C., when the prophets Zechariah, Isaiah, Hosea, Amos, and Jonah were alive. Zechariah and Uzziah were probably the closest of friends, and it was probably Jeremiah who caused Uzziah to seek the God of Israel and do right before God. Later on in his life, after the death of Jeremiah, Uzziah became prideful and stopped seeking God for instruction as to how to lead God's people. He began to feel as if he were above the law of God. One day, he decided to enter the Temple and light the candles of incense, a job reserved for only the priest. Eighty priests tried to stop him that day, but he stubbornly refused to submit to their authority in his life. The moment he reached out to disobey God, leprosy struck him. Realizing what had happened, he ran. He spent the rest of his life abandoned because of leprosy. His son reigned on his behalf from another location. Uzziah is referred to in the inscribed stone seals of two of his servants, Abiyaw and Shubnayaw, and in his second burial inscription from the second Temple.

He is biblically referred to in 2 Kings 15:34.

23. King Ahaz (Achaz, Jehoahaz)

King Ahaz was the son of Jotham and reigned during the 8th century B.C. He started this reign at the age of 20-25 years of age. His son was Hezekiah and, as both a father and a leader, was by all accounts an evil king. He gave two of his sons to be burned alive in child sacrifices on the altar of Moloch. He had the holy utensils of the Temple cut into pieces and locked its doors so no one could worship the true God. He misled and abused his power for 16 years. He is referred to in Tiglath-pileser III's summary where he is referred to as Jehoahaz of Judah. He is also referenced by many other Assyrian inscriptions, one of which was the seal of Ushan.

He is biblically referenced in 2 Kings 15:38.

24. King Hezekiah

Hezekiah reigned between 715 and 686 B.C. He took the throne at the age of twenty-five and ruled for twenty-nine years. He was a good and righteous king for Judea. He outlawed the idolatry worship practices of previous kings. He brought strict reformation to the kingdom of Judea. The prophets Isaiah and Micah lived during his time. Hezekiah led many construction projects, two of which were the building of a broader wall in Jerusalem and the Siloam tunnel, often referred to as the Hezekiah tunnel. He had a son named Manasseh. He is referred to in antiquities by the Rassam Cylinder of Sennacherib, the Oriental Institute and Taylor prism, and the Bull inscription from the ancient palace of Nineveh.

Hezekiah is referenced in 2 Kings 16:20.

25. King Manasseh

Manasseh began his rule at the age of twelve. He reigned between 697 and 641 B.C. He worked very hard during his reign as king to undo the righteous acts of his father Hezekiah. He brought back the pagan practices, and he even worshiped the celestial gods of the sun and stars. He sacrificed his children to the god of Molech upon a fiery altar. His pride and arrogance led him to kill many innocent people and shed much blood. This same pride and arrogance led to his discipline when the Assyrians captured him and placed a ring in his nose, then led him back to Babylon. Manasseh cried out to God and repented, and a merciful God heard his cry and freed him from the Assyrian bondage. Manasseh returned to God, repented of idolatry, tore down the pagan temples and dismantled its practices. He lived out the rest of his life as a righteous king. Manasseh is referenced in the inscriptions of Assyrian king Esarhaddon written on a prism. He is also referred to in the secondary source of the Ashurbanipal records.

He is biblically referred to in 2 Kings 20:21.

26. The High Priest Hilkiah

Hilkiah was a high priest who served in the Temple. It is probable that he was the father of the prophet Jeremiah (Jeremiah 1:1). Nevertheless, he led during the time of King Josiah who brought back worship of the one true God and major reform back to the Temple. Hilkiah was the high priest who was in charge of leading the cleansing and reorganization of the Temple in which he found the "Book of the Law" (2 Kings 23:24). He led between 640 and 609 B.C. Hilkiah and Josiah brought great reforms to Jerusalem and the southern kingdom. He is referenced in secondary sources, outside the Bible. One is the City of David bulla of Azariah, son of Hilkiah.

He is biblically referenced in 2 Kings 22:4, 8.

27. Shaphan, scribe during the time of Josiah.

Shaphan was a scribe to the reforming King Josiah. He led between 640 and 609 B.C. Once the law was rediscovered in the Temple, Shaphan was the one who took it to the prophetess Huldah. Shaphan's grandson, Gedaliah, later became the governor of Judea when he was appointed by King Nebuchadnezzar. Shaphan's family was very influential and pro-Babylonian. He is referenced in secondary sources outside the Bible; thus, his existence is confirmed by a "City of David" bulla of Gemariah, son of Shaphan.

He is biblically referred to in 2 Kings 22:3.

28. Azariah, High Priest During the Time of Josiah

Azariah was the son of Hilkiah, the high priest. He led between the years of 640 and 609 B.C. Little is known about him personally, and there are multiple people with this name in our Hebrew Bible. He is referred by ancient documentation in the City of David bulla of Azariah, son of Hilkiah.

His biblical reference can be found in 1 Chronicles 9:11.

29. Gemariah, Official of Jehoiakim

Gemariah was an official during the reign of King Jehoiakim. He led between the years of 609 and 598 B.C. He is the son of Shaphan the scribe to Josiah. He was a Levite in the Temple during the time of Jehoiakim. He accompanied Shaphan with tribute money on behalf of Zedekiah to King Nebuchadnezzar. He also brought a letter to the Jewish captives (Jeremiah 29:3-4). He is referred to in the secondary source of the "City of David" bulla as Gemariah, son of Shaphan.

He is biblically referred to in Jeremiah 36:10.

30. Jehoiachin (Jeconiah, Coniah), King of Judea

Jehoiachin began his rule at the age of 18 as the son of King Jehoiakim. He reigned between the years of 598 and 597 B.C. He ruled only three months and ten days, as an evil king. Nebuchadnezzar attacked his kingdom and deported him to a Babylonian prison in 597 B.C. He spent 37 years in a Babylonian prison (2 Kings 24:16). The prophet Jeremiah prophesied his removal from the throne in Jeremiah 22:24.

After the death of Nebuchadnezzar, Evil-Merodach began to rule Babylon and showed Jehoiachin mercy by allowing him to sit at the king's table. Jehoiachin's exoneration until the time of his death is a metaphor for the mercy of God. We can spend our whole lives doing wrong and paying the high price that comes with such decisions; yet, through repentance and favor, we see the mercy of God until the time of our deaths (Jeremiah 52:32-34).

He is referred to through the secondary sources of the Babylonian Administrative Tablets. There are multiple tablets all referring to him distinctively and with different titles.

He is biblically referenced in 2 Kings 24:5.

31. Shelemiah, Father of Jehukal

Shelemiah was the son of Jehukal, a palace officer for King Zedekiah. His father is probably the one who tried to have the prophet Jeremiah killed at the order of King Zedekiah. Shelemiah, his son, is confirmed by the Lachish Ostracon from 589 B.C.

He is referred to in the biblical reference of Jeremiah 37:3; 38:1.

32. Jehukal (Jukal), Official During Zedekiah's Reign

Jehukal was an official during the reign of King Zedekiah. Jehukal led between the years of 597 and 586 B.C. He was sent to the prophet Jeremiah, along with Zephaniah to ask for prayer as Nebuchadnezzar attacked the city. He is referred to in a bulla discovered in the City of David and elsewhere.

He is biblically referenced in Jeremiah 37:3; 38:1.

33. Pashhur

"belonging to Jehucal son of Shelemiah son of Shovi"

"Gedaliah son of Pashur"

Pashhur is the son of Malchiah and was a priest who worked during the time of Jeremiah the prophet as an advisor to King Zedekiah. Pashhur suggested having Jeremiah killed for his prophetic words.

He is referred to in antiquities in a bulla from his son, Gedaliah who is referred to in Jeremiah 38:1.

34. Gedaliah, Son of Pashhur

"belonging to Jehucal son of Shelemiah son of Shovi"

"Gedaliah son of Pashur"

Gedaliah was a political opponent of Jeremiah and worked for King Zedekiah. Gedaliah also tried to have Jeremiah imprisoned for his prophetic word against Jerusalem. He is referred to in a bulla from the City of David.

He is biblically referenced in Jeremiah 38:1 as well.

35. Tiglath-pileser III (Pul)

Tiglath-pileser III was a very powerful Assyrian king who ruled during the eighth century between 745 and 727 B.C. He built a royal palace in Kalhu, the former biblical city called Nimrud. He is mentioned in multiple places outside the Bible such as the correspondence of Tiglah-pileser III and Sargon II from Calah/Nimrud.

He is biblically referenced in 2 Kings 15:19.

36. Shalmaneser V (Ululaya)

Shalmaneser V was king of Assyria between the years of 727 and 722 B.C. His original name was Ululayu, which he changed when becoming king. He fought Hoshea, king of Israel. He is referred to in antiquities in the Neo-Babylonian Chronicle.

He is biblically referenced in 2 Kings 17:2.

37. Sargon II

Sargon II was the king of Assyria who built a vast palace during the time he reigned between 721 and 705 B.C. His son, Tiglath-pileser III, ruled the Assyrians after him. Sargon II utterly defeated the Israelites.Many skeptics used his name and biblical reference to prove that the Bible was not true since he was mentioned only in Scriptures. This was only until they found the royal palace he built! He is referred to outside the Bible in numerous inscriptions such as the correspondence of Tiglath-pileser III and Sargon II from Calah/Nimrud.

He is biblically referred to in Isaiah 20:1.

38. Sennacherib

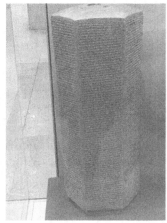

Sennacherib ruled Assyria as one of the most powerful monarchs in the world. He was the son of Sargon and reigned between 704 and 681 B.C. His palace was considered one of the Seven Wonders of the World and a "palace without rival." It was in this kingdom with hanging gardens that his two sons plotted to kill him. In 2 Kings 19:6-7, the prophet Isaiah prophesied Sennacherib's destruction as king. Then in 2 Kings 19:37, the Bible records his death. He is referred to outside the Bible in many places—one of these is his own inscription in the Taylor prism.

He is biblically referenced in 2 Kings 18:13.

39. Adrammelekh (Ardamullissu, Arad-mullissu)

Adrammelekh was one of the two sons who murdered their father, Sennacherib, in the Temple of Nisrock at Nineveh. Adrammelekh reigned during the early seventh century. He can be found outside the Bible in a letter sent to Esarhaddon.

He is biblically referred to in 2 Kings 19:37.

40. Esarhaddon

Esarhaddon was the youngest and favored son of Sennacherib. Esarhaddon was the third king of the Sargonid Dynasty. He rebuilt Babylon, and his rule lasted thirteen years. He is one of the most powerful kings of the Assyrian Empire. His contemporary was the Judean king, Manasseh. He is referenced in many inscriptions outside the Bible, one of which is the Succession Treaty.

He is biblically referred to in 2 Kings 19:37.

Babylonia

Babylonia was a small Amorite-ruled state that arose in existence around 1894 B.C. Babylonia made its capital in Babylon. Hammurabi brought it to great power and rulership. The Jewish people were exiled in this land, often referred to as "the land of Shinar," for seventy years. Babylonia is mentioned in the Bible as early as the list of the Table of Nations. It is also biblically referenced in 2 Kings 24:13-14.

41. Merodach-baladan II (Marduk-apla-idinna II)

Merodach-baladan II was king of Babylon twice—721–709 B.C. and then again for half a year in 702 B.C. He was a Chaldean prince who overthrew the throne in 721 B.C. He was a contemporary to King Hezekiah of Judah and the prophet Isaiah. He is referred to outside the Bible in the inscriptions of Sennacherib, as well as other places.

He is biblically referenced in 2 Kings 20:12.

42. Nebuchadnezzar II

Nebuchadnezzar II was a ruthless, powerful, and brutal king of Babylon. He is the longest reigning king of the Neo-Babylonian Empire. Nebuchadnezzar was known as a master builder and as Jeremiah called him, "the destroyer of nations" (Jeremiah 4:7). He destroyed both Judah and Jerusalem during the time of his reign from 604 to 562 B.C. Nebuchadnezzar was used for decades by critics to attack the Bible as accurate history. Literally for thousands of years, the Bible was the only piece of ancient literature that even mentioned his name. Today, nothing could be further from the truth. His named is etched in multiple dozens of artifacts, inscriptions, cuneiform tablets, etc. He is referred to in his own inscriptions and in the Neo-Babylonian Chronicle.

He is biblically referenced in Daniel 1 and 2 Kings 24:1.

43. Nebo-sarsekim, Chief Official of Nebuchadnezzar

Nebo-sarsekim, was a chief official for the king of Babylon—Nebuchadnezzar. He led during the early sixth century. He is mentioned outside the Bible in a cuneiform inscription on a Babylonian clay tablet.

He is biblically referenced in Jeremiah 39:3.

44. Evil-Merodach (Awel marduk, Amel Marduk)

Evil-Merodach is not to be confused with the English word "evil." More appropriate would be Ewil-Merodach. Merodach was the principle deity of Babylon. Evil-Merodach was the son and successor of King Nebuchadnezzar, yet he reigned only two years—562–560 B.C. He is referred to outside the Bible in various inscriptions such as the Babylonian tablets.

He is biblically referred to in 2 King 25:27. He is remembered in Bible history as the Babylonian king who showed mercy to the Judean king, Jehoiachin.

45. Belshazzar, Son and Coregent of Nabonidus

Belshazzar was a Babylonian king who ruled sometime between the years of 543 and 540 B.C. He is the eldest son of Naboidus, the last king of the neo-Babylonian Empire. He is referred to outside the Bible in multiple places. One such place is the Nabonidus Chronicle. Decades of skepticism referred to the Book of Daniel as imaginary literature or worse yet, pure fiction. However, within these last decades archaeological finds have discovered much to confirm the Book of Daniel as accurate history.

He is biblically referenced in Daniel 5:1.

Persia

Persia is the setting for the Book of Esther and the opening setting for the Book of Nehemiah. It is an empire in Southeast Asia created by Cyrus the Great during the sixth century. It was later destroyed by Alexander the Great in the fourth century. King Xerxes ruled over 127 territories for many years, according to Esther 1:1. This vast region once reached from India to Greece and from the Caspian Sea to the Red Sea.

46. Cyrus II (Cyrus the Great)

Cyrus the Great was the king of Persia between 600 and 530 B.C. He is mentioned by name in the Bible more than 23 times. He sanctioned Nehemiah to rebuild the wall around Jerusalem. Cyrus the Great controlled most of the world's kingdoms during his reign and was praised by the Jewish people as a righteous king. He had tremendous military power and was known as a king of high moral and ethical character. He delivered the Jewish people by ending the Babylonian captivity. He is referred to outside the Bible in various inscriptions, one is known as the Cyrus Cylinder.

He is biblically referred to in 2 Chronicles 36:22.

47. Darius I

Darius I was the fourth king of the Babylonian Empire. He reigned 36 years during the years 550–486 B.C. The Persian Empire reached a climatic peak of success during his reign. He is mentioned outside the Bible in multiple places. You can find him referenced in his own inscriptions, one of which is called the trilingual cliff inscriptions at Behistun.

Darius is referred to in Daniel 9:1.

48. Xerxes I (Ahasuerus)

Xerxes I was a king of Persia, and he is referred to as Ahasuerus in the Book of Esther. He led a failed invasion of Greece, even though he was a master builder of great buildings and monuments in the Persian Empire. His mother was Atossa, the daughter of Cyrus the Great. He was assassinated, along with his son, by one of his own ministers. He is referred to outside the Bible in many places such as bowls, other inscriptions, and documents from the time of his reign.

He is biblically referred to in Esther 1:1. Esther was married to Xerxes.

49. Artaxerxes I Longimanus

Artaxerxes I Longimanus was king of Persia between the years 425 and 404 B.C. He was also called Longimanus because his right hand was longer than his left hand. He commissioned Ezra and was the king who asked Nehemiah, "Why are you so sad?" He sent Nehemiah back to Jerusalem. He was the son of Xerxes and was considered a good and kind king. He is referred to outside the Bible in multiple inscriptions and documents during the time of his reign.

He is biblically referenced in Ezra 4:6-7.

50. Darius II (Nothus)

Darius II was the king of Persia and came to rule when Xerxes II was murdered by his brother Secydianus. Ochus, his illegitimate brother, rebelled, fought, and killed him. Ochus then adopted the name Darius II. Some Jewish traditions suggest that he is the only son of Queen Esther. He is referred to outside the Bible in the Elephantine Paypyri and other documents.

He is biblically referenced in Daniel 6:25.

So, you can clearly see that Dr. Lawerence Mykytiuk, the associate professor of Library Science and Historical Literature at Purdue University was correct. As a matter of fact, Dr. Lawrence now suggests that there are 53 documented people! His later articles include three more names—Tattenai, Persian administrator for Darius the Great, Nebuzaradan and Negal-sharezer, two Babylonian warriors who fought for Nebuchadnezzar in the destruction of Jerusalem. Dr. Mykytiuk says, "If you get the person's name, his or her father's name, and the person's office or title, that doesn't verify that they did certain things. However, it can sometimes show that they were in a position to do the things Scriptures say they did."[3]

Now, if the Bible can correctly identify 53 real people by closing itself and then looking toward secondary sources to prove their existence, how much more is the story of John 3:16 in all probability, true also?

---

[3] "Patterns of Evidence, Researcher Uses Evidence to Confirm Existence of 53 People in Bible," September 8, 2017, accessed July 17, 2018. *http://www.patternsofevidence.com/blog/2017/09/08/researcher-uses-evidence-of-53-people-in-the-bible/.*

Lethal Faith

Chapter 3

Gods and Cities of the Old Testament

The trustworthiness of the Holy Scriptures goes much deeper than naming 53 dead people whose names are found on ancient rocks. It even defines correctly the worship of other gods and the cities mentioned in the Bible! The Bible is an amazingly accurate historical document. And if it can be proven to be historically accurate in its description of other gods and biblical cities, then the probability of its spiritual message logically becomes more applicable.

The Bible is also amazingly accurate in its description of the ancient worship of other gods. However, the Bible is clear that there is only one God. Early Israelites were taught the Shema at a very early age. It is the question that we should first train our children, students, and leaders to ask and know: How many gods are there? The answer is, "Only one." This belief is called monotheism. The oldest fixed daily prayer in Judaism is a monotheistic prayer called the Shema. It is found in Deuteronomy 6:4-9: "Hear, O Israel: The Lord our God, the Lord is one!" (v. 4 NKJV). This Jewish prayer was spoken daily as an affirmation of God's singularity. It is considered by many to be the most

73

essential prayer in Judaism. It is part of the climatic end-ing to the prayer on Yom Kippur, and it is the last prayer prayed before death. It is the most essential declaration of the Jewish faith. Isaiah the prophet made it crystal clear when he spoke for God by saying, "I am the first and I am the last; besides me there is no god" (Isaiah 44:6; 45:5 ESV). The psalmist wrote in 86:8, "There is none like you among the gods, O Lord" (ESV). Therefore, when a monotheistic book accurately names the practice of other ancient gods, we should take note.

So, would you not find it interesting that a book which claims there is no other God but Him, could get the worship of other deities correct? Name them by name and describe in detail their principles and places of worship? The Bible even gets the names of its arch-enemies correct!

There are approximately 34 gods mentioned in the Old Testament that were worshiped at different times with-in the history of man. It is important to keep two things in mind when studying the ancient gods. First, there are some possibilities of overlap due to spelling differences in other languages, as well as the transference of gods into differ-ent cultures. Second, "Many of these gods were not simple effigies, but rather a personification of elements of observ-able reality."[1] This is to say that many times a real human such as an emperor or pharaoh was worshiped (deified) as a god. Therefore, take a look at their names, the people who worshiped them, and notice how the Bible mentions certain characteristics of their worship or features. The Bible, on the topic of other gods, is remarkably accurate!

---

[1] Louis Ginzberg and John Deyneley Prince, "Adrammelech," *Jewish En-cyclopedia*, accessed September 12, 2018, *http://www.jewishencyclodpedia.com/articles/856-adremmelech.*

74

1. Adrammelech (old Semitic god)

This god was an idol named Adrammelech and was referred to as a sungod. It was worshiped by the Sepharvites, as recorded in 2 Kings 17:31. This passage mentions the distinct worship of this god, requiring the burnt human sacrifice of infant children. Interestingly, this god is always featured as an idol with a human torso, a mule's head, peacock tail, and limbs of a mule or peacock who offered warmth (sun) and protection for a few burnt infant sacrifices.

This is one god to watch for in archaeological digs since the present literature and archaeological discoveries are extremely limited. "The utmost that can be said is that the word "Adr" occurs in Phoenicia as a god-name in the form יתנאדר, "Itnadr" (Baethgen, "Beiträge zur Semitischen Religionsgeschichte," p. 54), and that "Adr" appears as an epithet in connection with another divine name in the proper name Adarbaal (Baudissin, "Studien zur Semitischen Religions-geschichte," i. 312). There is no essentially Syrian god Adar."[2] That is to say, scholars have yet to discover it's worship and hermeneutically understand the passage historically.

2. Amon (Egyptian god)

This god was a god in human form that came to be seen as a tripart being, (Amon, Ptah, and Re). *Amon* means "hidden one" and was often seen painted in blue, denoting his invisibility. Amon was an Egyptian deity, sun-god, or "god of the wind." He was thought to be one of eight principle deities worshiped in Hermopolis. Amon was characterized as having been self-created,

---

[2] Louis Ginzberg and John Deyneley Prince, "Adrammelech," *Jewish Encyclopedia*, accessed September 12, 2018, *http://www.jewishencyclodpedia.com/ articles/856-adremmelech.*

a champion of the poor, and a god of fertility. Amon was often seen in the image of a ram's head or a ram. Jeremiah 46:25 mentions Amon. As the princes of Thebes revitalized its worship, they connected Amon to the political well-being of Egypt. Archaeologists have confirmed its worship in multiple places and on multiple objects as a stele of worship seen at the Petric Museum of Egyptian Archaeology in London, the temple of Dier el Medina, and Amenhoteps III's statue at the British Museum in London. In addition, there is a Granite statue of Amon in the form of a ram protecting King Taharqa of the 25th dynasty, 690–664 BCE, as well as a dioritic statue of a priest of Amon from Thebes, Egypt, 381–362 BCE in the Brooklyn Museum in New York.[3]

3. Anammelech

See Adrammelech: Anammelech was the female counterpart to the god Adrammelech. She was considered to be the "moon goddess." Her name meant "Anu is King"; descriptively, she had the same characteristics as Adrammelech. She is referenced in 2 Kings 17:31. While there is debate as to whether the Babylonians ever engaged in child sacrifice, scholars know that child sacrifice was a reality during ancient biblical times, and the Bible places this ritual with the Samarians.

> [Anammelech was] a god worshiped by the Sepharvites in Samaria under the Assyrian régime, along with the god Adrammelech (2 Kings, 17:31). Anu was the chief of the old Babylonian trinity, Anu, Bel, and Ea; and if Sepharvaim (compare *ib.* 24) is Sippara in North Babylonia (not Sepharvaim in Syria, 2 Kings, 19:13), as is very probable, there is no difficulty in supposing that Anu was there and worshiped under this appellation.[4]

---

[3] Britannica Encyclopedia, eds. "Amon, Egyptian God," *Britannica Encyclopedia,* accessed September 15, 2018, *http://www.britannica.com/topic/Amon.*

[4] J. Frederic McCurdy, "Anammelech," *Jewish Encyclopedia*, accessed 9-12=18, *http://www.jewishencyclopedia.com/articles/856-anammelech.*

The worship of this god is attested to in the Babylonian Talmud. The Talmud teaches (Sanh. 63*b*) that Adrammelech was an idol of the Sepharvaim in the shape of an ass.

4. **Asherah (Asherim)**

Asherah was the Canaanite mother goddess that has been worshiped by many people within the Mediterranean world. She is referenced in Judges 6:25-26, 28, 30; 2 Chronicles 19:3; 1 Kings 14:23, Exodus 34:13 in both male and female plural forms. Usually, she is characteristically associated with lions, serpents, and sacred trees. As the mother of Baal, she was often carved into the image of a wooden pole. Her name and image is mentioned in the Old Testament more than 40 times, often being referred to as the "Queen of the Sea" or the "Queen of Heaven" (Jeremiah 7:16-18). Some were erroneously led to suggest that she, because of Israel's polytheistic rebellion, worshiped her with Yahweh; thus, they concluded that Asherah was the wife of God. Her features are found in archaeological artifacts such as on the pithos sherd, found at Kuntillet Arjud, on many Asherah poles, which can be seen at the National Maritime Museum in Israel, as well as the "Four Tier Cult" stand found at Tanaach, seen in the Israel museum.

Originally, the name Asherah in the Old Testament did not refer to a goddess, but to an object, since its name means an object. The discovery of the Ras Shamra material, "which definitely established the identity of a goddess Asherah. Indeed, most scholars hold this view."[5]

5. **Ashima**

Ashima, the male god, is often referred to as the "god of fate." The Hammath in Syria worshiped him and often referenced him as a "short-haired goat." He is mentioned only once in the Old Testament and is still today very elusive, since little is known about its worship, characteristics, or features outside what is mentioned in 2 Kings 17:30.

It is probable that Ashima was related to the goddess Damkina, Shimti, and Ishtar in the Akkadian culture. "The late Assyrian Gotteradressbuchl locates Ea-the king, Damkina, Ishara,

---

[5] Judith M. Hadley, *The Cult of Asherah in Ancient Israel and Judah: Evidence for a Hebrew Goddess* (Cambridge, UK: University of Cambridge, 2000), 7.

Qingu, Malik, and Urgurtu all in the house of Ea-the-king," thus locating its worship in one of many places."[6]

6. Ashtoreth (Ashtaroth)

This female deity is known by many names which all were grounded in the root word for her name. The root of Ashtoreth's name is "shame." She is called Aphrodite to the Babylonians, Venus to the Greeks, Astarte to the Hebrews, and Isis to the Egyptians. Her name was a familiar name to the Syrians, Phoenicians, and Canaanites. They worshiped her as the god of love, fertility, the evening/morning star, and war. She was often characterized with the features or image of a lion, horse, sphinx, dove, or a star within a circle. She is predominantly characterized as a beautiful, naked woman, often with a set of bull horns on her head which was a sign of dominance and power. She is mentioned in 1 Kings 11:5 as a god that Solomon reintroduced directly before his own death to the Hebrew people. Archaeology has confirmed these features in many places such as the Julia Maesa coin from Sidon, on a stele with King Thutmose IV, seen at the Petri Museum of Egyptian Archaeology of London, and a piece called "Lady Galera," at the National Archaeological Museum of Spain.

Historians say, "the identities of the three great Canaanite goddesses—Asherah, Astarte, and Anat—have become quite fluid. Indeed, this tendency toward fusion begins quite early, as evidenced, for example, on the Winchester College plaque published by I.E.S. Edwards."[7]

7. Baal

The name Baal means "lord" and appears in the Old Testament more than 90 times. He is also referred to by the name, "lord of the earth," "lord of rain and dew," "lord of heaven," "king of gods," or the "one who rides on the clouds." His root name is found in the meaning to "own or possess." It was the people of Syria, Phoenicia, and Canaan who worshiped him. He was characterized by standing on a bull as a sign of strength. His worship was characteristically seen as a symbol of a "sacred marriage." He was offered

[6] W.G. Lambert, *Babylonian Creation Myths* (Winona Lake, Indiana: Eisenbrauns, 2013), 224.

[7] "The Queen Mother of the Cult in the Ancient Near East," in *Women and Goddess Traditions in Antiquity and Today*, ed. Karen L. King (Minneapolis: Fortress Press, 1997), 189.

child sacrifices as the god of "lightning," "wind," "rain," and "fertility." His biblical features are confirmed, not only in 2 Kings 10:18-23, 25-28; Romans 11:4, but also in the arch stele of Baal at the ruins of Ugarit and discovered on a bronze figure found at Ras Shamra, which can be seen at the Louvre Museum.

The name Baal took on many different names as a storm god. You can see a stele rendering of this storm god on a "sixteenth–fifteenth century relief of the Great Stele of Baal" earthed at Ugarit and published by Claude Shaeffer...In a very broad sense, the Syrian storm-god is geographically and conceptually related to the other great storm gods of Mesopotamia and the Anatolian Plateau."[8]

8. Baal-berith (El-berith)

His name meant "lord of the covenant." He was worshiped by the people of Israel directly after the death of Gideon. Baal-berith is mentioned in Judges 8:33, 9:4 as being worshiped by the people of Shechem who lived in Canaan. He was characterized by being the god of fertility and vegetations. Worship to him was lewd and sexually vile as men would engage in sexual acts with temple prostitutes, believing that rain would come to the land when the semen of men flowed. His worship too was characterized by Baal-Zebub "lord of the flies." This Baal was worshiped as having the features of a fly. Those who worshiped him would carry around an icon image of a "fly," pulling it out of their pockets, and then kissing it for good luck. The temple mentioned in the Book of Judges chapter 9 has been discovered by archaeologists at the acropolis of Shechem where they spent nearly 50 years in excavations.[9]

---

[8] Alberto R.W. Green, "Syria: The Upper Country," in *The Storm-God in the Ancient Near East*, vol. 8, *Biblical and Judaic Studies Volume* (Winona Lake, Indiana: Eisenbrauns, 2003), 165.

[9] G.R.H. Wright, "Temple at Schechem," *Zeitschrift fur die Alttestamentliche Wissenschaft* 80 (January 1968): 1.

9. Baal-Peor

His name meant "lord of the gap." Peor was actually a mountain in Moab; thus, he was called "lord of the gap." The people who worshiped him were the Moabites, and unfortunately at times the Israelites, as mentioned in Numbers 25:3, 5. While there was no one characteristic of this god, scholars do know he was a symbol of vile, sexual perversion in worship. He was characterized as a sun god, or fertility god, and worshiped with obscene sexual rites. Some biblical scholars suggest that he was worshiped through the excretion of bodily fluids such as human feces. People assumed that since feces could be a fertilizer for an agricultural project, feces could then be a sacrificial offering to the god Baal-Peor. His features are confirmed in the writings found in the temple of Ugarit and in the Ras Shamra texts.

10. Baal-Zebub

The name *Baal-Zebub* means, "Lord of the flies," and it stands as one of the most well-known gods of the Bible. He was worshiped in Ekron by the people called the Philistines. His characteristic image is interesting because of its possible dualistic meaning. On one hand, he is the "lord" who watches over the flies and protects the people's crop production as their god. However, he is a god of the flies, which lends itself to the use of the word as a possible insult to the Philistines by the Hebrew people, "god of the flies." Further, insulting them because of their dung sacrifices to the god of Baal, which in return attracts flies with its dung. He is characterized as the "lord of the dung." He is featured in 2 Kings 1:2-3, 6, 16; Matthew 12:25-28. He is even used as a proper name for Satan himself in Matthew 10:25. Baal worship is well confirmed in the history of archaeology, yet much is yet to be discovered as to its rites and practices.[10]

11. Bel

The name Bel is thought to be a shorter term for Baal and means "lord" or "master of the house." However, there are some scientists who believe that Bel, even though it was the basis for Baal worship, was a distinct divinity. He is referred to in Isaiah 46:1 and Jeremiah 50:2 as being the principle god worshiped by

---

[10] T. Gaster, "Ras Shamra 1929-39," *Antiquity* 13 (January 1939).

the Moabites, Babylonians, and Ammonites. The people of Assyria and Babylonia worshiped this god from the earliest of times. Bel was the leading god among the Phoenicians. Later, Bel merged with the worship of Marduk and became the same entity. There was a temple of Bel located in the Syrian city of Palmya. The Palmyrenes associated the sun and moon gods with the worship of Bel in an almost trinitarian form. Bel was said to be the "god of order" who presided over the movement of the stars. The archaeological remains of Bel worship are many. However, due to the unfortunate rise of ISIS in Syria, much of the Temple of Bel in Palmyra has been destroyed. "In addition to his own name, Marduk takes on many others, for example, those of other divinities with whom he was identified. The most important are Asalluhi, the name of an ancient Sumerian divinity of incantations, one of the sons of enki; and the Semitic title Bel, meaning "lord," which became almost a proper name of Marduk in the first millennium."[11]

12. Castor/Pollux (Dioscuri: twin brothers)

These Greek gods were half-twins and named Castor and Pollux. Castor was identified by horsemanship as Pollux was identified by boxing. In mythology, their father was Zeus and their mother was Leda. In Latin, the twins were known as Gemini—the two brightest stars in the galaxy. When Castor was killed, Pollux asked Zeus if he could own Pollux's immortality by combining their two spirits. Thus, he transformed them into the constellation Gemini. They were worshiped by the Greeks and Roman people. They are characterized in Iconography as being associated with horses, sailors, horsemanship and referred to in Acts 28:11 as having been carved on the front of ancient ships. Their features are confirmed in many places in antiquities. Such features are found in ancient symbolism for twinhood, like, two-upright pieces of wood connected to two crosses, pairs of shields, bottles, or snakes. In some images they are portrayed wearing skull caps, which are images of egg shells which came from the myth that they were hatched from the womb of Leda.

---

[11] Ivan Hrusa, "Principles of Mesopotamian Divinities," in *Ancient Mesopotamian Religion*, trans. Michael Tait (Buch-und Medienhandel GmbH, Munster: Ugarit-Verlag, 2015), 57.

The Temple of Castor and Pollux can be seen in Rome, as well as their images in multiple museums throughout the world.

In the annals of antiquities, scholars found a victory poem written by Pindar in praise of a wrestling match by Theaius of Argos during a festival of Hera at Argos. Pindar "tells the story of the friendship of the divine twins Castor and Polydeuces, who had once been entertained by ancestors of Theaius and whose patronage of his family might enable him to win a victory at Olympia."[12] This is just one of the many ways history confirms the worship of this god.

13. Chemosh

The name Chemosh means "handling, stroking, or to take away." His name implied, "destroyer, subduer, or fish god." He was worshiped by the Moabites and Ammonites (1 Kings 11:7). King Solomon, at the request of some of his wives, caused him to bring the worship of Chemosh to Jerusalem and build a temple in his honor. He was characterized by human sacrifices. He is attested to in the Moabite Stone where he is mentioned nearly nine times. This stone was discovered in Dibon and can be seen in the British Museum. In this Moabite Stone, "Chemosh receives mention as the deity who brought victory over the Israelites to the Moabites."[13]

14. Dagon

The name Dagon is believed to mean "grain." However, this has been a hotly debated subject for many years since others believe that Dagon was a "fish god," because the name Dagon is similar to the Semitic word for fish. He was known too as the "god of gods." The people who worshiped him, such as the Amorites, Philistines, and the people of Ebla and Ugarit, saw him as a fertility god related to grain and agriculture, while the sea people saw him as the fish god. He is characterized in Scripture as being the god of the temple which Samson pushed down by the pillars (Judges 16:22-29; 1 Samuel 5:2-5, 7). He was often characterized as a "plowman." He

---

[12] Simon Price, *Religions of the Ancient Greeks: Key Themes in Ancient History* (Cambridge, England: Cambridge University, 1999), 43.

[13] *The Britannica Encyclopedia of World Religions*, ed. Jacob E. Safra (London: Britannica Encyclopedia, 2006), 196.

is featured in historical artifacts such as being on the walls of Khorsabad, and on the slabs of Konyunjik as half fish and half man.

There has been much debate as to the plural paternity of Baal in archaeological thought; however, the Ugaritic tablets also speak of Baal as "son of Dagon."

> The designation "Baal, son of Dagan" thus served the Ugaritic author of the Baal Cycle to distinguish Baal from El's family—as well as making Dagon Baal's "positive" father— albeit only in the most nominal sense, without playing any active role. In Ugarit, however, these circumstances occurred only in the Baal Cycle.[14]

Once again, ancient history proves the worship of the god, Baal of Dagon.

15. Diana/Artemis

The name Diana was also famously known as Artemis and meant to be "prompt" or "safe." Her name is synonymous with the name Artemis, and the two names came to be known interchangeably in mythological worship. Her name in Latin means "sky" or "daylight," which may explain why some would come to see her as being related to the moon and connected to Luna. She was worshiped by the people of Ephesus in Greece (modern-day Turkey) and seen as a patron to the lower-class citizens called plebeians. It was also in Ephesus where a Temple of Diana was built, taking at least 220 years to build. This may be one reason why they called it one of the "Seven Wonders of the World." She is characterized in multiple ways such as a virgin goddess who never married, thus the god to whom women prayed for protection as they conceived and gave birth. She was seen as a fertility god, whose statues are covered in multiple breasts. This may be one reason why the people of Ephesus so gravitated to Christian worship, because John moved Mary to Ephesus.

Diana was seen also as the goddess of the wild animals and the hunt. It was believed that she had the power to speak to them and control their behaviors. As the twin of Apollo she was featured as youthful and beautiful, often being carved, painted

---

[14] Noga Ayali-Darshan, "Baal, Son of Dagon: In Search of Baal's Double Paternity," *The Journal of Oriental Studies* 133, No. 4 (Oct-Dec 2013), 651–57.

in a short tunic and hunting boots, with a crescent moon worn as a diadem. Many times she is featured by hunting with a bow and quiver, accompanied by a deer or hound. This virgin goddess is mentioned in Acts 19:24, 27-28, 34-35.

The worship of Artemis is attested in both the Odyssey and the Illiad. A temple was dedicated to her worship in the ancient biblical city of Ephesus which the early church used her stones to build much of the church of Saint John.[15]

16. Gad

The name Gad means "fortune" or "happiness." Gad was eventually called simply "Fortune." This god was worshiped by the people of Israel which was characterized by the making of vows, providing protection, thus being strong and exalted as a father and a king. He is featured in Isaiah 65:11 and can be seen on a relief discovered in Dura-Europos, as well as a fresco found at the Palmyra Temple. These Dura-Europos exhibits related to Gad are usually found traveling the country after a Harvard archaeologist discovered them in the late 1920s.

Interestingly, "an altar from Nabataean Hauran was found in the 19th century that included a dedicatory inscription by individuals who refer to themselves as Rhmygd "friends of Gad" (Littman 1904:93-94). Significantly, Gad here is simply "the Gad," not Gad of so and so. His identity is thus obvious enough for the educators that no further specifications was necessary."[16]

17. The Golden Calf

The worship of the golden calf is believed to have originated in the land of Egypt, where Israel began its worship after the Exodus (Exodus 32:4). Its worship is mentioned throughout the Bible in Nehemiah 9:16-21; 1 Kings 12:26-30. The original worship of the golden calf is founded upon the calf worship of Egypt, whose chief deity was called Apis. The worship of Apis, the bull, was consecrated in the region of Memphis as a bull who was con-

---

[15] Emily Kearns, *Ancient Greek Religion* (Chichester, West Sussex: Wiley-Blackwell, 2010), 45, 57, 336.

[16] Ryan Thomas, "Gad," Religion of Ancient Palestine, accessed September 25, 2018, *http://www.religionofancientpalestine.com/?p=488*.

ceived by a "bolt of lightning from heaven." Both the Egyptian people and children of Israel were found to worship the image of a calf. The golden calf Apis is often characterized by the image of a bull with a sun-disk between its horns. Apis was seen as the manifestation of the god Ptah upon the earth. Therefore, it featured the elements of strength, fertility, and a fighting spirit of a king. The Egyptians worshiped the calf deity with furious loyalty and extravagant measures, celebrating both its birth and death days on the calendar. Once the bull reached the age of 25, it was killed and thrown into a well. Then lavishly mummified and defied at great cost. Its image is well-featured in the annals of antiquities in multiple places. Two such places are the bronze features found in the British Museum and a statue located at the Louvre museum.

Recently, a team of Harvard archaeologists made history by discovering something the world had never seen—a golden calf. "The small icons were central to the Canaanite religion that flourished in Ashkelon and Israel during the second millennium B.C. And as the Old Testament makes clear, calf worship was anathema to the early Jews. Yet until now, no modern scholar has actually seen a bull-calf idol of this kind. That changed dramatically recently, when a team of Harvard University archeologists announced the serendipitous discovery of a tiny statue in the ruins of the ancient Canaanite city of Ashkelon. The figurine, just four and a half inches tall and made from bronze, copper, and silver was found almost perfectly intact in the rubble of a buried temple. Lawrence Stager, leader of the Harvard team, declared it the finest piece of Canaanite metalwork ever recovered in Israel. After studying the relic, the researchers will turn it over to the Israel Museum in Jerusalem."[17]

18. Jupiter

The god Jupiter became synonymous with the god, Zeus. The name *Jupiter* means "father that helpeth" or "heavenly father." The word Jupiter refers to the "god of the heaven or sky and is rooted in the more simple form of "jove." It is this word from

---

[17] Newsweek, "Yes, Virginia, There Was a Golden-calf," *Newsweek* 116, no. 6 (8/6/1990), 7.

which we get our English word "jovial"; hence, Jupiter's align-ment with the idea of "jolly, jovial, optimistic." Jupiter is actu-ally where we get our present form of the word for Thursday. Often known as the "king of gods," Jupiter was the twin of Juno and worshiped as the supreme god of both the Greeks and Ro-mans. In mythology, Jupiter was the chief member of the Capi-toline Triad. He is characterized by a thunderbolt, eagle, light-ning, and is referenced in Acts 14:12. The features of Jupiter are unique because it is a god who has a distinct moral concep-tion. Jupiter was seen as being the god of "oaths, treaties, and leagues." The priests of Jupiter were present during marriages as a representation of such a god of laws and orders. Jupiter's features can be confirmed in multiple places, two of which are the Neo-Attic relief, at the National Archaeological Museum in Madrid and in the form of statues seen at the Vatican Museum.

As previously stated many gods morphed into other names and into other cultures, Jupiter was no exception. "For the Ro-mans, Jupiter Optimus Maximus was the most important god of Rome, the ultimate protector of the city, whose favor was re-sponsible for the growth and might of Rome. Her image can be found throughout the old Roman Empire...The largest temple (in Corinth) flanking the main square was almost certainly a temple of the Capitoline triad, Jupiter, Juno and Minerva."[18] Not only does the Scripture get the worship of Jupiter correct, even the cities of the Bible confirm she was worshiped among the ancient people.

19. Kalwan (Chiun)

The name Kalwan is actually uncertain; however, some believe that it is rooted in a word meaning, "detestable things" or "ped-estal" and "idol." Kalwan (Chiun) was worshiped by the people of Babylon with the characteristics of being the "king of gods," and "ruler of heaven of all other gods." To the Greeks, Chiun was proba-bly the worship of the planet Saturn. The Phoenicians offered Chi-un both human and child sacrifices. Star worship is well-attested to in many archaeological finds such as the 11,000-year-old Gobekli Tepe, located in modern-day Turkey where they worshiped the dog star known as Sirius.

---

[18] Price, *Religions of the Ancient*, 150,157–58.

20. Meni (Destiny)

The name *Meni* means "to number, count, appoint, or tell." Its name furthermore, carries the idea of destiny. Meni was worshiped by the Israelites and was considered with his counterpart Gad, to be apostate Jews. Little is known about these two gods, and they are practically unknown in extrabiblical sources (sources outside the Bible). The backslidden Jewish people would sit both wine and food in front of the idol as a sacrifice. However, older writers believed that this was a sun god.

> The word Meni, which has produced the Greek (ynv), is derived from a Hebrew root, which signifies to number, because the motion of the sun serves to number time. And because the moon serves for the same purpose, it is derived from the same root for its Greek name of (Myvn). To prove further that Meni is the sun—the first king of the Egyptians—from whom came the religion of the Greeks, was named Men, according to Herodotus, Book 2, Chapter 9 and 99, and that first king of the Egyptians was the sun, according to Diodorus, Book one, from when the Egyptians gave the name Men or Menis, to the god Orus, which is the sun.[19]

It is important to note that when one finds a place, person, thing, or cultural practice in the Bible and such things have not yet been confirmed by extrabiblical sources, do not let it damage one's faith. The truth is that every time this has happened in the past, the spade of the archaeologist eventually ends up falling on the truth of the historical narrative of the Bible. Just ask about the Hittites!

21. Mercury/Hermes

The name *Mercury* in Latin means, "commerce, merchandise, trade, wages"; therefore, he is called the "god of commerce." He is worshiped as Mercury among the Romans and known as Hermes among the Greeks. He is characterized by snakes intertwined on his staff, winged sandals, and with the powers of being swift. He serves as the guide of souls to the underworld,

---

[19] David Henry, "Explanation of Gad and Meni, Mentioned by Isaiah," *The Gentlemen's Magazine: and Historical Chronicle* 41 (January 1771), 10–12.

and had no priest assigned to him as a god. He was believed in mythology to have invented the lyre. He is featured in Acts 14:12 and in history in many places. Two such places are the ruins of the Villa of the Papyri, where they found a statue of a seated Hermes and a Kriophoros Hermes seen at the Barracco Museum, as well as at the Louvre in Paris, where one can see a Mercury statue that shows his winged sandals.

Originally, he was a god of riches, but became a patron of travelers and thieves. The French for Wednesday, *mercedi*, derives from his name. His main annual festival, the Mercuralia, took place in Rome in May, and his statues were frequently placed as boundary markers. [20]

22. Merodach/Marduk

Merodach means "bitter" or "contrition." His name was originally Ea. His name was to mean "calf of the sun" or "solar calf," indicating his power came from the sun. He was the patron god of the Babylonians and was seen as the war god, or god of the canals, or possibly even the planet Mars. He was said to have defeated all earlier gods to form and populate earth. He is often characterized by tongues of fire which proceed out of his mouth, with a horned creature at his feet, a symbol of Ea. Considered to be the wisest of all gods and thus linked to more than fifty additional names. He was referred to by the Babylonians, especially Nebuchadnezzar. He is featured in Jeremiah 50:2, and in multiple inscriptions. The Nebuchadnezzar inscription found at Babylon mentions Merodach multiple times and is now housed in the India House Collection. His more primitive form is found in the Seven Tablets of Creation, housed at the British Museum. Furthermore, worship of Marduck is attested by the celebration of his main festival, the akitu, "performed at New Year, which continued up to as late as 200 B.C. It was performed by the Persian ruler Cambyses circa 538 B.C. Marduk's sanctuary in Babylon is the Esagila and the E-temen-anki ziggurat."[21]

---

[20] Michael Jordan, *Encyclopedia of Gods: Over 2,500 Deities of the World* (New York: Facts on File, 1993), 163.

[21] Ibid., 158.

23. Milcom (Malcham, Malcam)

Milccom is the god of the Ammonites and means "their king." He is characterized by a bronze statue of a calf-head, adorned with a royal crown and seated on a throne. He is mentioned four times in the Bible (1 Kings 11:5, 33; 2 Kings 23:13; Zephaniah 1:5), three of which are by Solomon who brought its worship to the Israelite people. There are some who say that Milcom is the same god as Molech, but this doesn't appear to be true in the Scriptures, because they are worshiped separately. While it may be possible that Milcom is another form of worship of a god named Molech, the two are separated here for study. Milcom worship included both human and child sacrifices among the Ammonites. In Ammon (Jordan) today, there has been recent discoveries that confirmed such practices.

24. Molech (Moloch)

The name *Molech* is believed to mean "king." Molech was worshiped by the Ammonites as the "destroyer," "consumer," or "fire god." Molech was characterized by the face of a calf, ox, man, and head of a bull or owl. Molech was known for child sacrifices, and the biblical references point toward "passing children through the fire" (2 Kings 16:3). In the ancient city of Carthage (Tunisia), an altar was found where they sacrificed children to Molech. In addition, a thirteenth-century B.C. temple has been discovered in Amman, Jordan, where skulls of both adults and children were discovered at the altar.

It is usually assumed that the cult of Molech involved sacrificing the children by throwing them into a raging fire. Our point here is not whether there were child sacrifices in ancient Israel, but whether this particular sacrifice existed, i.e., throwing them into the fire. It is not denied that children were at one time sacrificed as whole offerings: 2 Kings 3:6, where the writer evidently believed that such sacrifices were effective, even if made to a god other than the God of Israel.[22]

---

[22] N.H. Snaith, "The Cult of Molech," *Vetus Testamentum* 16, no. 1 (1966), 123–24.

25. Nebo (Nabu)

The name *Nebo* means to "call" or to "elevate." The origins of this word brought the meaning of "elevation," or "height." Nebo was worshiped by the Chaldean people of Babylon and Assyria. He was characterized by being the "god of writing" and was believed to be the inventor of writing. His symbol was that of a stylus that rested on a tablet, wearing a horned cap, with hands clasped. This gesture of the hands is typical of a portrait of a priest. Nebo was the god of writing, speech, literature, and arts. Nebo was the ancient deity of wisdom and writing, and he is featured in the Bible in Isaiah 46:1 and Jeremiah 48:1. Such features can be seen at a temple ruins at Birs Nimrud and as a statue of Nebo found at Calah, now shown at the British Museum. "A major deity in neo-Babylonian times from the eighth century B.C. onward, with an important sanctuary at Borshippa, near Babylon, known as Ezida."[23]

26. Nehustan

Nehustan is a name of a god which means "a mere brazen thing," or a "piece of brass." This bronze image was a derogatory name given to the snake on a pole that Moses lifted up (2 Kings 18:4). The people of Israel worshiped this image and its characteristics have been found in multiple pre-Israelite cities found in Canaan.

> Two bullae are believed to date from late eighth-century Judah that feature the winged uraeus (serpent). Each seems to have been the royal seal for a specific city named in the bulla. The one on the left reads: "Tza'ananim, belonging to the king") and the one on the right reads ("[A]pheka, belonging to the king"). Both cities are mentioned in the Bible.

Credit: Robert Deutsch, "Six Hebrew Fiscal Bullae from the Time of Hezekiah.[24]

---

[23] Jordan, *Encyclopedia of Gods*, 174.

[24] Richard Lederman, "Nehustan, the Copper Serpent: Its Origins and Fate," Torah: A Historical and Contextual Approach, accessed October 10, 2018, *http://www.thetorah.com/nehustan-the-copper-serpent-its-origin-and-fate/*.

27. Nergal

The name *Nergal* means "dunghill cock." He was worshiped by Mesopotamian people of Akkad, Assyria, and Babylon. He is characterized in 2 Kings 17:30 and is often seen in the image of a cock or a "destroying flame." He was also seen as a war and hunting god, a lion, or a specific sun god of noontime. This "king of the sunset," over time the "King of the underworld," was often symbolized by a male figure, carrying a scimitar or a mace, often topped with a double lion's head. He is featured in fragments of vessels found in the Temple of Nergal in Nineveh. One can see these fragments at the British Museum. Furthermore, one can see these mythical images at Kudurru of the Kassite, King Meli-Sipak at the Louvre Museum, and in the remains of his sanctuary in Mari (Tell al-Harir). [25]

28. Nibhaz

Nibhaz is a name which means "the barker." Nibhaz was worshiped by the Avvites and is referred to in 2 Kings 17:31. While little is known regarding Nibhaz, it is believed that such worship started in Egypt since they worshiped the deity of a dog too, (Anubis). This Avvite's god took the form of a dog and man. His head and feet were that of a dog, while his legs and arms where that of a man. His thighs and legs were covered with scales and he was crowned with a tiara on his head. His arms were crossed upon his breast and his fingers were clinched, all of which were known symbols of Nibhaz. There is archaeological evidence that this god was worshiped.[26]

---

[25] Ancient Mesopotamian Gods and Goddesses Project, "Nergal (god)," Ancient Mesopotamian Gods and Goddesses, accessed October 10, 2018, *http://www.oracc.museum.upenn.edu/amgglistofdeities/nergal/index.html*.

[26] D.T. Potts, *The Archaeology of Elam: Formation and Transformation of the Ancient Iranian State* (Cambridge, UK: Cambridge University, 2016), 296.

29. The Queen of Heaven (Ishtar, Inanna, Astarte)

Ishtar originally meant to "lead one," or "great lady of An." She was one of the most attested goddesses in ancient Mesopotamia where she originated as Inanna. She was worshiped by the Akkadians, Babylonians, and Assyrians as the goddess of beauty, sex, love, desire, fertility, war, justice, and political power. She was known as the "Queen of Heaven," never to be mistaken as a "Mother-goddess," since she was often seen as a jealous, vengeful god who would go to war, destroy fields, and make creatures infertile. This patron god of the Eanna temple in Uruk was often associated with the planet Venus. She was characterized by a lion, or eight-pointed star, and at times within a reed bundle gatepost. Furthermore, characterized by sexual temple prostitution that was referred to in antiquities as "sacred prostitution," with a meaning we still are trying to understand today. Such sexual prostitution is believed to possibly include homosexual transvestite priests, since the remaining artifacts point to genderless priests. She is well-featured in history in dozens of places such as the fragment images of Inanna at Nippur, entire front columns of the Babylonian temple of Ishtar discovered at Uruk, boundary stones at Meli-Shipak II, and lion plaques that made up the gates of Ishtar constructed by Nebuchadnezzar II (Pergamum Museum, Berlin). She is featured as well in Jeremiah 7:18; 44:17, 18, 19, 25. This myth closely follows "the Semitic descent of Ishtar to the Nether Regions" inscribed on Akkadian tablets dating from the first millennium B.C.[27]

30. Rimmon (Ramanu)

The name *Rimmon* originated as a name in Hebrew for pomegranate and as thunder in Akkad. Rimmon was worshiped by the Assyrians as the weather god. Often known as the god

[27] E.O. James, *The Ancient Gods: The History and Diffusion of Religion in the Ancient Near East and the Eastern Mediterranean* (New York: G.P. Putnam's Sons, 1960), 79.

Baal, lord excellence, he was the god of storms and thunder and a version of Hadad. He is featured in only 2 Kings 5:18 and other knowledge about him is illusive. The city Rimmon, a city named after this god, has been discovered, 1 km south of Tell Halif. However, his name is greatly attested in ancient literature.

> The Kurkh Monolith and Black Obelisk refer to the campaign of (Shalmeneser II) . . . Now, the first two characters from the well-known group expressing the name of the air god, Rimmon...The number of names by which the god Rimmon was known in Assyria and Babylonia was very great, and one list gives no less than forty-one words, all expressing this god.[28]

31. Sikkuth

The name *Sikkuth* is believed to have originally meant, "tent or booth." Some scholars suggest that it came from the Hebrew word Sukkot-Benoth, "daughter's tent," since this deity is female. Sikkuth was worshiped by the Babylonians as a Saturn god and star deity. Little is known about this deity mentioned in Amos 5:26 where some had identified her as the god Ninurta, or the Syrian war god, Adar, also called Sakkut.

> Because of a mistaken belief that the god Sikkuth was not introduced until after the Assyrian conquest (see 2 Kings 17:30), there has been an attempt to amend the Hebrew so that the text is read "shrine" or "abode" of the king. In fact, Amos's statement probably reflects the degree of cultural influence exercised by Aramean merchants and other travelers known to the Israelites. Sikkuth or d SAG.KUD is associated with Ninurta in Ugaritic sources and specifically with the planet Saturn.[29]

---

[28] Society of Biblical Archaeology, *The Proceeding of the Society of Biblical Archaeology: November 1882–June 1883* (London: Harrison and Sons, 1883), 71–72.

[29] The IVP Bible Background Commentary, "Amos Background Commentary," Rochester PDF, accessed October 10, 2018, http://www.pas.rochester.edu/~tim/study/Amos%20IVP%20Background%20Commentary.pdf.

32. Succoth-Benoth

The precise meaning of the name Succoth-Benoth is unknown. However, the primitive meaning is "booths of daughters." She was worshiped by the Babylonians as a goddess of baby deities. Similar to so many other gods, Succoth-Benoth was rooted in sexual perversions using temple prostitutes and the worship of phallic feasts. Succoth-Benoth was known as a place where women abandon themselves to impure rites under "booths" or "tents." The names of many gods can be confusing due to the Hebrew practice of mutating or mutilating their names as a way to express disgust. Her features are referred to in 2 Kings 17:30. Interestingly, while there is no cuneiform archaeological evidence of this god today, this passage contains the most gods listed in one place! Whereas all the other gods have been confirmed by the archaeological evidence. So look for this god, Succoth-Benoth to show up soon in the evening news!

33. Tammuz (Dumuzid)

The name *Tammuz* in its root means to "conceal or to consume." Tammuz carried the meaning as the "sprout of life." He was worshiped by the Babylonians, Samaritans, and eventually the Greeks in a different form. This god was originally known as Dumuzid or the "sun-god." He is characterized later as a fertility god, "the flawless youth," the "power of grain," and symbolized as an array of vegetables, matter, honey, and varieties of food. This symbolism of vegetation was what enforced the belief that Tammuz was the god of death and resurrection. Death being winter and spring/summer being resurrection—a time when fruit and vegetation would arrive again safely. It was this part of the myth that led people to mourn Tammuz's death. Tammuz was believed to be the lover and consort of Ishtar. Ishtar mourned his death when he was killed as a beautiful shepherd who was slain by a boar, the symbol of winter. It became a custom to weep for Tammuz among Babylonian women on the second day of the fourth month. Ezekiel 8:14 confirms this practice of weeping for Tammuz. Tammuz is featured in antiquities in multiple places such as the Erotic terracotta, Sacred Marriage relief, the Amorite, Ancient Mesopotamian relief which is housed at the Louvre museum in Paris, as well as in the Tammuz alabaster relief from Ashur,

Staatliche Museum in Berlin. Furthermore, in S. Langdon's book from 1914, he looks at the writings of an ancient Babylonian community, and their writings clearly demonstrate the worship of Tammuz.[30]

34. Tartak

The name *Tartak* means to be "chained, bound, or shut-up." Tartak came to be known as the "prince of darkness." He was worshiped by the Avvites in the form of a donkey. While he is mentioned in 2 Kings 17:31, a real historical understanding of him is illusive. While modern archaeology does not speak of him, early archaeologists do speak of having identified him. He has been identified by Hommel as being listed with the deity Dakdadra, an Elamite deity.[31] This is yet another god to keep a look out for as the archaeological spade will once again prove the Bible's historical narrative to be true.

At our best estimation there are 34 gods mentioned in the Scriptures. There are at least three that remain obscure by the archaeological spade. Therefore, 31 gods or idols mentioned in the Scriptures can be confirmed by history. The Scripture is an amazingly accurate book as it describes the ancient practices of worship.

Cities mentioned in the Scriptures are also amazingly accurate.

---

[30] S. Langdon, *Tammuz and Ishtar: A Monograph Upon Babylonian Religion and Theology: Containing Extensive Extracts from the Tammuz Liturgies and All of the Arbela Oracles* (London: Oxford University, 1914), 21–22.

[31] Editor James K. Hoffmeier and Alan Millard, *Future Biblical Archaeology: Reassessing Methodologies and Assumptions* (Grand Rapids, Michigan: Eerdmans Publishing, 2004), 263.

The Amazing Accuracy in Naming Biblical Cities

If the Bible were not true, we would see its error through the many cities, cultures, and towns it mentions. How does a book with multiple different authors on three different continents and languages not make a mistake regarding the existence of specific cities? How can 39 books accurately define specific cities within the Bible? The very fact that the Bible mentions the existence of 85 cities in just the Old Testament can lend credence to its trustworthiness.

There are at least 85 cities mentioned in the Old Testament. "Because of archaeology, and the discovery of ancient monuments and scrolls; and because scholars can now read cuneiform and hieroglyphics, startling new dimensions help us to see Moses, Joshua, Nebuchadnezzar, Antiochus Epiphanes, and others in a new way. . . They almost enable us to see and smell such now-disappeared cities as Sodom, Babylon, and Nineveh."[32] The archaeologist's spade, the geologist's meter, and the science of histography have all definitively discovered 70 of the 80 cities mentioned in the Old Testament. The number may be higher, because there are several cities in which the historians are "sure," but "not sure enough" to confirm their discovery.

A list of these cities is found below, followed with the specific Bible verses where they are mentioned as being a real city. Keep in mind that if the city is proven not to be mystical then there is an increased probability that the stories connected to them were often literal and not mythical in nature.

So, let's do a little family exercise. Go get your laptop, smart-phone, tablet, or family computer and go to your

---

[32] Charles Ludwig, *Ludwig's Handbook of Old Testament Rulers and Cities* (Denver, Colorado: Ancient Books, 1984), 7.

favorite search engine, such as Bing or Google. Place each name listed below into your search engine and see just how many cities you can locate today! Sometimes it helps to place the word 'archaeological discovery', or 'biblical city of...'' to expedite your search.

Cities of the Old Testament

A

Acre (Akko), Israel: Judges 1:31

Ai (Canaan): Genesis 10; Numbers 34; Joshua 7:2

Amam (Bible): Joshua 15:26

Tel Arad: Joshua 12:7, 14

Archites (Arkites) (Old Testament): Joshua 16:2

Arvad: Genesis 10:18; Ezekiel 27:8, 11

Ashdod: 1 Samuel 6:17

Ashkelon: Joshua 13:3; 1 Samuel 6:17; Amos 1:8

B

Beersheba: Genesis 21:14

Beit El (Bethel): Genesis 28:19

Beit She'an (Bethshean): 1 Samuel 31; 1 Kings 4:12

Beit Shemesh (Bethshemesh): Joshua 15:10; 19:38; 21:16

Beth Dagon: Joshua 15:41; 19:27

Beth-zur: Joshua 15:58; 2 Chronicles 11:7; Nehemiah 3:16

Bethharan: Numbers 32:36

Bethlehem of Galilee: Joshua 19:15

Bozkath: Joshua 15:39; 2 Kings 22:1

Bozrah: Genesis 36:31-33

C

Cities of Refuge: Numbers 35:32-33; Joshua 20:7-8 (Golan, Ramoth, Bosor, Kedesh, Shechem, and Hebron).

D

Dothan (ancient city): Genesis 37:17; 2 Kings 6:13

E

Eilat: 2 Chronicles 26:2; 1 Kings 22:49-50; 2 Kings 16:6

Ekron: Joshua 13:2-3; 1 Samuel 5:10

Etam (biblical town): 1 Chronicles 4:32; 2 Chronicles 11:6

Ezion-Geber: Numbers 33:35; 2 Chronicles 20:36

G

Gath (city): Joshua 11:22; 1 Samuel 5:7-10; 6:17; 1 Kings 2:39-40

Gath-hepher: Joshua 19:13; 2 Kings 14:25

Gaza (city): Judges 16:21

Geba (city): 1 Samuel 13:3; 2 Kings 23:8; Nehemiah 11:31

Gezer: Joshua 10:33; 21:21; 1 Chronicles 7:28

Giloh: Joshua 15:51; 2 Samuel 15:12

Golan: Deuteronomy 4:43; Joshua 20:8; 21:27

H

Halah: 2 Kings 17:6; 18:11; 1 Chronicles 5:26

Hebron: Genesis 13:18; 23:2; 23:19; 35:27; Numbers 13:22; Judges 1:10

Heshbon: Numbers 32:37; Joshua 21:39; 1 Chronicles 6:81

Hethlon: Ezekiel 47:15; 48:1

Horonaim: Isaiah 15:5; Jeremiah 48:5

I

Iim (Ijim; Iyim): Joshua 15:29; Numbers 33:45

J

Jabesh-Gilead: Judges 21:8-14; 1 Samuel 31:8-13

Jazer: Numbers 21:32; 32:1, 35; Joshua 13:25

Jericho: Deuteronomy 34:1; Joshua 2:1-3; 4:13

Jerusalem: 2 Chronicles 25:27

Jeshanah: 1 Samuel 7:12; 2 Chronicles 13:19

Jezreel (city): Joshua 19:18; 1 Kings 18:45; 21:1

K

Kabzeel: Joshua 15:21; 2 Samuel 23:20

Kartan: Joshua 21:32

Kedesh: Joshua 15:23; Judges 4:6

Kir of Moab: Isaiah 16:7; Jeremiah 48:31

Kirjath-huzoth: Numbers 22:39

Kirjathaim: Numbers 32:37; Joshua 13:19; Ezekiel 25:9

Kithlish: Joshua 15:40

L

List of surviving and destroyed Canaanite cities

M

Tel Megiddo: Joshua 17:11-12; 1 Kings 9:15; 2 Kings 23:29; Revelation 16:16

Mizpah (Judah): Joshua 13:26; 15:38; 18:26

Moresheth-Gath: 2 Chronicles 11:8; Jeremiah 26:18; Micah 1:14

N

Tell en-Nasbeh Netophah: 2 Samuel 23:28-29; Ezra 2:22

Nineveh: Genesis 10:11; 2 Kings 19:36; Nahum 1:14; 3:7

O

Ofra Ophel inscription: 2 Chronicles 27:3; 33:14; Nehemiah 3:26; 3:27; 11:21

Ophrah: Joshua 18:23; 1 Samuel 13:17

Q

Khirbet Qeiyafa

R

Ramah in Benjamin: Judges 19:11-15; 1 Kings 15:17-22; 2 Chronicles 16:1-6; Matthew 2:18

Ramoth (Issachar): Joshua 19:17, 21; 1 Chronicles 6:71-73

Ramoth-Gilead: Deuteronomy 4:43; Joshua 20:8; 21:38

S

Secacah: Joshua 15:61

Shaaraim: Joshua 15:36; 1 Samuel 17:52

Sharuhen: Joshua 19:6

Shechem: Genesis 12:6-8; Judges 9:1-45

Shiloh (biblical city): Genesis 49:10; Joshua 18; 1 Samuel 3:21

Sidon: Genesis 10:15, 19; 49:13; Joshua 11:8; 19:28; Judges 1:31; 1 Kings 5:6; Matthew 11:21-23; Acts 27:3

Susa: Nehemiah 1:1; Esther 1:2, 5; 2:3, 5, 8; Daniel 8:2

T

Tahpanhes: Jeremiah 2:16; 43:7, 8; 46:14

Tanis: Exodus 2:3-6; Ezekiel 30:14

Tekoa, Gush Etzion: Amos 1:1; 2 Samuel 14:2, 9

Tel Lachish: Joshua 10:3, 5, 23, 31-35; 2 Chronicles 11:9; Micah 1:13; Jeremiah 34:7

Tell es-Sultan: Luke 19:1-4

Timnah: Judges 14; Joshua 15:10

Tuqu': 2 Samuel 12:1-6; 14:2, 4, 9

Tyre, Lebanon: Matthew 15:21; Mark 7:24; Luke 6:17

Y

Yalo (Aijalon): Joshua 10:12; Judges 12:12; 1 Samuel 14:31; 1 Chronicles 6:69

Yavne (Jabneel; Jabneh): Joshua 15:11; 2 Chronicles 26:6-8

Yibna (Jabneel): Joshua 19:33; Acts 8:40

Z

Ziddim: Joshua 19:35

Zoan: Numbers 13:22; Isaiah 19:11; Ezekiel 30:14

Zorah: Joshua 15:33; 19:41; Judges 13:25; Nehemiah 11:29

At least 85 cities have been identified in the Old Testament. There are seven cities with no archaeological evidence or speculation available to us today. This many change in the future. There are seven with "some" or "very likely" evidence of its existence. Out of 85, we can certainly identify 71 cities. There are another seven cities containing some archaeological evidence and/or speculation which could suggest as many as 78! How does a book written more than 1,600 years ago with multiple different authors speak of 85 cities and have archaeologists confirm at least 78? The Scriptures are amazingly accurate as to the names of ancient cities!

Chapter 4

Those Silly Bible Stories We Tell Our Children

Do you really believe that in the beginning a snake had two legs or that a man and a woman ate a piece of forbidden fruit? Furthermore, are you so naïve as to believe that the world was flooded or that men built a Tower of Babel, which caused everyone's language to change? If so, you probably also believe a king named Nebuchadnezzar actually threw three Hebrew boys into a fiery furnace and a man named Daniel was almost eaten by the lions?

History or Myth?

Are the Bible stories history or myths? This is the debate facing us today as we look at our early Bible stories in the Pentateuch (the first five books of the Bible). The Book of Genesis is the first of these books and contains the story of creation. Creation is the debate within the cry of a lost world asking the questions: "Where did I come from? Is there a purpose for my life?" Ironically, these are the questions that all religions and every human being struggle to discover. This may be one reason why all religions have a creation story. In light of this, do you know that Christianity and

103

Judaism are not the only religions that believe the earth was filled with nothing but water in the beginning? In addition, there is an Egyptian religious story regarding a world where a "god" spoke the world into existence. Likewise, Assyrian stories tell of one man and one woman who lived first and a story where this woman was tested in her faith, thus causing corruption. Are these stories history or myth? If they are myths, what does this mean for the Bible stories we cherish as truth? How does a myth relate to the similar stories in the Bible? What does the science of archaeology have to say against the stories being mythical? What do the oldest fossil records tell us about snake-like creatures? Archaeology has much light to shine on additional biblical stories found in the Pentateuch.

Moving forward into the biblical account, we might ask: Is it possible that there might be scientific evidence that the world was flooded during the biblical date of Noah? Furthermore, why do all religions have a flood story where one man takes his family into an ark? After the ark, do you think it might be possible that other religions held to the account that all men came from one direction and eventually were dispersed at a tower where everyone originally spoke the same language? In light of these questions, one must ask if the stories in the first five books of the Bible (the Pentateuch) are history or myth. Should we teach our Bible stories as truth?

Truth, Myths, Legends, and Lies

The Bible is a book of truths with an accurate historical account of the records of man. The creation story is a record of the beginning of man. This Bible story of creation and its destruction by water can be a slippery slope. This naturally leads us to the question: "Is the Book of Genesis, history or myth?" This question is at the center of a hotly debated argument. The creation of the universe and its accompanying question—"Was the earth ever flooded?"—is the Achilles heel to many in this debate. Biblically, Saint Peter prophesied thousands of years ago that in the "last days," the argument against the Scriptures would be based upon whether the earth had ever been flooded. The Scripture tells us in 2 Peter 3:5-6:

> They deliberately ignore this fact, that by the word of God heavens existed long ago and an earth was formed out of water and by means of water, through which the world of that time was deluged with water and perished (NRSV).

But, what if I told you the real argument was not whether most ancient civilizations believed in a flood, but whether Moses obtained his information from ancient religious myths or through historical facts? Surprisingly, this is the question we must first answer before we can resume the archaeological evidence for the plethora of Bible stories which will follow. This new question, "Are the Bible stories borrowed from ancient myths?" or "Did the Bible speak from its own historical uniqueness?" leads some to seriously question the reliability of Scripture. Are these Bible stories, history or myths? That is the wall we now face in our faith becoming truly lethal.

Worldviews, Skeptics, and Bible Stories

Worldviews are important. It is important to begin our exploration with an assumption that is rooted in our biblical worldview. The Bible is the absolute, accurate Word of God. Thus, the Bible stories contained in the Bible are historically true. This is our "worldview." As someone who believes the Bible to be the Word of God, he or she must realize that there are competing worldviews with skeptics who do not believe the Bible is the Word of God. Whenever skeptics in our modern society critically analyze the Bible stories in the Scriptures, they do so based solely on the information available to them at the time of their writings.

These same skeptics said the Bible stories of Nebuchadnezzar, Daniel, and Pontius Pilate were probably mythical or exaggerated in Scripture. They said they were mythical because they had little or no archaeological evidence. Thus, they assumed that the Bible was wrong in its historical description regarding the days of Daniel or the man who judged Jesus Christ. Therefore, skeptics attacked the Book of Daniel and Pontius Pilate because of the previously, extremely limited archaeological evidence available regarding the events. Therefore, skeptics assumed that their interpretation of the biblical story was the correct one, and the actual biblical description was incorrect. Later, we can clearly see where their assumptions against the accuracy of the Bible were dismantled by an archaeological spade.

Recent archaeological discoveries have once again proven the historical accuracy of the Scriptures, especially the Book of Daniel and the existence of a man named Pontius Pilate. King Nebuchadnezzar, Cyrus, Darius, the New Testament, and Pontius Pilate have all been confirmed by scientific, archaeological evidence. Therefore, as we begin to wrestle with the question, "Is the Book of Genesis a book of history or myths?" we do so with a firm biblical worldview that holds a high authoritarian allegiance to the Bible as the Word of God. While there may be gaps today, the likelihood of the archaeological brush eventually filling in the gaps and strengthening the biblical account is most probable. This has been true for so many biblical stories that space does not allow for further elaboration. With this conviction firmly established, we now look to answer the question, "Did Moses write the first five books of the Bible (the Pentateuch)?" And then, "Did Moses use ancient history or myth to write these early Bible stories?"

Moses and the Early Bible Stories

Moses wrote the Book of Genesis around 1400 B.C. While some scholars say that Moses did not write the Pentateuch, but that "he borrowed his stories from ancient Near Eastern myths," the Bible confesses otherwise. We can see clearly in Exodus 17:4; 24:4; 34:27; Numbers 33:1-2; Deuteronomy 31:9-11; John 5:46; and 2 Corinthians 3:15 that Moses did write these books. The Bible tells us clearly who wrote the Book of Genesis and the rest of the Pentateuch. The idea that Moses borrowed his creation stories from ancient myths is now the center for our argument against the skeptics dismantling the Pentateuch as myths—an argument that denies the authorship of Moses.

Since the seventeenth century, man has seriously challenged Moses' authorship of the Pentateuch (the first five books of the Bible). It began when, "Benedict Spinoza voiced his denial of it in his Theological-Political Treatise (1677)."[1] This theory was the basis for what came to be called the documentary hypothesis or JEDP theory. By the nineteenth century, this became the prevailing thought among liberal theologians. The JEDP theory said, "The Pentateuch was written by various people whom (were called), 'Jehovist (J, also known as Yahwist), Elohist (E), Deuteronomist (D), and Priestly (P), each one supposedly distinguished by their literary characteristics. Thus the name JEDP theory refers to the various sources hypothesized."[2] The problem with this theory is the Bible tells us plainly who wrote the Pentateuch—Moses! (Numbers 33:1-2). Furthermore, to date there is NO SCIENTIFIC evidence for JEDP, yet archeology continues to point its spade as a compass to the authorship of Moses. Unfortunately, this is only the beginning of this argument, because they say that Moses borrowed the stories in the Pentateuch from Assyrian, Egyptian, and Babylonian sources. This argument against the authorship of Moses now takes an even deeper turn away

---

[1] Joseph M. Holden and Norman Geisler, *The Popular Handbook of Archaeology and the Bible: Discoveries That Confirm the Reliability of Scripture* (Eugene, Oregon: Harvest House Publishing, 2013), 57.

[2] Ibid.

from biblical authority when it attributes the writings to other religious sources, whose stories seem eerily similar to the ones Moses was said to have written. What makes matters seemingly worse is that they are said to have been written at least eight hundred years before Moses penned the Pentateuch. What is an Evangelical to do now?

Remember, we start with the fact that the Bible is the Word of God and is inerrant in its original forms. Therefore, we will proceed to the house of our critics. So, is it true that the Assyrians, Egyptians, and the Babylonian Persians wrote stories similar to our Hebrew Bible? The answer is "Yes." However, be careful what seems to be similar may not be similar when further investigated! Many times our skeptics are only armed with the argument. They say to us, Egyptian gods named Ptah, spoke and it was by using the word of his mouth to create the world. This Memphite theology does have a striking similarity to Genesis chapter one. "In examining this account called the Memphite theology, one finds that the god Pthah thought. There was a thought process involved, and then he spoke. But Yahweh-Elohim of Scripture does not go through a thought sequence. In creating, He is all-knowing at all times! What is actually happening is that this "new" god, Ptah, the god that put Pharaoh on the throne, is better than previous gods. The purpose of this myth, then, is to vindicate the new Pharaoh's right to the throne."[3] One can add to this story the Enuma Elish Creation Epic where earth was created by Marduk, god of Assyria, or the Babylonian Creation Epic. In addition, there are stories within these religions of "women giving birth to children without distress"; "where man spoke one language"; and where "a man built a boat when the whole earth flooded, saving his family as they were guided by god." However, a careful consideration

[3] David Livingston, "Ancient Days: Comparison of Genesis with Creation Stories of the Ancient Near East," Ancient Days, accessed September 1, 2018, *http://www.davelivingston.com/creationstories.htm.*

of the whole story has a much different outcome which will not advocate similarity, but actually dismantle it. This is because a biblical worldview differs drastically from what other ancient religions wrote about god.

Learn More:

HERE's Some HELP! This is a fantastic book to buy at *www.neverbefore.tv* to LEARN MORE on this subject!

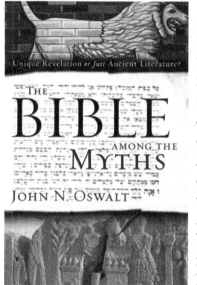

What seems similar is not similar at all. "Any straightforward comparison must conclude that beneath any possible surface similarities are radically different ways of thinking."[4] Dr. John N. Oswalt has written an outstanding book called, *The Bible Among the Myths,* and he outlines several points to rebut the argument about the creation stories of the Near East being similar to the Bible stories in the Old Testament. I would like to use these points to lead you through a quick snapshot of just how different the biblical creation stories are compared to the myths of the Near East. Are there similarities? Yes. However, the simple comparison of speaking the world into existence, a male and female breaking the laws of God via a piece of fruit, childbirth bringing pain, the world being flooded, a tower being built or languages being divided is simply where it stops in its similarities (the skeptics will never bring this up). So, how are the Bible stories different from myths? One difference is the facts. We will come back to that defense

---

[4] John N. Oswalt, *The Bible Among the Myths: Unique Revelation or Just Ancient Literature?* (Grand Rapids, Michigan: Zondervan, 2009), 63.

shortly. However, for now, the stories of the Bible differ greatly from the ancient mythical stories of the Near Eastern world. The following 16 rebuttals will give answers as to why the stories in the Pentateuch are not really that similar to the stories of ancient Near Eastern cultures. Oswalt, in his brilliant books, gives these 16 arguments to help his readers see the truth.

1. Obsession With Fertility and Potency

The ancient world logically placed their gods as fertile, potent, sexually reproducing divine beings. Through reason, the divine is in charge of fertility and potency. The gods are in charge of reproducing life. That seems exactly what the Bible teaches us—"That God is in charge of having reproduced life." But, that is not true at all.

It is no shock that the ancients considered the centrality of sexuality and sexual behavior as key components of their "gods." To humans who created these gods with their hands, it follows that sex and sexuality would be their ultimate reality. Just take a look at the Egyptians and Israeli's concept of worshiping bulls (golden calves). Or in the god segment of this book, did you notice how many of them were potent animals or contained ritual prostitution among the gods? Most of them use the reproduction of life only by the concourse of sexual potency.

Our God never reproduced sexually because God is asexual. He has no definitive sexuality. He created by the spoken word only or by the power of His Spirit in a barren womb of a virgin. Thus, he is much different than the other gods who use natural logical means to sexually reproduce, which makes sense when you know that a human has made these gods with their hands. The only natural way for them to be reproducible is natural means.

The ancient Near East was an agrarian society—rains, the earth, the elements of the weather were crucial for life to go on. So, the gods man created must be "fertile" and "potent" or else life could not reproduce. Our God is not seen as a fertile, potent God by sexual means. He is reproducible and potent with the natural use of sexuality.

2. Denial of Boundaries

When it comes to ancient gods, not only were they fertile and potent sexually, but also they engaged in incest, bestiality, and prostitution. There were no boundaries between humans and animals. These were theological statements about their gods. The Christian God has always set boundaries to sexuality. He set sexuality inside the life of man connected to responsibility. If you reproduce, you are responsible for your creation. The laws of marriage were set up to do just that, protect women from men who created children without responsibility. God knew that a boy needed a father in the home. God knew that a young girl needed a mother. He also knew that girls needed a daddy and boys needed a mother. He has always had a plan for sexual union to produce definitive churches and communities of excellence. This is under attack today, yet this is what made us different thousands of years ago and what apparently is making us different than the world today. Our God is a God of sexual boundaries for the purpose of protecting women, children, and the proper propagation of life to the fullness.

3. Polytheism/Monotheism

There are many gods within the myths of the Near East. In Hinduism alone, there is a reported base of 35 goddesses, and 50 male gods, combined into more than 33 million gods in all. So, one thing needs to be understood very clearly: The gods of the ancient Near East were all polytheistic. This means there was more than one god, which is the reason this book began early in communicating that as Christians

111

Lethal Faith

we are monotheistic, (one God/Shema) not Polytheistic (many gods). Why are there so many gods in the Near East? There is one god for the underworld (Hades), and a goddess for fertility (Diana), and another god that required child sacrifices—(Marduk)." This is because to the ancients, many different forces are needed in the world, thus the need for many gods. They needed one god to protect them in the rain, another one to protect the land and its fertility, still another to protect them from the storm (remember they are being created by man).

Multiple needs; multiple gods. Yet, for Christians (Jewish and Islamic people: all of which came from the stories of the Bible!), we are clearly and have always been commanded by God to be monotheistic. Israel struggled with this concept for thousands of years. We struggle with it today, albeit through new idols, (golf, soccer, family, work, etc.). The ancient Near East created many gods to meet their many needs. We need only one God who meets all our needs according to His riches in glory! (Philippians 4:19).

4. Images

The gods of the ancient Near East are represented by images. It is a representative of continuity, which is part of nature. Idols which represent these myths were made from wood, stone, or some natural material. In other words, they used natural symbols as the key to expressing divine concepts. Their gods come in the shape of this world—in human form and ritually driven. So, these gods are divine, human, and from nature. When we do it to the idol, we do it to the god and to the natural forces he/she inhabits.

By contrast, our God is not made by human hands out of natural things. Our God is the one who created nature and the human hands. He has no shape. He is omnipresent (everywhere), omnipotent (all powerful), and omniscient (knows everything).

112

5. Eternity of Chaotic Matter

To the ancients, the source of life has always been the cause of conflict. So, the creation of life is conflicting. In the mythical stories of the ancient, life is created only by much chaos. They assume the fundamental element of this world has always existed. For them, chaotic matter is first, not GOD. In all their creation stories, there is first matter, then conflict. So, the first issue that comes to the gods to handle is to turn chaos into present order. Notice that this god is usually a female. Why? It is because naturally and logically, females are needed to reproduce offspring. But this god is never personal or caring. Their personality is not essential to reality. Personality is not found in their gods, but only in humanity. You see spirit, but not personality.

Lastly, chaos is the source of life. Nothing, absolutely nothing, could be further from our belief. Our God finds nothing, and then out of love, creates man with no chaos. Yes, there was a Fall, but creation had no chaos in its story; the only chaos in our story is the chaos of what man created! This makes the story much different. Our God then did not come to handle chaos, but to take nothing and make it into something beautiful. Our God is asexual, not female. Unlike the god Ptah, our God doesn't need the semen of men or the womb of a fertile female to create. No, this God speaks and order appears. Furthermore, He not only speaks and order and peace appear, but He also does so out of love and personality with purpose and care.

6. Low View of the Gods

Many people fail to realize that ancient myths hold a low view of their gods. They are temperamental, untrustworthy, and seek their own. They certainly do not appear to care for humans in particular. Only a fool would call Isis or Hades, a "Shepherd." These gods are not only self-seeking, but also they are constantly fighting with each other. If it were not enough that the gods created in chaos, instead of out of chaos, they fight each other over extremely petty matters. They are fearful of losing power, intimidated by each other's greatness. They are not omnipotent; they are actually subject to magic, and to those who worship them with their magic. These gods can be controlled by magical powers of the people they created! They are not absolute authority; they are weak, with sexual desires, and not all-powerful. And what frightens these Eastern gods the most? Death—they are afraid of dying! Not our God!

We hold a high view of our God. He is, after all, "High and lifted up" (Isaiah 6:1), and the psalmist proclaims, "Exalt Him!" (Psalms 99:5). Our God is seen as a trustworthy, patience, kind being (Romans 2:4). This is not to say that God has not or will not bring discipline (Hebrews 12:4-13) or judgment (Exodus 34:7; 2 Timothy 4:8) upon human beings. But his declarations are just and fair! (Romans 12:12-16). However, throughout Scripture God is separated, and high above the men and women He rules and created. He is a caring, good, kind God who is strong, loving, and sovereign. He has the power to do what He wants to do and when He wants to do it. No man, or other weak, timid, manipulated god can dethrone Him (Isaiah 14).

7. Low View of Humanity

Not only are the Eastern gods weak and temperamental to humans, but they also hate humans, even though they were created to serve the gods. The creation of human beings was an afterthought. They were not important on the radar of their selfish gods. In one Egyptian account of creation (and there are several, depending upon what new pharaoh was in power), "Humans are merely the tears of Atum (god) that fell into the dust during his struggle with Chaos (god)."[5] Thus, humans are insignificant to gods. Furthermore, humans have no real control over their destinies. So, choice seems to be an illusion. Not so with our God!

---

[5] Oswalt, *The Bible Among Myths*, 60.

Our God doesn't hate human beings or see us as a nuisance of which to rid the world. No, you know John 3:16: "For God so loved the world that he gave his one and only Son that whoever believes in him shall not perish but have eternal life." Our God loves us (Deuteronomy 7:9; Romans 2:4; 5:8, 1 John 4:7-8). As a matter of fact, our God loved human beings so much He gave his best to them, simply to redeem them. What ancient god can you find that would ever sacrifice himself for a human being? None, absolutely none! But our God has a high view of humans. David told us that God created man a "little lower than the angels" (Psalm 8:5; Hebrews 2:7). Furthermore, we were created in the image of God (Genesis 1:27). Nowhere do we find ancient gods caring enough for the humans underneath their power. Nowhere do we find ancient gods giving their lives or using their powers for the benefit of someone other than themselves. No, our God loves human beings and made us in His image.

8. No Single Standard of Ethics

Ancient Near Eastern gods, and gods from all myths, have another thing in common—there is no single standard of right and wrong. Polytheism makes a central ethical system impossible. There are so many gods and goddesses there can't be a unifying ethical system. They vary in too many ways, likes, and dislikes. Because the visible world did not come about through a divine purpose, there is no possibility of right and wrong. This is important for the stability of civilization; whereas, different laws morph and change. Killing an innocent human being is considered wrong in most civilizations. Paul tells us that God wrote a basic moral law, stating what is right and wrong upon our hearts (Romans 2:14-16). Many skeptics of the Scriptures love to point out the earlier law codes such as the Code of Ur-Nammu in 2050 B.C. or the Hammurabi Code of Law from Babylon (1754 B.C.), which preceded our Ten Commandments. Hammurabi was a Babylonian king. The point is, civilizations developed into mass migration of cities (Genesis 4: 17). This is why Mesopotamia and Hittite societies developed a Law Code, so that people could get along with other people who were now living in close quarters (cities). However, while there are similarities, there again are major main differences.

Archaeologists have now discovered at least five "law codes" that preceded Moses, many by a thousand years. Again, there are similarities like a law that calls for justice, civil order, Lex Talionis (eye for an eye), kidnapping, and stealing. There again are major differences. In contrast, mercy and the sanctity of life—protecting the poor and the oppressed over the wealthy and elite—are present in the law, and these laws are tied to an ethical morality. Just because a critic gives precedent to something old having a higher authority than something written later doesn't mean that what was written first or what the oldest writings were, are truth. Furthermore, similarities do not prove plagiarism.

Consequently, the Old Testament Law of Moses is definitively religious in nature. The Law of Hammurabi was not. The Babylonians believed that the god, Shamash gave Hammurabi the law so people could get along with one another. This is the exact opposite of the Mosaic laws. The Mosaic laws were not given so that people could get along with each other, but so that people could get along with God. Accusations of similarities are usually, simple and not similar at all when rationally inspected.

9. Cyclical Concept of Existence

The ancient myths told a story of a life that is seen only through the experience of cycles. The problem with this reasoning is that life then will not show progress. Life starts from nowhere and goes nowhere. Coincidentally, the Book of Ecclesiastes suggests such a cycle (3:15). Yet, the past is a record to a way forward unlike the ancients who believed that the past was to help us understand a reality that does not move forward, but repeats itself.

We serve a God that has a forward-moving plan for the complete redemption of man. Our past experiences are there to warn and guide us to learn from our mistakes. There is clearly a consummation to biblical theology. That means that God is moving time and people forward for a purpose. That purpose is definitive. It is a purpose to re-unite man and God, expel sin, and reestablish a vibrant relationship with man. For the ancients, time has no purpose; it's all meaningless repetition. Yet, our God is a God of purpose with a divine plan to move humanity forward to an ultimate future.

10. Iconoclasm

God may not be represented in any created form, because God is not identified with this world. You can't find an ancient idol of a god that is not found in the shape of something from this world.

On the contrary, our Bible says in Exodus 20:4-5: "You shall not make for yourself an image in the form of anything in heaven above or on the earth beneath or in the waters below. You shall not bow down to them or worship them." Why does the Bible say this? Because, God is not of this world. He cannot be identified with the world or the things in this world. A piece of wood cannot compare to His majesty. Thus, He cannot be manipulated by the world. We serve a God not made by human hands (2 Corinthians 5:1; Acts 17:25). However, our God actually says the exact opposite of the Near Eastern myths. They were made out of natural elements by the hand of man. Paul told this to the silversmiths in the city of Ephesus (Acts 17:25). Not only do we not serve a god made by human hands, we serve a God who says, "My hands made you!" (Isaiah 64:8).

11. The First Principle Is Spirit, Not Matter.

In the ancient Near East, it is clear that matter came first. To a Christian, it was the Spirit of God, which always was and is prior to everything. This Spirit created matter. The world believes that matter is the source for every living thing. We as Christians do not believe this because we believe in a God who created everything from nothing, thus creating matter.

The Near East gods find themselves wrestling with matter upon the earth; however, our God does not "wrestle with matter." In fact, it is quite the opposite. Our story does not contain the chaos of matter continually trying to destroy the creation. Our story is one of peace and submission. God spoke, and matter obeyed. Matter is seen as calm, good, peaceful, and under the sovereign control of God, rather than matter controlling God.

12. Absence of Conflict in the Creation Process

The origin of the Pentateuch is very different from that found in Near Eastern myths. As it relates to ancient Near Eastern gods, it is conflict that is crucial to creation. In contrast to Christian belief, the world began because God wanted it to! Matter was without form and void (Genesis 1:2). There was no resistance in the creation story of the Bible. God fought no one to create. Evil only entered the world through willful disobedience.

Furthermore, after creation was complete, God was never threatened by the presence of evil. The ancient gods were always threatened by someone else. In the Bible, it is only man who is threatened by evil. He deals with Adam and Eve, treating them as accountable and responsible. As a matter of fact, God only offhandedly speaks to Satan. Satan (evil) is not equal with God. There is no fight; there is no threat. Conflict with evil has nothing to do with the creative acts of God. Creation was the purpose and will of God. Creation and Creator are clearly separate.

13. God Is Suprasexual.

One of the most important points to remember about just how different the Judean/ Christian God is, is the fact that our God is not sexed. Sexuality has nothing to do with God's ability to reproduce or create.

In contrast to the ancient myths, all gods came into existence through sexual means. Why? The ancients are once again making a world reflective of their sexuality. In ancient myths, gender and sexual activity are required attributes for creation. If something is to be created, it naturally, logically, and scientifically requires two distinctly different species of human beings, who come together sexually—one with an egg, the other with sperm. This is how life is created in the world. However, this is not how God created life. Outside of Israel, all gods were sexed and sexual. Our God doesn't have sex with anyone to create. Their gods all have sexual intercourse to create. Gender for us is an attribute of the creation of God, but doesn't have one role in the production of creation. An asexual God creates without sexuality. This is not true of any of other gods.

14. Sex Is Desacralized

In the Near East myths, sex between two humans had the power to influence the will of the gods they served. In our Bible, nothing happens to God when men and women are sexually active. The God of the bible is asexual and cannot be manipulated by sexual acts on earth.

119

15. Prohibition of Magic

The gods of the Near East are magical gods who work their incantations. However, in the Bible, all sorcery is forbidden (Leviticus 19:26). According to our Bible, we don't have to manipulate God to have our needs met. He meets our needs out of a divine love for humanity (Philippians 4:19; Matthew 6:31-32).

16. Ethical Obedience as a Religious Response

Since we cannot relate to God in magical ways, the way in which we relate to our God is through reflecting the character of God.

Therefore, to our Bible stories, God is not the cosmos; He is transcendence. God is radically other than His Creation and cannot be manipulated by the forces He created. We are monotheistic, which means we believe in one God, existing in three persons—the Father, the Son, and the Holy Spirit (1 Timothy 2:5). That is why we do not make idols of God; we don't want to suggest that God is part of this world or can be manipulated through this world.

Similarities are not really similarities at all. What seems similar on the surface and is often a clever rebuke to the history of Christianity, isn't similar or a rebuke, but a clarification. The ethics of our Bible and our God is not the same as the ethics of the Near Eastern religions. As a matter of fact, one cannot appropriately address ethics with the other gods of this world, because there is no unifying ethic that aggregates the will of the gods. This is because to those gods there is no specific purpose in their world. Not true of our God, because we can speak of a behavior (ethic) that is overarching in its specific principles (thou shalt not steal or murder). The Bible treats its characters as real human beings, and it never, unlike the Egyptians, covers up the failure of its people. These broken people are not the enemies of God, but the friends of God (James 2:23). The humans in the Bible are rooted in a significant relationship with their God. This relationship is further established by their choices, which play a major part in the relationship.

In contrast, these are similarities on the surface of the stories. Similarities in earlier law codes which preceded the Ten Commandments can be found, as well as gods who "spoke the world" into existence. There are similarities as to worldwide floods and virgin births.

Below are the final words from Oswalt's outstanding book on this subject.

> In light of these kinds of evidences, should we not say that Hebrew religion is just a variant of the general Western Semitic religion of its day? We should not, because these similarities are not the key issues when it comes to describing Hebrew belief. What is significant is the way in which the Israelites utilize these features in a belief system that is radically different from anything around them . . . the whole way of thinking about reality is unique and it is absolutely thorough throughout the Bible.[6]

There is nothing like the Bible in all of Near Eastern religions. The Bible is a unified theological journey of man wandering away from God and of God's redemption of wayward man. Whereas, the Near Eastern gods are already propagandistic to ensure the power and control of some new leader who wanted the masses to believe he was a god. The Bible is unified, both ethically and in its admonishment of character, rooted in absolutes where there is a right and a wrong. Not true anywhere in the Near East religions. God has an overarching plan; the gods of the east have no plan except for their own narcissistic survival.

---

[6] Ibid., 150.

Chapter 5

Historical Evidence for a Worldwide Flood and the Tower of Babel

When I was young, I believed that Santa Claus visited my home when I was nearly five. I was instructed by my mother and father to wait up for Santa Claus and say hello to him as he walked into my house. All night I lay by the rocking chair, ready to sneak up on Santa. To my surprise, he walked right into my house through the front door that night. I saw him in his full glory with a bag full of toys. I remember being scared to move. Finally, my mother and father brought him over to the chair that I was hiding behind and introduced me to this amazing "Saint." Looking back on this event, I would have sworn I "saw Santa Claus" one Christmas night. And, I did swear that I saw Santa Claus, but I did so on the limited knowledge I had as a five-year-old boy. As I have grown older, I learned that my parents had asked one of my father's friends to dress up like Santa and make a house call that night!

As ironic as it sounds, this same argument is what the skeptics often use to disprove the existence of God. They

123

are often heard, or we read of them saying, "Now that you are more intellectually mature and have all the facts, you should know that God and Santa Claus both come from the gene pool of your imagination!" But, hold on here. I came to know that the man I met was not Santa based on the facts I have learned since the event. I knew that the guy who visited my house that night was not the real Santa Claus based on eyewitness knowledge! The point is this, it's one thing to know by fact that the Santa Claus which visited my home was only his "helper," and not the real one. Why? Because my mother and father told me later in life the truth as eyewitness to the facts. That scenario is the one thing that plays out in my mind about so many "Christian kids" who have been told there is no God just like there is no Santa Claus, Easter Bunny, or Great Pumpkin. They are told in school, often in the name of education, that the Bible is not "real" history; because the facts prove it! Well, no, the facts regarding the historical reliability of the Bible are different. We will pursue what historical pieces we can know today based on our own limited knowledge of the facts. And we shall do so, despite the plethora of skeptical theologians who deny its inherent historical accuracies.

Before beginning the journey into the beginning pages of the Bible, there is one point that needs to be made very clear! You can't assume there is no God, based solely on the information you have heard just during the *time you have lived*. I can't help but think about the day I read a book called *Sex Symbolism in Religion: Volume One* by James Ballantyne Hannay. My heart broke for such a keen intellectual mind. The book was first written in 1922 at the precipice of German Higher Criticism, which believed that much of the Bible was symbolic, not literal history. He made many assumptions about God and the history of the Bible based on the limited knowledge of *his times*.

The same is true for a man who was once Billy Graham's closest friend, the former evangelist, Charles Templeton.

Charles preached to tens of thousands of people as they packed arenas all over this world. One day, he, like you and me, had a roadblock arise in his faith. Charles too lived during the period of German Higher Criticism; and he began to believe its interpretation of biblical history, which said it could not be trusted because its lessons were to be taken only as myths that developed moral character. Charles lost his faith; he became an atheist (apostate). Charles's faith was further aggravated by the explosion of the predominantly new science of archaeology. A science that was just coming into its middle school years at the time. So, Charles based his future faith on the current knowledge of his time. He believed that evolution brought man into existence, not God. He did so because he believed the same thing Darwin believed, that the human cell was nothing more than a very simple piece of tissue. He also interpreted the historical narrative in the Bible as myths and not historical truths because of the limited knowledge that archaeology had during his time. This was a knowledge that said that Nebuchadnezzar never existed and that there was never a man named Pontius Pilate in "real life." Things that we knew for a FACT are NOT true for us today but seemed true at the turning of the twentieth century.

Here is the point: Both James and Charles have made conclusions based upon the limited knowledge available to them at the time during which they lived. Since the time they lived, major advancements in science, archaeology, and world history have been uncovered. Therefore, when James Hannay, the man I previously wrote about, said, "The tale of Jesus is the work of the priesthood, and was written for a purpose, and the gospels are just as much fiction as any of the popular semi-historic or mystic novels."[1] He did so before the avalanche of archaeological finds, confirming the gospel narratives of Saint Luke's history.

---

[1] James Ballanytne Hannay, *Sex Symbolism in Religion, 1* (Amsterdam, The Netherlands: Fredonia Books, 1922), 235.

Charles Templeton decided to leave his Christian faith and become an atheist, before Darwin's idea that the human cell was simple and insignificant could be dismantled by science and strengthened by the discovery of DNA and the genomes that hold them! We must realize that although our faith today does contain gaps within its own history, and there are characters mentioned in the Bible in which we have no present archaeological evidence for their existence, that doesn't mean that tomorrow's archaeological spade might not overthrow our current ideas with fresh realities! Today, not one archaeological discovery has ever controverted a biblical passage. However, there are dozens of examples where skeptics have "assumed" that the Bible was wrong, but then later they were proven wrong and the Bible was correct! The simple truth is this: what we don't know today about biblical history, tomorrow we may well discover! Start out in the chapter with me by believing deeply that the Bible is the Word of God and can be fully trusted. Today, I believe the Bible is a historically reliable document based on the immense amount of evidence I have before me today. I do not simply believe that the Bible is God's Word because someone says so. I believe that the Bible is God's Word because the historical information of which it speaks can be verified by facts. The Bible's continuity tells a single story of God's search to rescue man whom He made in His image and His love for mankind—stories which involved hundreds of different cities, gods, peoples, and cultural information. Now, we will verify its historical stories by establishing factual evidence present in its stories.

The Creation of the Earth

The Garden of Eden

Is it possible that we could know anything of the world within its earliest moments of creation? Yes, it is. We will do so by looking at early stories that have been believed by multitudes of religions throughout the beginning of human creation. We are not the only ones who believe that the earth was created with an original man and woman, or that a worldwide Flood swept it all away. Another point to remember as we begin is this: What the biblical accounts of these same stories do for us is that they strengthen our stories by clarifying such truths through the Word of God. This is important, because the Word of God contains facts that can be tested such as when it says the Hittites lived during the time of Abraham. We can know that the biblical story is true based on objective facts in many cases. The Bible helps clarify these early stories and does so by specifically defining which God really created the earth, and then it clarifies the story by giving historical bits of information, which in turn, provide us with historical facts that can be confirmed. This is what makes the Bible stories of creation different from the mythical stories of creation from other religions. We will investigate what proof we have regarding early Creation, the Flood, and the Tower of Babel, so that we might make an informed decision as to their objective truths.

The Tigris and Euphrates Rivers

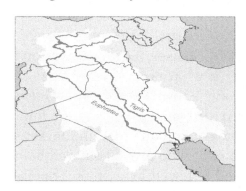

In Genesis 2:10-14, we are told that there are four distinct rivers that flowed from the Garden of Eden (Pishon, Gihon, Tigris, and the Euphrates). While, geological conditions over time would have changed the shape and nature of these rivers from a worldwide Flood, two of these rivers (Tigris/Hiddekel and the Euphrates) are names noted throughout the historical timeline (Genesis 24:10; Deuteronomy 23:4; Acts 7:2). These are probably not the exact rivers mentioned in the Genesis 2:8-14; however, they do prove the familiarity of their names to the people of the Middle East. Furthermore, the rivers Pishon and Gihon have long disappeared from any defined names in the Middle East. Even though the possibility of their existence is plausible. In a satellite image, two very large dry river beds were discovered in the Middle East, near the Euphrates and Tigris rivers by Dr. Juris Zarins, a Saudi archaeologist from Missouri State University in 1983, and reported in the *Smithsonian* magazine in 1987.[2]

The Story of Adam and Eve

A river is one thing, but a story of the first humans can be far-fetched. We can start by looking at other ancient civilizations and any possible connection to a story that may suggest that there was an original man and woman in a garden who sinned.

- **The Speiser Stone**

In Genesis 1:26-30; 2:4-7 is a story about a man and a woman who were deceived by a snake to eat fruit from a forbidden tree. An Assyriologist, Ephraim Avigdor Speiser, led an excavation to what is considered to be the oldest worship center in our known world—the Goebki Tepe site, near Nineveh. At this site, E.A. Speiser found a small seal made of clay measuring one inch in diameter. It pictures a man and a woman, who are considered being downcast and brokenhearted followed by a snake. Speiser dates the seal at 3500 B.C. and believed it to have highly suggested Adam and Eve.

[2] Dora Jane Hamblin, "Has the Garden of Eden Been Located at Last?" *The Smithsonian,* 18, no. 2 (May 1987).

- ## The Greenstone Cylinder

The original

The woodcut from Smith

This cylinder is often referred to as "The Temptation Seal" or "The Adam and Eve Seal." It is dated around 2200 or 2100 B.C. It has a naked man, woman, a tree, and shows a serpent by the woman. Originally, it was thought by the British Museum to be a reference to Adam and Eve, but now it is suggested to be a post-Akkadian banquet with the snake god, Nirah. The problem with this interpretation is the previous interpretation which suggested it was a reference to Adam and Eve is now "challenged by a specialist." Yet, there is no factual evidence to interpret this cylinder for sure in either direction. As well, the symbol is on an official government seal from Ancient Sumer who prayed kneeling not standing up. Nevertheless, it is an interesting piece of history to interpret.

- ## The Tetrapodophis amplectus

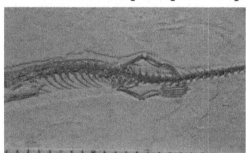

The Bible is clear, originally snakes walked on all fours, but because of the curse, started crawling on their bellies (Genesis 3:14). Recently, scientists found a fossil which they say is the oldest living fossil of a snake, called a Tetrapodophis amplectus. They are sure that it is a snake, because it has more than 150 vertebrae and scales which stretch along the width of its belly—two distinct features of snakes.[3] The most amazing fact is that this snake had four legs—just like the Bible clearly states.

---

[3] Sid Perkins, *Science Magazine*, Science, accessed October 2, 2018, *http://www.sciencemag.org/news/2015/07/four-legged-snake-fossil-stuns-scientist-and-ignites-controversy.*

- **The Epic of Enmerkar**

These clay tablets from ancient Sumer, some measuring only 23 x 23 cm, talk of an ancient place called Dilmun. These Sumerian tablets (from one of the oldest civilizations in the world) speak of a time and place where "the lion did not kill, and the lion and the lamb lived peacefully." Then one day, Enki and Ninhursag ate certain plants that contained a deadly curse. The story goes on talking about how everyone spoke one language to their god.

- **A Worldwide Flood**

As previously mentioned, 2 Peter 3:5-6, clearly tells us that during the "end times" the argument that the unbeliever will have with the Bible is whether the world was ever flooded. Saint Peter even says that they will "deliberately" do so. The word "deliberately" implies an active volition and purpose. What is important for us today is to realize that every major religion teaches historically that there was a worldwide flood.

- **The Ark Tablets**

These tablets were written in Old Babylonian cuneiform around 1900–1700 B.C. It tells the story of a Sumerian king, named At-ram-Hasis—a Noah-like figure. The tablet tells of a boat which was round and made of reeds that saved mankind from a global flood. A Mesopotamian god instructs him to build this large boat where animals were to enter it, two by two.[4]

---

[4] Mark Prigg, "Was Noah's Ark Round? 3,700-year-old clay tablet reveals giant boat was made out of reeds and bitumen," Daily Mail, accessed October 10,

- ## List of Sumerian Kings (Genesis 1-11)

The Sumerian Kings List was discovered in the Temple Library of Nippur and announced around 1906 to the public at large by Hermann Hilprecht. It lists the kings of this early civilization and comes to a place in its writings where it skips a king and simply reports: "The flood swept thereover." Since this initial discovery, there has been an additional eighteen lists found, detailing the Sumerian kings. Sumer is considered the earliest of civilized cities located in Mesopotamia between the Tigris and Euphrates rivers. The community of Sumer gave way to the Babylonian kingdom, and today it is known as Iraq, near Baghdad. [5]

- ## The Babylonian Epic, Enuma Elish (Isaiah 47:5; Daniel 5:1)

To date, this is considered the oldest creation story in the world. Often referred to as The Seven Tablets of Creation, these tablets were discovered at Ashurbanipal's library in Nineveh. They date to 1100 B.C. and speak of the beginning of the world where water was undifferentiated, swirling in chaos until a god became involved, separated

---

2018, *http://www.dailymail.co.uk/scienetech/article-2545941/Was-Noahs-Ark-ROUND-3-700-year-old-caly-tablet-reveals-boat-coracle-reeds-bitumen.html.*

[5] The Electronic Text Corpus of Sumerian Literature, The Sumerian King List: Translation, accessed September 14, 2018, *http://www.etcsl.orinst.ox.ac.uk/section2/tr211.htm.*

the water, and caused the chaos to come to rest. Henry Layard in 1849 discovered these tablets, and George Smith in 1876 published their accounts. Today, numerous copies have been found.

- **The Epic of Atra-Hasis**

This is an Akkadian story of both creation and a worldwide flood called the Epic of Atra-Hasis. These ancient clay tablets are dated to the eighteenth century B.C. They tell of a story where a god became displeased with humans and thus warned them that a flood was impending. A man named Atra-Hasis built a boat, but before the rain came, he gathered all kinds of animals in it. In the flood, all humanity was destroyed, except Atra-Hasis and his family. When Atra-Hasis left the boat after the flood, he made an offering to the god. Atra-Hasis was the Sumerian king of Shuruppak who ruled before the flood and was noted in the Babylonian Kings List.

- **The Eridu Genesis**

This Mesopotamia writing was found on cuneiform about the time of Abraham (2150 B.C.). The Eridu genesis speaks of a god who fashioned man from clay to cultivate the ground. Somewhere the gods decided to destroy humanity, and a man named Ziusudra was called by a god to build a large boat. He placed animals and his family on this boat. A great flood then swept the world.

- **The Writings of Gilgamesh**

This is perhaps one of the oldest books in the world. It is a Babylonian story that contains an account of a worldwide flood. Written within the third millennium B.C. on cuneiform it tells a story of a man named Utnapishtim that builds a boat to save his family during a huge deluge (rain). The gods had decided to destroy mankind for their wickedness. In this deluge, the earth was flooded. After the boat lands on top of a mountain, this Noah-like character releases a bird to identify if it's safe to go outside again.

- **Berossus, The Greek Historian**

Berosus Caldaeus

Berossus was a highly respected Greek historian around 200 B.C. and often quoted by later historians to the end of 325 A.D. Berossus wrote the book *Babyloniaca: The History of Babylonia*. In his writings, he speaks of stories similar to our creation story—a global flood and a tower located in Babylonia. He speaks of a list of ten kings; and when he comes to his description of the time during the eleventh king, he reports "the deluge of rain" came upon the land and flooded it. He then speaks of how a man named Xisuthrus built a boat to save his family and certain animals. Berossus is quoted by many other historians such as Abydenus, Apollodorus, Alexander Polyhistor, and Josephus. Josephus, a famous Jewish historian, quotes Berossus in 110 A.D. when he referred to how all the barbarian histories reported knowing exactly where the ark set on Mt. Ararat.[6]

---

[6] Search for Noah's Ark, Berossus: Babyloniaca, accessed October 14, 2018, *http://www.noahs-ark.tv/noah-ark-flood-creation-stories-myths-berossus-xisuthrus-babylonica-history-of-babylonia-abydenus-apollodorus-alexander-polyhistor-josephus-eusebius-georgius-syncellus-oannes-280bc.htm.*

- ## The Titanic

What does the Titanic have to do with Noah's ark or creation? Everything! Do you know who found the Titanic in the ocean? His name is Robert Ballard, and he is one of the most famous underwater archaeologists in his field. Ballard found the Titanic, and afterward he set out to find Noah's Ark. He made the statement that the probability of finding a boat made of wood is slim; however, if the world was really flooded, then that could still be proven to be true by finding an ancient civilization that was flooded instantly. So, he began to dig in the Black Sea at the base of Mount Ararat (Genesis 8:4). He dug 500 feet beneath the Black Sea and found a civilization flooded at 250 times the water force of Niagara Falls (Genesis 7:1). When he dated the ancient shoreline, it dated to about seven thousand years ago, just like the biblical timeline said! ABC's *Good Morning America* even has a wonderful video you can watch on YouTube! Go to: *https://www.youtube.com/watch?v=gilY0fTh7yg&t=29s*

- ## Jesus and Saint Peter in the New Testament and the Problem With Noah

As Christians, we have a problem. If we choose to believe that the story of Noah is a symbolic story of Creation rather than historical fact, a major theological problem arises. Both Jesus and Saint Peter refer to the Flood as a historical event (Matthew 24:37; Luke 17:26; 1 Peter 3:18-22; 2 Peter 2:5). Jesus specifically said that as "in the days of Noah," and Saint Peter calls Noah, a "preacher of righteousness."

The Creation stories in our Bible are not just stories that Christians believe, but also stories that many other religions and civilization believed to be true.

134

- **Now, the Rest of the Story: After the Flood**

  So, the ark landed, and Noah and his sons went out and repopulated the land. Is there any truth to this story that we find in our Bibles?

- **The Ebla Tablets**

Discovered in the late seventies, these tablets that number near 16,000 were written in a Sumerian script. They date around 2300 B.C. and include the territories of Syria, Damascus, and Southeast Turkey. Today, you can see the ruins that housed these clay tablets along the road to Allepo, Syria, at Tel-Mardikh. When they were first discovered, there was much debate as to whether they added to our understanding of the Bible. Some early scholars of the Ebla tablets, rushed to say, "no." However, today it seems that much has been learned since its early discovery in 1975. There are biblical scholars who argue that names such as Michael, David, Esau, Saul, Ishmael, Adam, Eve, and Noah can be found within the writings of these tablets. Cities such as Sodom and Gomorrah, Joppa, Canaan, Haran, and Urasalem (Jerusalem) are all thought to have been mentioned in these early writings, confirming even the cities mentioned in Genesis 14. The Ebla tablets, at the very least, confirm many of the cultural practices described in the Book of Genesis.

- **Mesopotamia After the Flood: The Table of Nations**

  There is a little passage in Genesis 10 that most Christians ignore, look past, or assume that it's just not that important. They are wrong! In Genesis 10, the Bible gives us the genealogical dispersion of mankind after

135

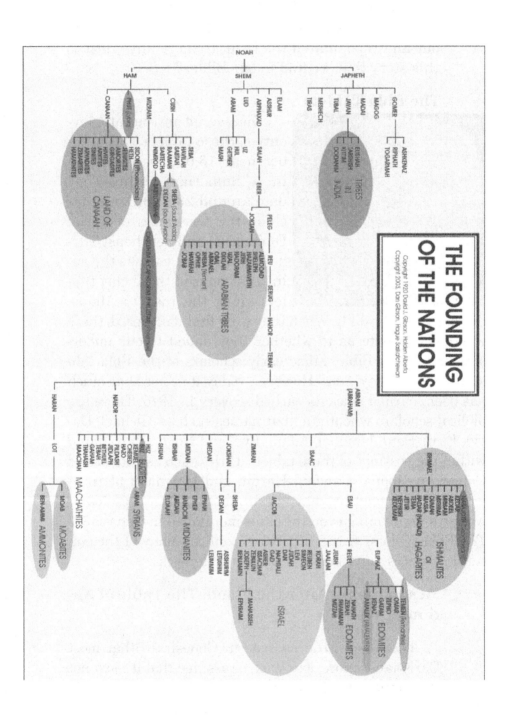

THE FOUNDING OF THE NATIONS

Copyright 1920 David J. Gibson, Holden Alberta
Copyright 2003 Don Gibson, Hague Saskatchewan

a worldwide Flood. It does so by naming men and their sons, which is dangerous if the Bible is not true. This process of reporting men and their sons is called Y-Chromosome and is scientifically called Y-Haplogroup. A Y-Haplogroup is defined by mutations in nonrecombining portions of DNA from Y-chromosomes."[7] When we talk about Haplogroups, we are speaking of a major branch of a family tree for Homo sapiens (humans). This group has characteristics of early migration populations as they spread out over the earth. Thus, they are often associated with geographic regions. The Bible is so bold as to tell us who these Haplogroups were and how they migrated in Genesis 10—called the Table of Nations. The Table of Nations is a migration record of ancient historic times. Acts 17:26 says, "From one man (or one blood) He made every nation of men, that they should inhabit the whole earth; and He determined the times set for them and the exact places where they should live" (NIV 1984).

The Table of Nations is important because the Bible tells us that it was the sons of Noah, Shem, Ham, and Japheth with their wives who spread out over the earth after the Flood. Now with the advent of genomes and DNA, science can use our DNA to help us know where we originated from across the earth. While there are some tensions between humans originating in the East Africa area compared to the region of Mesopotamia, there are many similarities with what science tells us about Genesis 10. Historical records, ancient literature, mythology, burial customs, archaeology, ethnography, ethnohistory, genetics, geology, sociology, and political histories, empires, and kingdoms all provide sources with strong evidence

---

[7] "Understanding Haplogroups: How are the haplogroups named?" Family Tree DNA, accessed November 4, 2018, *http://www.familytreedna.com/understanding-haplogroups.aspx.*

for the biblical account of Genesis 10. To read more about the effects of the Y-Chromosome in Genesis 10, go to this website: *http://www.soundchristian. com/man/* and https://aschmann.net/BibleChronology/Genesis10.pdf. To learn more about how ancient history aligned with the Table of Nations go to this website: *https://answersingenesis.org/genesis/josephus-and-genesis-chapter-ten/*

- **The Civilization of Sumer 2350-2300 B.C.**

On a cool fall afternoon, I stood in the Ford Theater in Washington D.C. staring at the hat of Abraham Lincoln. I remember being in awe as I connected the hat with this legend of American history. The hat was barely a hundred and fifty years old. Eventually, I found myself in Greece standing on Mars Hill looking up at the Greek Parthenon, thousands of years old. Americans don't always stop and realize just how young our civilization is compared to Greece? And because of our lack of reflection, we assume that "really" ancient history has very little proof that established its existence. Nothing could be further from the truth.

The Bible calls this region of Sumer—Shinar (Genesis 10:10; 11:2; 14:1; Zechariah 5:11). It was in the southernmost part of Mesopotamia and considered the cradle of civilization. The Sumerian people called themselves "the black-headed people," and were known in the region as "The land of the civilized kings." These people were the ones who invented the wheel, sailboats, and irrigation systems, along with the cuneiform style of writing. The Bible is accurate in naming this region as one of the first civilized cities in the world!

Ancient Sumerian Sites

- *The Shuruppak Tablet, 2100 B.C.*

One of the archaeological evidences of this region is a tablet that speaks of a worldwide flood that destroyed all of humanity. Furthermore, this region gave us the first development of urbanization (2800 B.C.) and of a government ruling by assembly (2900 B.C.).

- *The City of Erech (Uruk)*

This city is mentioned in Genesis 10:10 as the second city that Nimrod built. This city was discovered by William Kennett Loftus in 1849.

139

- *The Administration Tablets of Uruk*

Archaeologists have discovered administrative tablets from Uruk! (3100-2900 B.C.).

- The Tower of Babel

The Bible tells us a story of a tower being built in the land of Babel. It was in southern Mesopotamia that the Bible tells us in the land of Shinar (Uruk) in the province of Babel that a tower was built. Is there any archaeological proof that ancient southern Mesopotamia ever built such edifices to their gods? Yes, there is.

The Technology of Making Bricks

The development of baked brick technology took place in the region of Jamdet Nasr around 3100 B.C. This is important to the biblical story of the Tower of Babel because the Bible mentions the material in which men used to build this tower (Genesis 11:3): "The building materials described in Genesis are consistent with those used to build Mesopotamia ziggurats."[8] So we know that southern Mesopotamia used bricks to build towers to the gods. As a matter of fact, bricks with cuneiform writing have been found on Ziggurats! What is a ziggurat you ask?

- *Ziggurats in Mesopotamia*

---

[8] Holden and Geisler, *The Popular Handbook*, 212.

A *ziggurat* is a tower that the ancient people of Sumer, Babel, built as a tower to their gods. Archaeologists have even found more than 30 of these ziggurats in Mesopotamia, just like the Bible described.[9] King Shulgi of Ur, 2100 B.C. raised Sumer to its cultural heights. The oldest ziggurat is Tepe, Sialik, a ziggurat from the Proto-Elamite period, which is the oldest ziggurat known (3000-2900 B.C.) in Kashan, Iran.

While there is debate as to the Hebrew word *migdal*, and whether it means a tower or a fortress, there are enough stories in antiquities to attest to the belief that a tower was built to the gods in the Mesopotamian region of Babylon. Archaeologists can attest to the fact that there are numerous ancient stories where people built a tower to the gods and that a god confused their language.

- *Shinar / Nimrod*

---

[9] Ibid., 210.

In Genesis 11:2, the Bible says, after the Flood, men migrated to the land of Shinar to build a city. According to Genesis 10:8-10, Nimrod built a city in this region. Genesis 14 appears to suggest that Shinar was also a specific name of a kingdom with its own king. The name Shinar appears eight times in the Bible and is considered the name for the broad area of ancient Mesopotamia. Nimrod is believed to be by many King Sargon I. Nimrod might be Sargon because of Sargon's geographical origin, and first because of Kish, who is possibly associated with Nimrod's genealogical origin of Cush. Cush was the oldest son of Ham. Nimrod was the grandson of Ham, son of Noah. Second, both Sargon and Nimrod are credited with bringing Akkad into prominence. Third, Nimrod was involved in initial building projects in Assyria. Fourth, both Sargon and Nimrod had a lasting influence related to Assyria. Toward the end of Sargon's reign, he introduced the eponymic dating system in the empire. Fifth, the prophet Micah refers to the land of Nimrod with the land of Assyria. "And they will pasture the land of Assyria with the sword, and the land of Nimrod at its entrance points" (Micah 5:6). Here, Micah is equating the land of Nimrod with the land of Assyria. Therefore, Sargon and Nimrod could be the same person. Add to this thought, the fact that both Sargon and Nimrod were legendary for their military exploits and brutality, and Sargon's candidacy for being Nimrod is superior to that of Naram-Sin, the grandson of Sargon. However, for a number of scholars, Naram-Sin is either just as worthy of being the ideal candidate for Nimrod as Sargon is, or a better one. As Levin stated the case, "The identification of Nimrod with either Sargon or Naram-Sin has been brought up in the past," such as van Gelderen's suggestion in 1914 that Naram-Sin is to be equated with Nimrod. Moreover, not only does Naram-Sin come from the correct era and dynasty, which automatically makes this Akkadian king a legitimate candidate, but his exploits seemingly outshine those of his grandfather. You can see the bust of Sargon of Akkade at the Iraq Museum in Baghdad. To read more, go to this website: *https://israelmyglory.org/article/the-identity-of-nimrod/*

- *Etemenanki (Babylon)*

The world's most famous ziggurat is called Etemenanki in Babylon (Iraq) and was built to honor the god Marduk. Nebuchadnezzar II said it "reached to the heavens." The word *etemenanki* means, "House of the foundations of heaven on earth." At the Louvre in Paris, there is a cuneiform tablet from Uruk written in 229 B.C. that describes the making of this ziggurat, a seven-terrace tower with a ground floor of 91 x 91 meters! This tower has been confirmed by archaeologists. [10]

- *Enuma Elish*

In 1849, Austin Henry Layard, discovered in ancient Nineveh (Mosul, Iraq) at the Library of Ashurbanipal, seven clay tablets called the Enuma Elish. Since then, archaeologists have discovered more than 26,000 tablets. These tablets were written in an-

---

[10] Jeremy Norman, "Construction of the Etemenanaki Ziggurat: Later Known as the Tower of Babel," History of Information, accessed November 11, 2018, http://www.historyofinformation.com/expanded.php?id=154.

cient Akkadian cuneiform style and told the story of the Babylonian belief of creation. The Enuma Elish gave a detailed account of a huge tower in Babel and it "calibrates the Book of Genesis on a chief architect, builders, names, location, structure, materials, and purpose," of a tower in Babel.[11]

- *The Lord of Eridu*
  The story is told of a golden age where everyone spoke one language until the god Enki changed their speech (5400 B.C.). Eridu was the first city of the ancient Sumerians in which was built a ziggurat (tower of worship) called Amar-sin in the center of the city. [12]

- *Enmerkar and Lord of Aratta*

Enmerkar was the king of Uruk and lord of Aratta. This Sumerian Epic tells another story of a golden age when everyone spoke one language until there was a "confusion of tongue," at the construction of a temple of worship. It contains allusions to a unified language and the subsequent diversifying of language by the gods.

There are numerous stories of a creation, just like the Bible has stated. Also, there are plentiful chests of ancient documents that prove that the ancient world firmly believed that the world was once flooded. Too, there are stories which speak of a world where there is but one language and people who, because of God, were made to scatter throughout the earth. Today, science is adding to the fact of a catastrophic flood, regardless of whether the world acknowledges it or not. There is proof of towers built to gods in the regions of

---

[11] *Understanding Haplogroups.*

[12] Joshua J. Marks, "Eridu," *Encyclopedia of Ancient History*, July 20, 2010, accessed November 2, 2018, https://www.ancient.eu/eridu/.

Mesopotamia and scientific work among DNA specialists to prove their migrations. While we have not found the bodies of Adam and Eve, and probably never will, and while yes, there are "holes" (questions) that remain, and a mountain of hypotheses by the mathematical concept of probability, we might safely assume, at this point, that "something" is there. Deep within the Bible, truth is present!

Chapter 6

Abraham and Sodom and Gomorrah

Do you remember seeing your first picture of Abraham in Sunday school? I can imagine that it was unusual to see a man dressed like he was dressed. You must have had a certain feeling that he was very different from you and your time. This probably led you to believe, because of the place in the Bible where we find his story, we would never be able to go back "that far" tracing history. That is not true. As a matter of fact, the Sumerian communities that we have just explored have preceded Abraham.

- **Abraham**

    Abraham is an important figure in our Bible and a foundational history is given in the Book of Genesis (Genesis 11:27-28). While certain evidence that Abraham was a literal person is not available to us, information about the place he came from is changing that by way of the archaeological spade. In 2006, "The only suggested extrabiblical mention of Abraham is in the topographical list (Nos. 71-72) of Shoshenq I (Shishak) of Egypt in 925 B.C., giving what may be read as 'The Enclosure of Abram,' and which is fairly widely accepted. But this is not absolutely certain; it could be interpreted 'Enclosure of the Stallions' (`abbirim), although the Negev region where this place was located is not exactly famous for horses. However, the Negev is mentioned as one of Abraham's haunts (Genesis 12:9; 13:1, 3; 20:1; also Isaac, 24:62), which would fit well with a place being named after him."[1]

Today, things are changing even more for the cities in which the Bible uses to connect Abraham. The Bible makes it clear that he came from "Ur of the Chaldeans."

- **Ur of the Chaldeans**

Ur of the Chaldeans is the major landmark the Bible uses to connect the patriarch Abraham (Genesis 11:31) to this area. Archaeologists have recently found a wealth of information about this Sumerian city called Ur of the Chaldeans, known as the ancient city Ur Kasdim. Ur is the best known of the cities of Sumer, and the Bible tells us this is the birthplace of Abraham.

Ur was first discovered in 1854 by J.E. Taylor who started the excavation of the original ruins. Since then, many other archaeologists have excavated

---

[1] Claude Mariottini, "Abraham and Archaeology," Claude Mariottini: Professor of Old Testament, March 1, 2006, accessed November 1, 2018, *https://claudemariottini.com/2006/03/01/abraham-and-archaeology/*.

this site finding a golden "Ram in a thicket" piece of artwork—elaborate artwork—painted upon clothes, and even a house which has now been restored that existed during the time of Abraham.[2]

- ### Ur of the Chaldeans and Artwork: The Tomb of Ur

We have discovered artwork from this city from the ancient Tomb of Ur.

- ### A Skeleton From the City of Ur

Archaeologists have discovered the skeletal remains of a 6,500-year-old person from the city of Ur! This 6,500-year-old skeleton from the site of Ur in present-day Iraq was recently rediscovered in the basement of the University of Pennsylvania Museum of Archaeology and Anthropology. The skeleton had originally been uncovered in 1929–1930 during the joint British Museum/Penn Museum excavation at Ur led by Sir Leonard Woolley. For 85 years, the skeleton has been lying in a wooden box in the Penn Museum's labyrinthine basement; any associated documentation that may have once been attached to the skeleton or storage box has long been missing.

---

[2] Robert Silverberg, *Great Adventures: Archaeology: Edited and with an Introduction by Robert Silverberg* (New York: Dial Press, 1964), 256–57.

- ### The Golden Ram in the Thicket

The Book of Genesis 22:13, tells the story of Abraham as he was going to sacrifice his son Isaac to God on an altar. Thank God, he looked over and heard God say to him that he was to use the "ram caught in a thicket." While, this does not prove that Abraham lived, it does prove that the biblical description of Abraham's time contained the imagery of a "ram in a thicket." This ram was discovered by Leonard Woolley, a famous archaeologist, when he discovered the 'Great Death Pit' at Ur, the city where Abraham lived before he traveled to Canaan. In the pit, he found a pair of statuettes, gold and lapis lazuli, dating from about 2600–2400 B.C., showing what looked like a golden goat or ram caught in the branches of a thicket. Woolley thought there might be a connection between these objects and the story of Abraham and Isaac. Judging by the horns and coat of the animal in the statuette, some said it was just a goat—a symbol of fertility. The 'ram' or goat is shown reaching up to nibble at the branches of a shrub or bush—a common sight in the ancient Near East.

- ### The Time of Abraham

The time that Abraham lived is important and often hotly debated. However, it would be important for us to talk about this timeline before we proceed much further into this chapter. The logical and often biblical view of the timeline of Abraham must be defined within the chronology of ancient Mesopotamia. This chronology of Mesopotamia is as follows: (You may have already heard many of these names and places throughout this book already.). Also, notice how much work archaeologists have already completed by excavating these sites which actually PREDATE the life of Abraham. These times periods are as follows.

1. The Hassuna Period: 5800–5500 B.C.

2. The Halaf Period: 5500–4500 B.C.

3. The Ubaid Period: (Genesis 10) 5300–3750 B.C.

4. Protoliterate (James Nasr) Period: 3150–2900 B.C.

5. Early Dynasty I, II, III, IIIA, IIIB: 2900–2334 B.C.

6. Dynasty of Akkad (Sargon the Great): 2334–2154 B.C.

7. The Dynasty of Gutian (Kingdom of Gutium): 2217–2120 B.C.

8. The Reign of Utu-khegal: 2120–2112 B.C.

9. Ur III Dynasty: 2112–2004 B.C.

10. The Dynasty of Isin: 2017–1787 B.C.

11. The Dynasty of Larsa: 2025–1763 B.C.

12. The First Dynasty of Babylon (Hammurabi) 1894–1595 B.C.[3]

To read more about this, go to this website: *https://assets.answersingenesis.org/doc/articles/pdf-versions/arj/v5/abraham-chronology-ancient-mesopotamia.pdf*

---

[3] Matt McClellan, "Abraham and the Chronology of Ancient Mesopotamia," *Answers Research Journal*, no. 5 (2012): 141–50.

It was previously thought that Abraham lived during the reign of the First Dynasty of Babylon with the King Hammurabi. However, the current line of thinking today is that Abraham lived somewhere between the Ur III and Isin/Larsa Dynasties (Nos. 9–11 on the list). Notice how many artifacts have been discovered from time periods that exceed the story of Abraham by thousands of years.

- ## The City of Haran

We not only know a great deal about the city that Abraham was born in but also the city in which his Father Terah fled to when Abraham was young (Genesis 11:31; Acts 7:2-4). *Haran* means "road," and it was the strategic location of trade at the time of Abraham. Ancient Haran was discovered in 1950 in the country of Turkey, near the modern city of Urfa. At the site, there have been many excavations from several periods of time. One such discovery was the Temple of the moon god, called Sin. The early Sumerians worshiped it as a deity. A treasure trove of ancient Mesopotamian artifacts has also been found at the site.[4]

- ## The Hittites

At the turn of the eighteenth century, the majority of historians began to believe that a people called the Hittites did not ever exist even though the Bible mentions them more than 50 times. They pointed out that

---

[4] Algerim Korzhumbayeva, "Haran," *Electrum Magazine*: Why the Past Matters, (March 2, 2013), accessed November 1, 2018, *http://www.electrummagazine.com/2013/03/harran-ancient-crossroads-city-of-mesopotamia/*.

the Bible is the only place that mentions these people (Genesis 15:20, 23; Joshua 1:4; Judges 1:26). Newspapers made fun of the treaty which is spoken about in the Bible between the Hittites and the Egyptians which is called the Treaty of Kadesh. That was . . . until A. H. Sayce, in 1876, used the Bible to discover where this civilization might be located. Sayce did not find just one piece of information, but he found the capital city of Hattusa and more than 10,000 clay tablets from their library! Since 1876, Hugo Winckler from 1906–1908 further excavated this site, firmly establishing the realities of a people called the Hittites.[5]

- **Sodom and Gomorrah and the Cities of the Plain**

  While the names Sodom and Gomorrah are etched in history as famous places of judgment, the cities which were connected are often forgotten by time. The Bible says, Abraham lived in Canaan while his nephew Lot moved to "the valley of the Jordan," and "pitched his tent as far as Sodom," (Genesis 13:10-12). Genesis 19:15 tells us that Lot was living in this area when an angel (don't laugh yet), told Lot to get his family out of this city or, "you will be consumed" (Genesis 19:15 NRSV). The angels actually said, "Do not look behind you nor stay anywhere in the plain. Escape to the mountains, lest you be destroyed" (Genesis 19:17). The name "plains' is mentioned multiple times in the Bible and almost always implies the Cities of the Plain, of which Sodom and Gomorrah were two of five cities (Sodom, Gomorrah, Admah, Zeboim, and Zoar, Genesis 13:10). Four of these cities were never mentioned again by these names as an occupied city after their reported destruction in Genesis 19. These were Cities of the

---

[5] Fred H. Wight, "Highlights of Archaeology in Bible Lands," No name, Chapter Six: 1955, http://baptistbiblebelievers.com/LinkClick.aspx?fileticket=uz3E9va3Kgs%3d&tabid=456&mid=1433.

Plain. The word *plain* is the Hebrew word *Kikkar*, and means "a circle." This circle of cities (Kikkar) has for us a haunting question. A question that Dr. Steven Collins and Dr. Latayne C. Scott, the archaeologist who led the excavation of Sodom, raised: "Why did a civilization built upon one of antiquities' best-watered agriscapes at the crossroads of the region's main north-south and east-west thoroughfares suddenly collapse and literally disappear from history for seven hundred years?"[6]

- **Sodom**

The Bible tells us that Abraham could see the destruction of Sodom and Gomorrah by looking down upon the cities (Genesis 18:16) from the highpoint of Canaan, which is west of Jordan. Abraham probably lived during the time of the Middle Bronze Age II, and based on archaeology, geographical evidence, along with Genesis 19, Sodom has been identified as the city of Tall el-Hammam. This is the most logical place based on geological, archaeological, biblical, and historical experts. While there are many educated myths about its destruction such as the existence of "sulfur balls," tar pits under the city, oil and gas deposits, and volcanic eruptions as the reason this city virtually disappeared, seems to have been solidly disproved by science today. But before you say, "I told you the story was not true," you may want to grab your prayer journal, because what science has proven is a worst-case scenario than previously assumed, and proven by scientific methods.

---

[6] Steven Collins and Latayne C. Scott, *Discovering the City of Sodom: The Fascinating, True Account of the Discovery of the Old Testament's Most Infamous City* (New York: Howard Books, 2013), 156.

- ## The Witnesses of Sodom and Gomorrah

There are no eyewitnesses alive today to confirm the biblical story of Sodom and Gomorrah, but there are witnesses. Collins and Scott point them out by arguing with the vigor of honest scientists. They first point out there is a direct absence of evidence in the Late Bronze Age, found within this region, specifically in Tall el-Hamman (Sodom). They report: "In fact, there's no evidence of Late Bronze habitations at Tall el-Hammam . . . at all. This is true of all the other sites of the eastern Kikkar as well."[7] They continue to report that the "brick has been blown away, where a "sprawling city" once stood—a fortified city that would back up the fact that Lot was standing at the city gate (Genesis 19:1). In fact, there are few precious metals and other treasures such as pottery or jewelry present at Tall el-Hammam. While some point to grave robbers, there is great plausibility that a natural destruction so severe and enormous destroyed most of them instantly! All these pieces of evidence clearly support the biblical narrative of Sodom and Gomorrah. Are there more witnesses? Yes.

- ## Human Remains

Archaeologists and geologists have confirmed the remains of human beings at Sodom in the year 2011. What is fascinating and sobering is that "All archaeologists on site agreed that the skeletal remains were intrinsic

---

[7] Collins and Scott, p. 164.

to the ash layer, which dates to the Middle Bronze Age II, according to the ceramics...the human remains are mixed... with lots of ash."[8] They went on to report the positions of the two adults and one child, along with pieces of many others: "What we see are bodies wrenched around in a facedown position, as if they were thrown down in the process of turning away from something in an unconscious reaction, as if protecting themselves. ... One is charred off at mid-femur. Their condition at death attests to "extreme trauma."[9] These humans were found in the undisturbed matrix of destruction in which they died . . . instantly. What is even more amazing is that these skeletons have been dated to the Middle Bronze Age II—the time of Abraham!

- **It Was Trinitite Hot!**

These "witnesses" were found covered in twenty-inches of ash! What kind of heat happened during the destruction of Sodom and Gomorrah? The scientists who discovered Sodom took a piece of melted, greenish glass found at the site and pieces of pottery shards, with greenish, glasslike surfaces. (These were discovered at the Middle Bronze Age II level!) The scientists realized that what they had discovered could have never been the result of pottery being fired in a furnace because of the level of heat it took to make pottery. To make what they held in their hands would take an enormous amount of heat, much higher than what it took to make ancient pottery. They took the greenish glass, to the U.S. Geological Survey Laboratory on the campus of New Mexico Tech.[10] When the scientists

---

[8] Ibid., 178.

[9] Ibid., 179.

[10] Ibid., 206.

saw the perspective piece they said, "Oh, trinitite!" Trinitite is a glassy residue left on the desert floor after the plutonium-based Trinity nuclear bomb test. Simply said, its sand, rocks, and other minerals were melted together by an atomic bomb. Scientists suddenly realized that it contained pieces of pottery, which looked like trinitite, but could not have been trinitite. However, there is a similar material which looks like trinitite called impact glasses. The amazing issue here is that this was not trinitite nor was it melted by any normal means due to its chemical analyses. The piece of evidence from Sodom could have only been made in one way—a "sort of quick, superlatively hot event (occurring) over the air in the desert, converting exposed sand into chunks of rare, greenish substance...in twenty seconds."[11] This was not enough to melt quartz on the ground, creating glass!

The scientists discovered that "without an atomic bomb to create such an effect, the blame would have to fall on a meteor or other midair event producing heat so intense and fleeting that it could melt just the surface of the inanimate things exposed to it. Aside from the heat of these phenomena, the sheer force would be horrific, unimaginable force."[12] In other words, the only thing according to a scientist trained in the latest astrophysics impact, was fire from heaven.

• Abraham and the Ebla Tablets

What is an Ebla tablet? It's a gift rolled out from the rock of history given in clay form of 1,800 complete copies, 4,700 fragments, and thousands of pieces from ancient clay tablets. Inside these clay tablets you can find a complete dictionary—actually there are eighteen copies of over 1,000 ancient words.

---

[11] Ibid., 214.
[12] Ibid., 215.

Ebla was a city that today is called Tell Mardikh, which between 2400 and 2250 B.C. had a population of 260,000 people. It was an ancient Sumerian city that Paolo Matthiae from the University of Rome excavated in 1964. When word hit the news that this city had been found, there were many discussions and assumptions about what this archaeological treasure trove would eventually mean for biblical archaeology. And of course, the Ebla tablets still has their skeptics all these years later. However, we know a great deal more today than we did at the height of its arguments in 1975. We now know that there were eighteen copies of an ancient dictionary containing 1,000 words. Why is this important? It is important because the Sumerian dialect of Ebla is very similar to the Hebrew and Phoenician languages. In other words, it has a distinctively Semitic feel as many words are distinctively similar to the Semitic (Jewish) language. Similarities abound such as the Ebla word for man (*adum*) which, of course, is similar to the Hebrew word for man (adam). The similarities and distinctions don't stop here.

These Ebla tablets predate the biblical record attributed to Moses. However, many names, places, phrases, and cultural activities mentioned in the Bible are confirmed in the Ebla tablets. The Ebla tablets seem to point toward names in Sumerian similar to Hebrew (Semitic) names such as, "Melchizedek," "David," "Saul," "Ishmael," "Abraham," and El (God). The Ebla tablets identify places such as the towns of Hazor, Lachish, Megiddo, Gaza, Sinai, Joppa, Damascus, Urusalima (Jerusalem), and the Cities of the Plain, specifically Sodom and Gomorrah, just to name a few, are quite possibly identified in these ancient documents. You can find such familiar phrases as, "Ya has mercy on me," and "addad (God) is our shepherd." Along with these familiar phrases you can spot cultural activities like the mention of the Hittites, long before Abraham introduced them to us in the Bible. You can find information that attests to the fact that in the days of the Ebla tablets, there were prophets and ritualistic sacrifices. The Ebla tablets specifically mention distinctive codes of justice—something the skeptics have argued about for years. They said the Bible can't be true because they mention the Ten Commandments (codes of Justice/Laws). The skeptics said, "There were no specific codes of justice (laws) for these earlier peoples." Indeed there were, and the Ebla Tablets prove that eight hundred years before Moses wrote the Ten Commandments, such judicial laws existed. All these "likelihoods" build up to a mathematical probability.

The skeptics of the Book of Genesis have often criticized the Bible by suggesting that the words "the deep," were not in use at such an early date as the writing of the Book of Genesis. However, the Ebla tablets use this same phrase (the deep/*tehom*), as well as the word "Canaan." The Ebla tablets used (*tehom*) 800 years before Moses used it! [13]

• **Abraham, the Patriarchs, and the Camel**

The phrase, "Abraham, the Patriarchs, and the Camel," isn't necessarily something you are going to read about in the news tonight. It, however, is at the center of a vigorous biblical debate. The Bible says in Genesis 12:16, "Therefore he treated Abram (Abraham) well for her sake. He had sheep, oxen, male donkeys, male and female servants, female donkeys, and camels." Who would have ever thought thousands and thousands of years later that the little phrase, "and camels," would be at the center of many arguments as to whether the Bible was true or not?

[13] Clifford Wilson, "Ebla: It's Impact on Bible Records," Institute for Creation Research, April 1, 1977, accessed November 1, 2018, *https://www.icr.org/article/ebla-its-impact-bible-records/*.

The skeptics of the Bible have said that the Bible is not true because Abraham would not have had camels in Palestine due to the simple fact that camels had not been domesticated in that region during the biblical times of Abraham. Yet, the Bible says otherwise. The Bible says in Genesis 12:16; 24:10 that Abraham possessed camels. It says that Jacob did also (Genesis 30:43; 32:7, 15), as well as other patriarchs (Genesis 24:10-64) and Egyptians (Exodus 9:3). But as late as 2013, Israeli archaeologists at the University of Tel Aviv date the domestication of camels to the tenth century B.C. They say that the camel was not domesticated in Palestine until 1,000 years after Abraham lived. They support their argument by saying that camels do not appear as domesticated in the Near East until the ninth century B.C. However, there is a problem within their argument.

To argue that the camel was not domesticated until 1,000 years after Abraham lived is based on a faulty premise. The skeptics are assuming something that the biblical text does not say. The Bible does not say that camels were in "wide-spread," use in Palestine. It was saying that men like Abraham who came from Mesopotamia did have SOME camels. Furthermore, what, if any, does the archaeological evidence suggest about the earlier presence of camels before the Patriarchal times? Is there evidence for the earlier presence of camels before the time of Abraham? Dewayne Bryant does an amazing job of answering this question. Here is what he writes:

> Ancient texts mention the camel in passing, but do so in ways that indicate they had been domesticated early in Mesopotamian history. A lexical text found at Nippur, known as HAR.ra-bullum, alludes to camel milk (Archer, 1970, 127[505]:17).[14] This can't be an undomesticated camel, because you simply can't milk a wild animal.[15]

---

[14] Dewayne Bryant, "Abraham's Camel," Apologetics Press, 2014, accessed November 2, 2018, *http://www.apologeticspress.org/APContent.aspx?category=9&article=4800* .

[15] Gleason Archer, "Old Testament History and Recent Archaeology From Abraham to Moses," *Biblotheca Sacre* 127, no. 505 (1970): 3–25.

In addition, "the ancient city of Ugarit mentions the camel "in a list of domesticated animals during the Old Babylonian period (1950–1600 B.C.)," suggesting that it, too, was domesticated (Davis, 1986, p. 145)."[16] Also, there is "A fodder-list from Alalakh (18th century B.C.) which includes the line, "1 SA.GAL ANSE.GAM.MAL" (269:59), translated as "one (measure of) fodder—camel" (Wiseman, 1959, 13:29; translation in Hamilton 1990, p. 384)."[17] Animals in the wild forage for themselves!

There is an ancient seal from Syria which depicts two people on camels. "A cylinder seal from Syria (c. 1800 B.C.) depicts two short figures riding a camel." Gordon and Rendsburg state: "The mention of camels here [in Genesis 24] and elsewhere in the patriarchal narratives often is considered anachronistic. However, the correctness of the Bible is supported by the representation of camel riding on seal cylinders of precisely this period from northern Mesopotamia (1997, p. 121). While the riders on the seal seem to be deities, it nevertheless demonstrates the concept of camel riding (for illustration and discussion, see Gordon, 1939, 6[1]:21; Collon, 2000, Fig. 8)."[18]

Numerous discoveries of figurines depicting domesticated camels have been found from a wide range of locations in the ancient world. From the territory of Bactria-Margiana near present-day northern Afghanistan (late third to early second millennium), Terracotta models of camel-drawn carts (dating as early as c. 2200 B.C.) have been discovered at the city of Altyn-Depe in present-day Turkmenistan (Kirtcho, 2009, 37[1]:25-33). "Early in the twentieth century, excavations conducted by the British School of Archaeology at Rifeh, Egypt, explored a tomb and discovered a pottery figurine of a camel bearing a load of two water jars. Based on the pottery in the tomb, William Flinders Petrie dated it to the Nineteenth Dynasty (c. 1292-1187 B.C.) (Ripinsky, 1985, 71:139-140)."[19]

---

[16] Bryant, "Abraham's Camel.

[17] Ibid.

[18] Ibid.

[19] Ibid.

As it relates to Egypt and the presence of camels, here is yet another rock that is crying out. A rock inscription in hieratic (a type of Egyptian script) found near Aswan has an accompanying petroglyph of a man leading a dromedary camel. It is thought to date to the Sixth Dynasty (c. 2345-c. 2181 B.C.; Ripinsky, p. 139).[20] If interpreted correctly, this petroglyph gives evidence of the domestication of the camel in Egypt roughly 2300–2200 B.C., centuries before the patriarchs ever visited. Additional petroglyphs in the Wadi Nasib, Sinai, include a depiction of a man leading a dromedary. One author tentatively dates these petroglyphs to 1500 B.C. based on the presence of nearby inscriptions whose dates are known (Younker, 1997).[21]

Finally, a curious piece of evidence comes from the ancient city of Mari. A camel burial (c. 2400-2200 B.C.) was discovered within a house. Ancient people often buried their animals, and this could hardly be explained away as a wild camel wandering into a home and subsequently buried by the occupants."[22]

The evidence for the presence of camels, not the widespread domestication of camels is what the biblical text strongly suggests.

• **The Existence of Abraham**

We have not found a bag of goods in the ruins of the Sumerian regions of Ur with the name Abraham or a note that says, "If lost, please call..." Maybe one day we will find a physical piece of evidence with the name Abraham etched into it, just like archaeologists eventually found the name "Pontius Pilate,"

[20] Michael Ripinsky, "The Camel in Dynastic Egypt," *The Journal of Egyptian Archaeology,* 71 (1985): 134–41.

[21] Randall W. Yonker, "Late Bronze Age Camel Petroglyphs in the Wadi Nasib Sinai," *Near East Archaeological Society Bulletin* 42 (1997): 47–54.

[22] Wilson, *Ebla.*

"Nebuchadnezzar," and even "James, son of Joseph, brother of Jesus." Until then, it is not intellectually fair to write off Abraham as a real person, *if* there is circumstantial evidence to suggest that many other parts of the biblical story can be historically confirmed. And remember: "Just because we don't have the proof today, doesn't mean we might not find it tomorrow." Every time the skeptics, whether they are archaeologists, liberal theologians, historians, geologists, or anthropologists, have decided that the Bible has been proven wrong in a specific statement, they have regretted their words. Just ask those who mocked the existence of the prophet Isaiah. (This is addressed in the coming chapters.) Archaeologists have found the city named after Abraham's father and brother (Terah and Haran). We have located the "Cities of the Plain," Sodom and Gomorrah, the people he traded with called the Hittites, the camel, and other cities and names. The mathematical probability that Abraham lived is in our favor. One, history points toward his world as having been real places; second, the Bible says so—period!

Chapter 7

Joseph and the Land of Egypt

Joseph and the land of Egypt was a colorful tapestry which detailed the fascinating family history of Abraham, and his sons (patriarchs). What about Abraham's sons? The children's song says: "Father Abraham had many sons, and many sons had father Abraham...." Perhaps laying a quick foundation of the lineage of Abraham will help to transition from Abraham to Joseph. Abraham had two sons, Isaac (the promised son) and Ishmael (the one whom Abraham "helped" God to fulfill His promise); Isaac had twin sons— one named Jacob and the other named Esau. Esau sold his birthright (Genesis 25:29-34); therefore, Jacob, whose name was changed to Israel (Genesis 32:28), had twelve sons who later became the twelve tribes of Israel. These sons were:

1. Judah (Deuteronomy 33:7)

2. Issachar (1 Chronicles 7:1-5)

3. Benjamin (1 Chronicles 7:6-12)

4. Reuben (1 Chronicles 5:1)

5. Naphtali (Numbers 2:29)

6. Manasseh (1 Chronicles 7:14-19)

7. Ephraim (Numbers 1:33)

8. Gad (Genesis 46:16)

9. Asher (1 Chronicles 7:30-40)

10. Simeon (Numbers 1:23)

11. Dan (Numbers 1:39)

12. Zebulon (Judges 1:30)

Now, you will notice that the tribe of Levi (Levites) is not here. They were not included in the inheritance of the Promised Land (Genesis 29:34). Perhaps you are wondering where Joseph is in this table. He is found under the lineage of Ephraim and Manasseh, which are both listed as two of the twelve tribes of Israel (Ephraim and Manasseh were Joseph's sons). These twelve sons became the foundational lineage to the establishment of the people who would later be known as the twelve tribes of Israel. So, is there archaeological evidence for Joseph and his brothers—the twelve tribes of Israel? There is some, but not much, because these sons were predominantly herdsmen. They would have been unknown by most of civilized society. It is highly unlikely that these common herdsmen would be mentioned by the elites of society. However, there are some things we do know about the family history of Joseph and the twelve tribes of Israel.

We do not have early physical evidence today of the majority of the twelve tribes of Israel. However, we do have some early evidence for at least four of them: Dan, Gad, Asher, and Judah.

• The Tribe of Dan

The tribe of Dan is mentioned in Genesis 49:16. The city known as ancient Laish (Judges 18:5) was renamed Dan later. In 1 Kings 12:28-29, Dan is mentioned as the "high place," set up by Jeroboam, a wayward king of the Northern Kingdom. This "high place" was excavated in 1976 by A. Biran in 1977—"[where] a very important discovery was made from the Hellenistic period (third and second centuries B.C.).[1] A dedicatory inscription mentioning Dan was found some 17 meters south of the high place."[2]

• The Tribe of Gad

There is a famous stele called the Mesha Stele which was found at Dhibon in Jordan, dating from the ninth century B.C. The tribe of Gad is mentioned in this stele when they used the phrase "Men of Gad."

• Asher

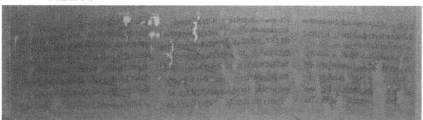

In Genesis 49:20, the tribe of Asher is mentioned. During the rule of Rameses II, (1279–1212 B.C.),

[1] A. Biran, "City of the Golden Calf," *Bible and Spade* 5 (1976): 22–27.

[2] Bryant G. Wood, "Is There Archaeological Evidence of the Sons of Jacob, the Tribal Leaders of Israel?" Christian Answers, 1998, accessed November 2, 2018, *www.christiananswers.net/q-abr/abr-a028.html.*

several groups of people were conquered. A list has been found which mentions Asher ('Isr) among these conquered people. In a papyrus of Anastasi I during the end of the 13th century, there is a novice scribe, whom the god Hori chides and says, "Qazardi, ruler of Asru ('Isr). [3]

- ## Judah

In Genesis 49:10, the name Judah is introduced. Judah was the most well-known tribe and became the greatest of all the twelve tribes. It was an immensely political and important tribe, so there are numerous references in history to it. One of the oldest is a reference to King Ahaz of Judah, dated around the eighth century. This reference was found in a bulla (clay sealing) which reads, "Ahaz (son of) Jotham, king of Judah."[4]

- ## The Arrival of Joseph

The Patriarchs (Abraham, Isaac, and Jacob) are coming to a close in our historical search of the Book of Genesis. The remaining thirteen chapters of Genesis begin to unfold a story of the Jewish people. While they have not reached the status of an empire or even a nation, they are beginning to be seen as a separate group of people. The story in Genesis is now moving from the region of Mesopotamia and Canaan, to the national empire called Egypt.

---

[3] K.A. Kitchen, *Ancient Orient and Old Testament.* (Downers Grove, IL: InterVarsity Press, 1993), Inside Inscription.

[4] H. Shanks, "Strata," *Biblical Archaeology* 23, no. 2 (March/April 1997): 8.

It is important to note here that the timeline of Joseph, Egypt, and its Pharaohs have been the source of hotly debated arguments. The arguments are over the exact timeline of the Dynasty of Pharaohs, which in turn, greatly influence the time in which we believe Joseph, Moses, and Aaron, lived. We don't know for sure how these timelines play out within the biblical text. However, we can know the probability of such timelines because there are some logical assumptions based on the timing of certain events in biblical history.

• **Joseph**

Abraham was Joseph's great-grandfather. Jacob was Joseph's father and moved his family into Egypt (1876 B.C.) about 215 years after Abraham entered Canaan (2091 B.C). For the most part, Joseph's family dwelt in tents since they kept livestock. It is possible that Joseph was born during the Egyptian reign of Pharaoh Amenemhat II (1919–1884 B.C.).[5] Joseph later became a ruler in Egypt around (1878 B.C.) as the Pharaoh Sesostris II was coming into power is another plausible time. However, Joseph was living in Canaan with his brothers and father Jacob when he had a dream (Genesis 37:1-12). Joseph's brothers were offended by his dream that portrayed them bowing down to Joseph (Genesis 37:8). One day when his brothers were in Shechem, Jacob sent Joseph to look for them. Joseph eventually ended up in Dothan. His brothers saw him coming, and they stripped him of his coat of many colors (Genesis 37:3, 23). The brothers sold Joseph into slavery to the Ishmaelites for twenty shekels of silver (Genesis 37:28). His brothers went back to Jacob and told him that Joseph had been killed. The Bible

---

[5] Ashby Camp, "Israel, Egypt, and the Exodus," *Outlet*, 2016, accessed November 5, 2018, http://www.theoutlet.us/Israel,Egypt,andtheExodus.pdf.

eventually leads us to the fact that Joseph had been taken down to Egypt and sold to the Egyptian officer, Potiphar, who was the captain of the bodyguard (Genesis 39:1). The Bible then tells us that Joseph became very successful, having first been placed as the personal assistant in Potiphar's household (Genesis 39:2-5). What evidence do we have that the Bible was correct about the story of Joseph?

According to Genesis chapters 33 and 46, the patriarchs—Abraham, Isaac, Jacob, and Joseph—traveled often to Egypt for business and safety (Genesis 12:10; 33; 46:28-34). This travel of the Asiatics mentioned in the Bible is of great importance. The word "Asiatics" was a catchall word which the Egyptians used to describe the people of Syria, Palestine, and Mesopotamia. In murals, the Egyptians would paint them yellow to note their difference. In Egypt, there is a burial place known as Ben Hasen. Inside Ben Hasen, is the tomb of the Pharaoh Khnumhotep II. In this tomb, there is a unique mural on the walls. It is a mural that depicts the Asiatic nomads from Canaan traveling to Egypt for business. While this is not a specific picture of the biblical patriarchs, it does clearly show the practices of Asiatic people traveling to Egypt during this time were a reality.[6]

---

[6] Christiane Amanpour, "Joseph of Biblical Times: Archaeologists Seek Ancient Famine Evidence," ABC News, December 21, 2012, accessed November 12, 2018, *https://abcnews.go.com/2020/video/joseph-biblical-times-archeologists-seek-ancient-famine-evidence-18042343.*

• The Tale of Two Brothers

In an Egyptian papyrus scroll, dated from the thirteenth century, we find a folklore tale told within the Egyptian culture. This papyrus scroll is called "The Tale of Two Brothers," and alludes to the story of the Egyptian man named Potiphar and his wife. Susan Tower Hollis who has written extensively on this ancient scroll believes that it may "contain reflexes of an actual historical situation."[7]

• Famines in Egypt

The Bible speaks of two famines in Egypt. One during the time of Abraham (Genesis 12:10), and a second one after the season Joseph was in jail for falsely being accused by Potiphar's wife (Genesis 41). The Pharaoh called for Joseph in prison to come and interpret his dream (Genesis 41:14). It is highly probably that this was Sesostris I. Joseph described a seven-year cycle of plenty and a seven-year cycle of famine in his interpretation of Pharaoh's dream. There are three images that support this story.

a. The Famine Stele or "Hungry Rock"

There is a stele located on the Sehel Island in Egypt discovered by archaeologists who speak of a seven-year period of drought and famine. It also gives credit to Imhotep for interpreting the dream of Pharaoh and saving Egypt from the famine.

---

[7] Susan Tower Hollis, *The Ancient Egyptian "Tale of Two Brothers": A Mythological, Religious, Literary, and Historico-Political Study* (London: Bannerston, 2008), 110.

b. *Fragment of a Fifth-Century Dynasty Relief*

In the causeway leading to the valley temple of King Unas (Wenis), that dates to 2500 B.C., there is a relief of what many believe to be emaciated[8] Egyptians with protruding ribs.

c. *A Statue of Sesostris III*

Many people believe he is the most probable king during the time of the famine.

- **Sleeping Stones**

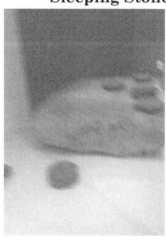

Do you like to sleep on pillows? So do I—lots of them. My wife calls them "a fortress." I can't image the words found in Genesis 28:11: "He took one of the stones of the place and put it under his head, and lay down in that place" (NASB). Sleeping on a stone! Preposterous! Well, that is exactly what the Bible says, and that is exactly what archaeologists have confirmed. It was the custom of Jacob, Joseph's father, to

---

[8] Hoerth, *Archaeology and the Old*, 150.

sleep on stones! The stones in the picture are from the British Museum in their exhibit from Egypt.

- **Twenty Shekels: The Laws of Hammurabi**

The Bible tells us the price paid for Joseph in Genesis 37:28 was twenty shekels. The price of slaves is well-known; it is an attested fact in history from 2400–400 B.C. In the laws of Hammurabi, it specifically states that the price for a slave is twenty shekels. In Genesis 37:28, the Bible tells us that Joseph, around the age of 17, was sold into slavery for that specific amount.

- **Joseph Shaved: Ancient Egyptian Razor**

In Genesis 41:4, we are told that Joseph prepared to meet Pharaoh by first shaving. In the picture, you can see an ancient Egyptian razor and an Egyptian statue of a clean-cut servant, giving us insight into the hygiene of the Egyptians.

- **The Land of Ramses: Genesis 47:11; 50:13**

You may not realize what you are seeing right now—it is a mummified corpse. However, it is a special corpse. This is the only picture in existence of any actual human directly mentioned in the Bible. This is the mummified body of Pharaoh Ramses II.

173

• The Tomb of Joseph

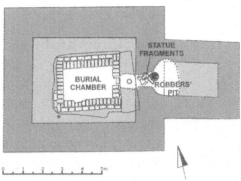

The Bible tells us that Moses took the bones of Joseph with him (Genesis 50:25; Exodus 13:19). So, it is reasonable to think that few ever thought they would find his grave in Egypt. Traditionally, since the fourth century, it was thought to be located near the ancient city of Shechem. However, recent archaeological discoveries in Egypt itself are changing the story. Again, according to the Book of Genesis, Joseph's bones were to be brought out of Egypt by Moses. Surprisingly, archaeologists have recently found another tomb they are attributing to Joseph.

In the city of Tell el-Dab'a, which is also known as Avaris, archaeologists have discovered an ancient city they believe to be the former capital of the Hikos people. This city is sitting in the middle of the land of Goshen. The people who inhabited this site were sometimes referred to as Asiatics. This again, was a catchall phrase for those who were understood to have come from the Levant (region of Canaan/Semitic). It was most improbable that they could have settled in this area without Egyptian consent. In this area, archaeologists found Hebrew tombs, and a great palace with a garden tomb designed with both Egyptian and Semitic styles. This palace belonged to a non-Egyptian ruler of Avaris. Many reputable archaeologists believe this to be the house of Joseph in the land of Goshen.

• A Possible Statue of Joseph Himself

Inside the previously mentioned palace, "One of the tombs in the village cemetery included a large statue, almost two times the size of a person, of a

seated Asiatic dignitary . . . the skin was yellow, the traditional color of Asiatics in Egyptian art. It had a mushroom-shaped hairstyle, painted red, typical of that shown in Egyptian artwork for Asiatics. A throw-stick, the Egyptian hieroglyph for a foreigner, was held against the right shoulder. The statue had been intentionally smashed and defaced."[9] The statue was dressed in a coat of many colors as a leader in Egypt, by the authority of Pharaoh, in the image of a Semitic person, and in the land of Goshen. The tomb and the statue were dated to the time of Joseph's probable death (1805 B.C.). To learn more, watch the movie which is being acclaimed by historians and archaeologists called, "Pattern of Evidence: Exodus." It speaks of a home and the statue itself! Go to the Internet and watch this video about Joseph and Egypt from ABC news! *https://abcnews.go.com/2020/video/joseph-biblical-times-archeologists-seek-ancient-famine-evidence-18042343*.

- **The Egyptian Linguistic References**

    The titles which are given by the Bible to Joseph were distinctively Egyptian and can be confirmed in antiquity. Such titles as "Lord of Pharaoh's House," (Genesis 45:8), meant "Chief Steward of the King"; the title "Father to Pharaoh," (Genesis 45:8), meant "Father to Pharaoh"; the title, "Ruler Throughout All the Land of Egypt," was often a term regulated to a vizier (Genesis 45:8). Skeptics of the Bible argue that no one man held two of these three titles at the same time. But, there are no facts on which to base this information. It is possible

---

[9] Manfred Bietak, *Egypt and the Levant: The Egyptian World* (New York: Routledge, 2002), 422.

that at this time during Egypt's history, a man might have held at least two of these three titles.

- ## Egyptian Embalming

In Genesis 50:22-26, it mentions that Joseph was embalmed. The Bible not only stated many cultural cues correctly, but it also understood the process of burying in Egypt. "The reason for embalming was that the ancient Egyptians believed the dead could only enter the afterlife if their bodies were preserved."[10]

- ## Goshen: After the Death of Joseph

After Joseph was embalmed, his people, the Hebrews, continued to live in the land of Goshen. The Jewish people eventually found themselves living in a world where, "Now a new king arose over Egypt, who did not know Joseph" (Exodus 1:8). The Bible says that Jacob passed (Genesis 50) and was buried at Machpelah (Genesis 50:12-13). After this, Joseph stayed in Egypt until his death (Genesis 50:24-26). The Egyptian people would grow to fear the success and growth of the Asiatic people in the land of Goshen.

---

[10] Stephen Leston, *The Bible in World History: Putting Scripture Into a Global Context* (Uhrichsville, Ohio: Barbour Books, 2011), 50.

Chapter 8

The Foundation for Moses and the Exodus

Why do we need a foundation for Moses and the Exodus? There are few biblical subjects more debated or controversial than the timing or the event of the Exodus. The Exodus is the name we give to the Asiatic people in Goshen when they left Egypt and headed to their Promised Land which God had given Abraham (Genesis 12). This was a time when the Israeli/Asiatic/ Semitic people were leaving slavery in Egypt. It's a powerful story of freedom which has rung in the ears of even our American revolutionaries. However, today's skeptics, who number from the ranks of authors, university professors, television documentaries, and even Jewish rabbis, all resound with the same voice regarding the Exodus. It either did not exist or it existed during the time of Rameses, which would place the date into the New Kingdom.

The problem is with the New Kingdom date which was a time of immense prosperity in Egypt. It is also a late date for Asiatic populations in Egypt. Furthermore, this is the date that is assumed by almost all Egyptologists and historians for hundreds of years. This assumption has created a great divide between the evidence and the belief that the Exodus took place in the New Kingdom. There is no evidence within the New Kingdom for an Exodus and certainly not a devastating blow caused by ten natural disasters from on high! As Brian Fagan, professor of anthropology, UCLA, writes: "The mortuary temple of King Seti I outside the Valley of Kings epitomizes the power of New Kingdom pharaohs. Ahmose, Amenhotep III, Seti I, Rameses II—the names of the mightiest New Kingdom monarchs are a litany of greatness."[1] While another period of weakness followed Egypt later, it's much too late for an exodus of Semitic people, and the archeological evidence is very clear regarding the establishing of "the People of Israel," as a civilization outside Egypt. To help you understand our journey, you must have a small grasp on the time periods of the Egyptian pharaohs. This time period referred to as the New Kingdom is the one most accepted by scholars; however, it contradicts the Bible narrative. It is the disagreement of this timeline which is used to attack the historical accuracy of the Bible. The time periods for the New Kingdom are:

1. Late Predynastic Period: 3100 B.C.

2. Early Dynastic: 2950–2575 B.C.

3. Old Kingdom: 2575–2150 B.C.

4. First Intermediate Period: 2125–1975 B.C.

5. Middle Kingdom: 1975–1640 B.C.

6. Second Intermediate Period: 1630–1520 B.C.

7. New Kingdom: 1539–1070 B.C. (The time of Rameses the Great II).

8. Third Intermediate Period: 1075–715 B.C.

9. Late Period: 715–322 B.C.

10. Greco-Roman Age: 332 B.C.–395 A.D. [2] (Time of Alexander the Great and Ptolomy II).

---

[1] Brian Fagan, *Egypt of the Pharaohs* (Washington, DC: National Geographic, 2001), 176.

[2] Ibid., 256–57.

There are scholars as well who are both Christian and agnostics who are beginning to believe that a different chronology of Egypt is required which fits the biblical narrative much better. While these scholars are in the minority, their scientific credentials are impressive and their assumptions to the timeline fit perfectly within the biblical narrative. The biblical chronology in simple form looks like this:

1. Predynastic and Old Kingdom: Mizraim (son of Ham, Noah's son, Egyptian line), Abram

2. Middle Kingdom: Joseph, Moses (the time of the Exodus)

3. New Kingdom: Solomon, Rehoboam, Asa, Ahab

4. Third Intermediate and Late Periods: Hezekiah, Josiah, Jeremiah

You may be asking, "Why is all this important?" Again, it is important because it's the timeline that causes the current disagreement between "the experts" and "the Bible." However, what is so fascinating about this argument is a difference of only two to three hundred years! If we move the chronological order of the Egyptian pharaohs by as little as 200–250 years, the biblical narrative and the current accepted Egyptian timeline fit perfectly. You may be asking, "Then why is this timeline not changed?" The answer is twofold: Manetho and a Bible verse.

• *Manetho and the History of Egypt*

Manetho was an Egyptian priest from the city of Sebennytos, Egypt, who lived during the Ptolemaic Kingdom, which was the early third century B.C. Ptolomy II asked Manetho to compile a history of Egypt, which he did. Manetho's account of the pharaohs is the reason why most people in the scholastic community believe in the late (New Kingdom) timeline rather than the earlier timeline (Middle Kingdom). But, "Manetho lived some 1,500 years after it all happened."[3] Yet, Manethos is the primary influencer for the chronology of Egyptian Dynasties. He "gives us the basic structure or skeleton of Egyptian chronology that we use today . . . Great reliance is placed on Manetho—no full text of his work survives."[4]

Manethos' chronological timeline was never intended to be a chronological account of Egyptian history. Secular scholarship has made it their structure for the Egyptian Dynasties. The ancient church historian Eusebius, the fourth-century historian says, "Several Egyptian kings ruled at the same time. . . . It was not a succession of kings occupying the throne one after the other, but several kings reigning at the same time in different regions."[5] Also, the current facts now being developed, point out inconsistencies in the later timeframe (New Kingdom) from our contemporary Egyptian sources today. Professor J.H. Breasted, author of *History of Egypt,* writes, regarding the history of Manetho, calling it a "late, careless, and uncritical compilation, which can be proven wrong from the contemporary monuments in the vast majority of cases, where such documents have survived."[6] Manetho is not the only problem, there is a Bible verse that archaeologists have used and interpreted, possibly in the wrong way for years.

- **That Pesky Bible Verse: Dating the Exodus**

    Genesis 47:11says: "Then Joseph settled his father and brothers in the land of Egypt and gave them property in the best part of the land, the land of Rameses, as Pharaoh had commanded" (CSB). Many Egyptologists

---

[3] John Ashton and David Down, *Unwrapping the Pharaohs: How Egyptian Archaeology Confirms the Biblical Timeline* (Green Forest, AR: Master Books, 2006), 66.

[4] Peter A. Clayton, *Chronicles of the Pharaohs: The Reign-by-Reign of the Rulers and Dynasties of Ancient Egypt* (London: Thames and Hudson, 1994), 9.

[5] W.G. Waddell, *History of Egypt and Other Works by Manetho* (Boston, MA: Harvard University Press, 1940), 9.

[6] D. Mackey, ""Sothic Star Dating: The Sothic Star Theory of the Egyptian Calendar," abridged thesis, Sydney, Australia, 1995, accessed November 10, 2018, *http://www.specialityinterest.net/.*

use the Bible as a guide to understanding possible history, and this verse has led many to assume that the Exodus was during the New Kingdom.

> This later date relies mainly on the evidence of archaeology. It is suggested that the reference in Exodus 1:11 to the store cities of 'Pithom and Ramesses' fits well the time of Pharaoh Ramesses II (1279–1213 B.C.) who built the city of Pi-Ramesses (the domain of Ramesses) commencing around 1279 B.C. Thus, the Pharaoh 'who did not know Joseph' (Exodus 1:8) eighty years before, would be Horemheb (1319–1292 B.C)."[7]

However, there is a problem which has only recently been revealed that may clarify some assumptions. Archaeologists began to dig in Goshen, which is clearly known as the Land of Rameses today; and what they found recently is intriguing.

The probable reason that Moses used the phrase, "The Land of Rameses," was by the time of his writing, the recipients of his book would have been very familiar with the "Land of Rameses," and where it was located. Furthermore, they would have known what lay beneath this region—the Semitic land of Avaris.[8]

• **Rameses Versus Avaris**

It is crucial that we revisit our previous discussion regarding the ancient city of Avaris and Joseph. We do so because it will add great clarity to our argument. It is our assumption that the Middle Kingdom fits the proposed biblical timeline better than the New Kingdom. Why? To start with, "The early date

---

[7] Clive Anderson and Brian Edwards, *Evidence for the Bible* (Leominister, England: Day One, 2014), 199.

[8] Timothy P. Mahoney, *Patterns of Evidence: A Filmmaker's Journey: You Never Know Where a Crisis of Faith Will Lead You* (St. Louis Park, MN: Thinking Man Media, 2015), IV: I.

 for the Exodus would mean that Joseph fits better in the Middle Kingdom (2040–1786 B.C)."[9] The Bible said that Joseph entered into this land with his family in "the Land of Rameses." This is known as the most fertile part of Egypt and as the land of Goshen—the place where the Bible says the Israelites inhabited. Archaeologists have dug for years excavating the "Land of Rameses." They found many monuments, tombs, inscriptions, all pointing to Rameses the Great (II)—items such as statues. "A statue of Ramesses II of the Nineteenth Dynasty groups the sun god in the form of a falcon and the pharaoh as a child."[10] What they have not found is any evidence of an Exodus. The timing of Rameses is clearly held within the New Kingdom period, not the Middle Period. This was a time of immense prosperity, not national economic decline and collapse. "Ramesses was also an impressive builder, and there are more monuments and temples to Ramesses than to any other Pharaoh...Ramesses was on the throne for sixty-six years."[11] It was the longest reign of any Pharaoh and arguably the most successful and powerful. This Egyptian timeline falls within the thirteenth century, within the 19th Dynasty of Egypt. It is improbable that the Exodus took place during this time of national achievements, both politically and socially. A biblical plague would have decimated the economy, the people, and the will of the Egyptian people. But here is the clincher—it was what the archaeologists have discovered under the New Kingdom of the "Land of Rameses" that has placed the historical community on the edge of their seats. They found a city called Avaris, in the region of Goshen.[12] This is the most probable reason why Moses refers to the entrance into Egypt as "The Land

---

[9] Anderson and Edwards, *Evidence for the Bible*, 199.

[10] David P. Silverman, *Ancient Egypt* (New York: Oxford University Press, 1997), 241.

[11] Anderson and Edwards, *Evidence for the Bible*, 23.

[12] Mahoney, *Patterns of Evidence*, V. I.

of Rameses." The audience of Moses would have known that this "Land of Rameses," was the previous known city of Avaris. "Though not continuously inhabited, it would become Pi-Ramesses, the impressive capital of Pharaoh Ramesses II...Ramesses expanded the city of Avaris . . . and made the delta city his principle residence."[13] Rameses was also used as a catchall name for a pharaoh. However, the point here is that underneath the "Land of Rameses," a highly populated city of Semitic people was found in a city called Avaris.

- **Avaris**

The archaeologists in Avaris are now discovering many things that provide evidence for an earlier timeline, namely the Middle Kingdom. They have excavated several things that are all challenging the thought of an exodus during the New Kingdom, such as the arrival of Joseph, the presence of a famine, the creation of wealth to Pharaoh, the multiplication of Semitic people, the presence of slavery, disease from malnutrition, the death of young males, judgment and sudden calamities, the exodus of a people who left quickly, and any apparent collapse in the Egyptian civilization. Is there evidence for these things? Yes, and more are appearing every year they dig in Avaris.

- **Abraham and the Patriarchs**

Repeating what was earlier written in the chapter regarding Joseph, Jacob arrived with his family into the land of Egypt. Remember, he had twelve sons, who would later become the twelve

---

[13] Jennie Ebeling, et al. *The Old Testament in Archaeology and History* (Waco, TX: Baylor University Press, 2017), 249, 254.

tribes of Israel. According to an agnostic Egyptologist named David Rohl, he believes that not only is the story of the Exodus true, but that the suggested biblical timeline is true.[14] He points out that at Avaris they have found evidence of houses built within the style that Abraham and Jacob would have known in the city of Haran. They found the presence of a simple house with this Canaanite/Semitic style that had been demolished. A large palace was built on top of it. This house had twelve pillars, twelve graves and a statue of a man wearing a coat of many colors. At the least, it's the highest form of irony; at best, it bears the plausible suggestion that this was the home of Joseph.[15] Here is why:

The major tomb was found in the shape of the Egyptian pyramids; only the pharaohs or persons with great power and influence are found buried in such a tomb. Whoever this was is most certainly buried with a king's burial. But do you remember what they found in the tomb? They found a huge statue!

This statue had all the Egyptian features used to paint someone of a Semitic race.[16] His face was yellow, his hair was in the form of a Semitic person, his arm held an emblem of power, and he was dressed in a coat of many colors (Genesis 37). The size of the statue suggests that this person was a very important person. The statue tells us his nationality, said the Egyptologist, Charles Aling.

So, here is a palace built over a home of Semitic architectural origins, complete with twelve tombs, twelve pillars, and a tomb of royalty with a Semitic

---

[14] Mahoney, *Patterns of Evidence*, V. II.

[15] Mahoney, *Patterns of Evidence*, V. V.

[16] Bryant G. Wood, "The Sons of Jacob: New Evidence for the Presence of the Israelites in Egypt," *Biblical Archaeology*, January 28, 2016, accessed November 5, 2018, *http://wwww.biblearchaeology.org/post/2016/01/28/The-Sons-of-Jacob-New-Evidence-for-the-Presence-of-the-Israelites-in-Egypt.aspx.*

person represented in the tomb dressed in a coat of many colors![17] Furthermore, it was excavated underneath the New Kingdom at the level of the Middle Kingdom in the old city of Avaris, which is now called the City of Rameses.

- **The Preparation for Famine**

   Is there any archaeological evidence for the presence of a famine at Avaris, the ancient land of Goshen? Bryant Wood, Archaeological Association for Biblical Research, believes that there is evidence.[18] The Bible tells us the reason that Joseph was brought out of jail and taken to the Pharaoh was to interpret the Pharaoh's dream (Genesis 39:19; 41:1-37). When Pharaoh heard Joseph's interpretation of the dream, the Bible says Pharaoh appointed Joseph over the plan to steward a season of famine (Genesis 41:31-41).

- **Fayum**

 There is a canal in Egypt, still to this day, called Fayum. It connects to the Nile River as a tributary. The name *Fayum* means, "Waterway of Joseph," and has been called that for thousands of years. Many Egyptologists who are changing their timelines believe that this waterway was cut by Joseph as a tributary to save and store water before a drought and famine ever occurred.[19] This leads us to ask the question as to whether or not great wealth changed hands, which would be a very logical question if the plan described by Joseph in Genesis 41 was ever actually activated.

---

[17] Robert Shiestl, "The Statue of an Asiatic Man From Tell El-Dab'a, Egypt," *Egypt and the Levant*, no. 16 (2006).

[18] Wood, "The Sons of Jacob."

[19] Mahoney, *Patterns of Evidence*, V. II.

- ## Changing of Wealth

  It was during the Middle Kingdom Eygpt was ruled by not one leader but a set of leaders called Nomes. These Nomes functioned like districts and held tremendous power and wealth. At some point, all of this suddenly changed in Egypt. The positions lost wealth and power. At the same time, it appears that all the wealth became centered and concentrated where the pharaoh ruled. In the history books of Egypt, there are no explanations. What would have caused such a social upheaval of political structures? Bryant Wood agrees. It appears that the wealth of Pharaoh became concentrated by Joseph's plan to take charge of the land (Genesis 41:34). This is a possible explanation for this social change. Genesis 47:20 tells us that Joseph purchased all the land for pharaoh. The Bible simply says, "So the land became Pharaoh's." Furthermore, the statue of Pharaoh Amenemhat III may speak to the coming season of famine.

- ## Amenemhat III

  This famine, under the Middle Kingdom timeline would have fallen under the reign of Amenemhat III. Take a look at his picture—a hard look—and notice his facial expression. All Egyptian pharaohs were painted and sculpted with a bland look upon their faces, but not Amenemhat. He is sculpted by ancient Egyptians with the look of deep worry on his face. He is portrayed as a king in distress. This is highly unusual for a pharaoh's sculpture. It is plausible that he was sculpted with a deep sense of worry because he held the reigns of leadership during a very troubled time of famine. Ironically, he built his pyramid right next to the waterway of Joseph.

186

The Multiplication of Semitic/Asiatic People

The Bible says these Asiatic people, the children of Israel, multiplied greatly in the land. We know the Avaris findings confirm a large population during the Middle Kingdom, around 20 to 30 thousand. This population is confirmed earlier than later. However, archaeologists have found proof that the city began as a small village of Semitic people.

In Genesis 42, we are told that the famine had arrived and was the cause of Joseph's family coming to Egypt to purchase grain. They came, Joseph reunited with them through the power of forgiveness, and Jacob and his sons lived in Egypt in the land of Goshen (Avaris) (Genesis 46 and 47). This was a land known by Moses as the "Land of Rameses." Genesis 47:27 tells us that Jacob/Israel lived in the land of Goshen and acquired land and became very fruitful.

The Book of Exodus starts out with the story of the multiplication of Egypt. Exodus 1:7 tells us after describing the death of Joseph that the Asiatic people of Goshen "multiplied and became extremely strong." Then, we find these dire words, "Now a new king arose over Egypt, who did not know Joseph" (Exodus 1:8). So, is there any proof of multiplication?

When archaeologists began to excavate in the land of Avaris/Goshen, they found an early habitation of a few houses numbering seventy or more. Then, this same village grew to become one of the largest cities in the world at that time. It was, however, a city of foreigners, not Egyptians.[20] There are several ways we know this to be true.

We know this to be true because the graves of these Asiatic people held knifes, and tools used in the Canaanite

---

[20] M. Bietak, *Avaris and Piramesse: Archaeology Exploration in the Eastern Nile Delta* (London: British Academy, 1986), 14.

region, and were not distinctively Egyptian. Their graves were found with donkeys which were buried with them and their goods—a practice that is most certainly not Egyptian. It is important to note that at this time it would be very difficult to distinguish between a Canaanite/Mesopotamian human and a Hebrew, and thus very difficult to know the difference, culturally. At this point, we are dealing with the ethnic aggregation of a race that would bring us the Jewish people as the nation of Israel. However, the facts are that they were Semitic and not Egyptian. They came from the region of Canaan.

John Bimson, tutor of Old Testament at Trinity College, in Bristol, says that the archaeological evidence clearly shows the only time Egyptian timelines show a massive amount of Semitic people is during the Middle Kingdom. During the time of Rameses, there is no evidence at all. There is "no sign of massive numbers of Israelites or Semites living in Egypt during this time (New Kingdom), especially centered on the city of Avaris/Rameses in the Nile/Delta area of Goshen. Some Semitic presence exists in all periods, but to fit the Bible's account, there needs to be signs of the exceedingly great multiplication."[21]

- **The Presence of Slavery**

This new pharaoh arose who did not know Joseph and quickly became intimidated with this ethnic population growing at leaps and bounds right in

[21] Steven Law, "Part 2-Ancient Graveyard of Slaves Discovered in Egypt—Could They Be Hebrews?" Evidence, Patterns of Evidence, July 21, 2017, accessed November 12, 2018, *http://www.patternsofevidence.com//blog/2017/07/21/part2-ancient-graveyard-of-slaves-discovered-in-egypt-could-they-be-hebrews/.*

his backyard. Exodus 1:11-12 tells us this pharaoh put these Asiatic people into slavery. He specifically demanded them to make bricks. What is so fascinating is what David Rohl, an Egyptologist, points out. The archaeological record shows that Avaris/Goshen began to show a decline in the lack of prosperity and wealth. We know this by the graves of the people of Avaris/Goshen which have been excavated.

- **The Graves Support Slavery**

    The archaeologists began to find graves with bodies that were appearing extremely malnourished by the presence of rickets. Rickets could be seen in legs especially, or curved long bones caused by vitamin D deficiency. The bones in the newer graves began to show a shortage of nutrients in the bones. This led the archaeologists to uncover the average lifespan of an Asiatic person in Avaris during this time. The average life span declined dramatically to thirty-two to thirty-four years of age. The obvious answer is slavery. But there are other evidences of slavery.

- **A Graveyard of Slaves Found in Egypt**

    Recently, a graveyard of slaves has been discovered in Egypt, but it's not just any graveyard; it's a graveyard of adolescents. Exodus 1:13-14, tells us that Israel worked with hard labor making bricks, and this process "made their lives bitter with hard service" (ESV). The graveyard numbers near 6,000 human beings. These slaves had worked to build the city of Amarna, Egypt's new capital under Akhenaten, which is in the period of the New Kingdom. However, these adolescent slaves were defined as people "in poverty, hard-work, poor diet, ill-health, frequent injury, and relatively early death."[22] Then, archaeologists found

---

[22] Steven Law, "Part 1-Ancient Graveyard of Slaves Discovered in Egypt—Could They Be Hebrews?" Evidence, Patterns of Evidence, July 14, 2017, accessed November 12, 2018, *http://www.patternsofevidence.com//blog/2017/07/14/ancient-*

another cemetery of even poorer human adolescents, located near the main stone quarry. Many humans were piled up on top of each other and buried, a practice that was most certainly not Egyptian. When they were analyzed by Dr. Gretchen Dabbs of Southern Illinois University, it was confirmed that "more than 90 percent of the skeletons had an age that ranged from 7–25 years, with most being under the age of 15."[23] It needs no elaboration to say that people at this age should not be dying in mass quantities.

> The majority of 15–25-year-olds had some kind of traumatic injury and around ten percent had developed osteoarthritis. It is conventional thinking that such osteoarthritis can be caused by a lack of vitamin D due to poor nutrition, since bones can become stronger when under strenuous exercise, unless the proper nutrients are absent. Even in the under 15s, sixteen percent were found to have spinal fractures along with a range of other abnormalities usually associated with heavy workloads.[24]

- **The Brooklyn Papyrus**

This ancient document is a listing of the names of about one hundred slaves in Egypt. The names are about 70 percent Asiatic. While this is one of the oldest medical writings in existence, its contents are from two of the tribes of Israel. Any historian realizes that when you have a text, you have a piece of history, unlike when you have a rock; you don't always know at the moment what you are holding. Of course, many scholars debate this list as having any relevance to the slavery of the Asiatic people; however, the

---

graveyard-of-slaves-discovered-in-egypt-could-they-be-hebrews/.

[23] Ibid.

[24] Ibid.

mathematical probability of evidence seems most certainly more than coincidental. And why do they reject it? The timeline!! This document was actually set in the Middle Kingdom (13th century), not 19th century B.C. of Rameses!

- ## The Tomb of Rehmire, the Vizier

On the walls of the tomb of Rehmire, the Vizier in Thebes, we find a mural dating to the time of Thutmose III with an Egyptian beating Asiatic slaves.

- ## Tomb of Menna

In the tomb of Menna, we find another picture of Egyptians beating Asiatic slaves.

- ## Thutmose III

When the date of the Exodus is changed by a few hundred years, it begins to fit nicely into the biblical narrative. While Thutmose is not mentioned directly in the Bible, he may be referred to as the "Pharaoh of the Oppression" (Exodus 1:8). It is likely that the Pharaoh of the oppression of Israel was Thutmose. Here is his mummified corpse.

- ## Bricks With Straw

Exodus 5:6-7, says: "Pharaoh "commanded the taskmasters of the people and their officers, saying, 'You shall no longer give the people (Israelites) straw to make bricks as in the past; let them go and gather

191

straw for themselves." In 1920, T. Eric Peet, an Egyptologist at the University of Liverpool, believed that the Bible was in error and its account was a show of ignorance from the person who wrote the passage. He believed that Egypt never used straw to make bricks, and said so publicly. Later, Dr. Joseph Free, wrote, "I have examined many mud brick walls surrounding ancient temples in Egypt and have noted the presence of straw in many of the bricks. John Wilson, the eminent Egyptologist of the University of Chicago, observed that straw was used as much as it was left out in the Egyptian brick making."[25]

- **The Tomb of Rehkmire, the Vizier in Thebes**

In the tomb of Rehkmire, a mural was discovered of Hebrews making bricks.

It is likely that the evidence does support slavery in the Middle Kingdom. Think about it. If this story is not true, then who in their right mind is going to create a mythical history of their lineage being that of slaves? Especially in a world where there are clear class distinctions accompanied by honor and disrespect, respectively. It doesn't make sense. It is furthermore likely the graves, the bones, the lack of prosperity after a great season of wealth all appear to be more than coincidental in the land of Avaris/Goshen. To the Semitic people, such things point to one culprit—slavery.

---

[25] Charlie Campbell, *Archaeological Evidence for the Bible* (Carlsbad, CA: The Always Be Ready Apologetics Ministries, 2012), 43.

- **The Death of Young Males**

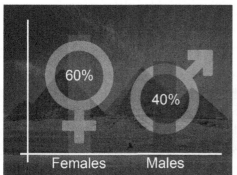

The Bible goes on to say that Pharaoh's way of stopping this Asiatic growth was to kill all the firstborn males. Hence, the reason Moses was placed in a bulrush and floated down the Nile River. Is there any evidence of massive deaths of young male children? Yes, there is.

The city of Avaris continued to increase in number during the Middle Bronze Age. During this time, the infant death rate was thought to be around twenty-five percent. When we jump in our timeline to the Middle Kingdom in the city of Averis/Goshen, we find something radically different. Archaeologists found in the graves of children that fifty percent died in the first three months of birth. Was this a disease? No, because when they looked at the graves of adults in this same span of time they found that women made up sixty percent of the graves, while males made up for forty percent of the graves. [26]

- **The Concept of Judgment**

Moses ended up being taken out of the basket and being raised by the Egyptians. He was raised as the stepson of the pharaoh. His half-brother became the pharaoh of the Exodus. In Exodus 5, we hear these famous words, "Let my people go." First, Pharaoh thought he was god. He believed that he had the power over the Nile, the fields, and most certainly the sun. Pharaoh's will did not bend easily. Finally, after the tenth plague, Pharaoh's firstborn son dies. This is the night that God told the people of Avaris/Goshen to place the blood of a lamb over their doorpost

---

[26] Mahoney, *Patterns of Evidence*, VII: IV.

for safety. When the death angel would see the blood of the lamb over the doorpost, the angel would pass over the house. This is why we call the Jewish feast, Passover.

As you know, Pharaoh changed his mind and chased Moses and the children of Israel into the Red Sea. Are these stories true? Let us look at two simple facts: (1) The celebration of Passover; and (2) An ancient document called the Ipuwer Papyrus.

Papyrus Ipuwer	*Exodus*
Papyrus 2:5-6: Plague is throughout the land. Blood is everywhere.	*Exodus* 7:21: ...there was blood throughout all the land of Egypt.
Papyrus 2:10: The river is blood.	*Exodus* 7:20: ...all the waters that were in the river were turned to blood.
Papyrus 2:10: Men shrink from tasting -- they thirst after water for they could not drink of the water of the river.	*Exodus* 7:24: And all the Egyptians digged round about the river for water to drink.
Papyrus 3:10-13: That is our water! That is our happiness! What shall we do in respect thereof? All is ruin!	*Exodus* 7:21: ...and the river stank.
Papyrus 4:14: Trees are destroyed. *Papyrus* 6:1: No fruit nor herbs are found.	*Exodus* 9:25: ...and the hail smote every herb of the field, and brake every tree of the field.
Papyrus 2:10: Forsooth, gates, columns and walls are consumed by fire.	*Exodus* 9:23-24: ...the fire ran along upon the ground. ...there was hail, and fire mingled with the hail, very grievous.
Papyrus 10:3-6: Lower Egypt weeps... The entire palace is without its revenue. To it belong wheat, barley, geese and fish.	*Exodus* 7:21: And the fish that was in the river died.
Papyrus 6:3: Forsooth, grain has perished on every side. *Papyrus* 5:12: That has perished which yesterday was seen. The land is left over to its weariness like the cutting of flax.	*Exodus* 10:15: ...there remained not any green thing in the trees, or in the herbs of the fields, though all the land of Egypt.
Papyrus 5:5: All animals, their hearts weep. Cattle moan...	*Exodus* 9:3: ...the hand of the Lord is upon thy cattle which is in the field... there shall be a very grievous murrain.
Papyrus 9:2-3: Behold, cattle are left to stray, and there is none to gather them together. Each man fetches for himself those that are branded with his name.	*Exodus* 9:19: ...gather thy cattle, and all that thou has in the field. *Exodus* 9:21: And he that regarded not the word of the Lord left his servants and his cattle in the field.
Papyrus 9:11: The land is not light...	*Exodus* 10:22: ...and there was a thick darkness in all the land of Egypt.
Papyrus 5:6: Forsooth, the children of princes are dashed against the walls. *Papyrus* 6:12: Forsooth, the children of princes are cast out in the streets.	*Exodus* 12:29: And it came to pass, that at midnight the Lord smote all the firstborn in the land of Egypt, from the firstborn of the Pharaoh that sat on his throne unto the firs born of the captive that was in the dungeon.
Papyrus 2:13: He who places his brother in the ground is everywhere.	*Exodus* 12:30: ...there was not a house where there was not one dead.
Papyrus 3:14: It is groaning that is throughout the land, mingled with lamentations.	*Exodus* 12:30: ...there was a great cry in Egypt.
Papyrus 7:1: Behold, the fire has mounted up on high. Its burning goes forth against the enemies of the land.	*Exodus* 12:21: ...by day in a pillar of a cloud, to lead them the way, and by night in a pillar of fire, to give them light; to go by day and night.

- **Passover**

  Why would a nation celebrate something for thousands and thousands of years if the story were not true? There must be a reason why this celebration has continued with such a long tenure in history. The original Hebrew people believed it to be true.

- **The Ipuwer Papyrus**

  In the Leiden Museum in the Netherlands, Amsterdam, there is an ancient piece of Egyptian literature called the Ipuwer papyrus. Ipuwer was the ancient Egyptian sage who wrote the document called "Admonitions of Ipuwer." It describes a unique biblical feature and a series of calamities written in the Egyptian language. Kenneth A. Kitchen also suggested that "The Ipuwer and the Exodus account were possibly referring to the same kind of natural phenomen."[27]

- **Ask for Silver and Gold**

  In Exodus 12:35, Moses tells the Israelites, "Now the sons of Israel had done according to the word of Moses, for they had requested from the Egyptians articles of silver and articles of gold, and clothing. . . . They plundered the Egyptians." In the Ipuwer Papyrus, there is a story of where the poor are suddenly wearing fine clothes, crowned in gold and silver. The papyrus said that the poor all of a sudden became rich. Exactly, how the Bible describes this time.

---

[27] Kenneth A. Kitchen, *On the Reliability of the Old Testament* (Grand Rapids, MI: Eerdmans, 2003), 250.

- ## The Ten Plagues

The ten plagues represented the ten gods to the Egyptian people. It was God's way of saying that I am in charge. But is there any evidence of these plagues? In the Ipuwer Papyrus, it details a story of calamity among the Egyptians. Take a moment and look at the similarities between the Ipuwer Papyrus and the Book of Exodus.

As you can imagine, the skeptics swear this has nothing to do with the Exodus. And why do you think they refuse this as evidence for the Exodus? The timeline is wrong. This "Admonitions of Ipuwer" was originally thought to be during the 19th Dynasty, around 1250 B.C. Today, that has changed; they believe that it dates to the Middle Kingdom. Furthermore, Brad C. Sparks claims that "90 Egyptian papyri demonstrate similar parallels to the Exodus."[28] How are we so sure that Israel was not living the Exodus at such a later date? The rocks are crying out the truth.

- ## The Merneptah Stela

The son of Rameses, Merneptah, had a stele erected which is known as the Merneptah Stela or the Israel Stela. It was a stela in his father's (Rameses) honor. It was discovered in 1896, at Thebes. At the bottom of the stele, a majority of archaeologists, including David Bohl, believe that there is a direct reference to Israel which reads, "Israel is laid wasted, bare of seed." This is the earliest mention

---

[28] Brad C. Sparks, "Egypt Text Parallels to the Exodus: The Egyptology Literature" at the recent Out of Egypt: Israel's Exodus Between Text and Memory, History and Imagination Conference. Host, Thomas E. Levy (San Diego, CA, 2013).

of Israel in antiquities. Merneptah reigned during 1215 B.C., after Rameses II. This would be the New Kingdom, where so much of modern scholarship believes that the Exodus took place, with no evidence at all. The point that begs to be mentioned is the fact that this stele is saying clearly that Israel was already known as a nation of people. This stele lists all the enemies of Egypt, and thus lists Israel as one of the many powerful armies Egypt defeated.[29]

The Bible makes it clear that the Israelites did not conquer Canaan until forty years after the Exodus. This makes it impossible for Rameses to have been the pharaoh of the Exodus. But there are other such inscriptions that can make the same point.

- **The Berlin Pedestal**

Clyde Billington, history professor at University of Northwestern in St. Paul, Minnesota, believes that the Berlin Pedestal at the State Museum in Berlin, Germany, shows a similar point—on a rock can be found Egyptian Hieroglyphics again. In the Egyptian language, there are three figures: Ashkelon, Canaan, and Israel. These three figures are bound, being the enemies of Egypt. The latest date given to this is 1360 B.C., which makes a late Exodus impossible. The Berlin Pedestal is earlier than the Merneptah stele.[30]

---

[29] David Rohl, *Pharaohs and Kings* (New York: Crown Publishing Group, 1996), 169–70.

[30] Peter van der Veen, Christopher Theis, and Manford Gorg, "Israel in Canaan (Long) Before Pharaoh Merneptah?" *Journal of Ancient Egyptian Interconnections,* 2, 4.

- **The Time of King Solomon**

The Bible, in 1 Kings 6:1, says plainly, "Now it came about in the four hundred and eightieth year after the Israelites came out of the land of Egypt, in the fourth year of Solomon's reign over Israel." Most scholars agree that Solomon began his reign in 970 B.C. What would that mean for the Exodus? It would place the Exodus in the Middle Kingdom, around 1450 B.C., two hundred years before Rameses the Great (II).

So, there is apparent evidence regarding the Exodus which contains numerous examples, ruling out mere coincidence. However, this leads us to another question: "Is there any evidence there was a mass exodus of people which took place where they left Egypt quickly and suddenly after the death of firstborn male children?"

- **Signs of Mass Exodus**

In the city of Avaris, archaeologists have found lots of pits dug into the ground suddenly. In these pits are bodies which were thrown one on top of the other. The burial was sudden and done *en masse*. There was no ceremonial goods, pottery, etc., in the graves. The graves were simply a sign of a sudden burial. Then the entire group of people living in the Avaris region suddenly leave. They left behind many of their personal Semitic goods. This took place in the Middle Kingdom. What could have caused this? A plague is a logical conclusion. Manfred Bietak, a highly respected Egyptologist, believes that it happened because of a plague which demanded a quick burial, due to diseases.[31] But is there any other evidence of a mass exodus during the time of the Middle Kingdom? Yes there is.

• Kahun

Kahun is a city located 120 miles away from Avaris. It was a Semitic settlement as well. In the city, archaeologists have found documents specifying slavery and an abandon township. The people of Kahun left overnight, leaving their goods and pottery in the streets. The city was found by the archaeologists exactly where people suddenly left them. The homes of Kahun still contained much of their original goods, streets were scattered with signs of life such as pottery, etc., Dr. David Rohl, attests to these facts pointing toward a sudden departure. Professor Rosalie David, an Egyptologist at the University of Manchester, UK, believes that the people of this town left quickly and without premeditation.[32]

Now, if all of these things actually happened, what do you think would be the end result? It would be total destruction and collapse of Egypt! Is there evidence of a sudden collapse in Egypt. No evidence in the New Kingdom, but there is in the Middle Kingdom.

• A Sudden Collapse of Egypt

In the writings of Manetho's history that we previously referred to, he says that Egypt was smitten by God. What is so interesting is that he uses the singular form of God not the Egyptian plural form of gods. What happened? Well, the Hyksos are coming.

---

[31] Mahoney, *Patterns of Evidence*, VII: IV.

[32] Ann Rosalie David, *The Pyramid Builders of Ancient Egypt: A Modern Investigation of Pharaoh's Workforce* (London: Guild Publishers, 1996), 191.

- **Hyksos**

The only time in a thousand years Egypt ever completely collapsed was during the Hyksos period. The Hyksos were a tribe of Semitic people from Asia who took the Nile region of Egypt during the 13th Dynasty B.C. According to most scholars, this was a complete time of devastation for Egypt. The Cambridge Ancient History states, "From their number, the brevity of their reigns, and the evident lack of any continuous dynastic succession, it would appear that the kings of the 13th Dynasty, dominated by a powerful line of viziers, were for the most part puppet rulers, holding their offices, perhaps by appointment or 'election,' for limited periods of time."[33]

The question that arises is how did someone defeat a superpower? Egypt certainly had the armies, personnel, protection, weapons, wealth, and strategic location to withhold the world's most powerful armies. The Hyksos enslaved Egypt, and again, it's the only collapse in a one-thousand year period, which happened in the end of the Middle Kingdom.

---

[33] I.E.S. Edwards et al. *The Cambridge Ancient History, Volume II, Part One* (Cambridge, UK: Cambridge University Press, 1980), 44.

- ### The Egyptian Amulet

This amulet is made in Egypt and has the name of the Hyksos king, Anopis.

- ### Neferhotep I

If the Exodus took place in the Middle Kingdom and not the New Kingdom then it is extremely plausible that Neferhotep I, Dynasty 13, was the pharaoh of the Exodus. The 13th Dynasty was a very troubled dynasty for Egypt. Neferhotep's son, Wahneferhotep did not succeed him to the throne, and scholars do not know why. It is plausible that he died in the plague, because his brother, Sobkhotep succeeded him to the throne.

While, the Exodus doesn't deliver us the archaeological jewels we hope to one day see as Christians, there is a rumbling going on in scholarship. Many scholars are not revisiting the timing of the Exodus, because the date of a New Kingdom does not fit with the archaeological evidence. This rumble is a rumble to rethink the timing of the Patriarchs and the Exodus to the Middle Kingdom. Recently, there has been no dearth of archaeological findings to support moving the date backward, instead of forward. The reasons are numerous as is the evidence. The current thought of a New Kingdom date for the Exodus does not fit in anyway. It was a time of great achievements in Egypt, there is no presence of a famine, a new creation of the Pharaoh's wealth as it relates to land, no multiplication or even presence of Semitic people in Egypt, no suggestions of Semitic slavery, malnutrition, death of young males, or judgement and collapse. All of these events can be found in the Middle Kingdom, which the Bible suggests is the date for the people of Israel and the Exodus of Moses. Furthermore, it is founded upon the fact that Israel was already a nation by the New Kingdom and could not have been known as a people at any time before the New Kingdom.

Egyptian culture is owed a great deal of gratitude for its ingenious contribution to civilized societies. Its chronology may always remain a mystery, but on the other hand, the archaeological spade may turn up within the soil of earth, answers not seen for thousands of years. No matter what date you believe that the Exodus happened, whether it be the Middle Kingdom or the New Kingdom, the important thing to keep in mind is the lessons it teaches us about freedom, human injustices, ethics, and history. While, the most probable evidence does seem to be in the Middle Kingdom, tomorrow may bring us additional fresh insights into this fascinating true story about how God created a nation of free people.

Chapter 9

Conquest and Early Activities of Israel

It is disturbing just how little average Christians know about their own history. Many assume that such an early history cannot be known, or worse yet, should not be known, and only accepted by faith. Still yet, there are those, often in places of influence, who tell frightened students that the Bible is a lie. There is no proof of a conquest of Joshua and the walls of Jericho, or King David, and certainly not his palace!! This statement is at the heart of our matter. The Bible is not a compilation of lies. It doesn't contain fiction, intermingled with moral lessons. The Bible contains moral lessons exemplified through the lives of real people. However, this thinking has been dismantled by the archaeological spade. It's so bad for the skeptics that they are spending more time arguing over the interpretation of the "rock," rather than proving the figure to be figurative. It seems like every week the science of archaeology is bringing to focus another piece of proof which undergirds the people of the Old Testament as being real, living, human beings, not moral lessons wrapped in mythological characters.

The Bible is a book of true stories. It is a historical account of ancient lives who were part of a grand narrative—

the love of God. This grand narrative is not fictional; the people of the Old Testament who played out this narrative lived lives in which the Bible is extremely forthright as it tells their stories of failures and successes—a truth that is often conspicuously absent in other religions' texts. The Bible treats its characters as real human beings, not gods, or semi-human beings. And for this reason, faith is expressed not through nature, like the rest of the Near East, but through a personal history. "Thus, the Hebrew does not bear witness to his faith by a reenactment of great cosmic or natural dramas for control purposes. Neither does he bear witness to his faith by retelling a fictional re-creation of the past for control purposes. Rather, he recited the ways in which God has intervened in the experience of the Israelites, both as individuals and as a nation, as interpreted by God through His own prophets."[1] Admittedly, there are still mysteries, problematic dating of timelines, proof for specific people missing, and so forth; but by faith, one day they will be answered and solved, just like previous issues with the Hittites, Nebuchadnezzar, Isaiah, Pontius Pilate, and multiple other people, places, and things mentioned in the Bible. This is not a blind faith, but a faith based on past scientific experiences, where questions are often eventually answered by a gavel that has repeatedly come down on the side of the Scriptural account of history. "In fact, the entire Bible is historical in that in its entirety it is an interpretation of the historical experience of Israel culminating in the life, death, and resurrection of Christ."[2] Looking at the personalities of the Old Testament and the events that shaped their lives should be very beneficial.

The Israelites have now fled the land of Egypt, heading for their Promised Land. The ending of the Book of Exodus, as well as the Books of Leviticus and Numbers established the religious customs for this new national identity. In front of them stood new territory with old gods and ancient

---

[1] Oswalt, *The Bible Among Myths*, 136.
[2] Ibid., 153.

people; yet, they knew the promise of God to Abraham and proceeded forth out of Egypt. Unknown to them, it was the beginning . . . the establishment of their identity as a nation. Their journey into the unknown regions out of Egypt into their Promised Land, headed for Canaan would be a story of conquest.

The Conquest

As it relates to the conquest of Israel leaving Egypt and beginning to conquer the lands and peoples who stood in their way of inhabiting the Promised Land, the real issue is elusive to many. "The problem of the conquest is not about what a tribe of Semitic people did or did not do in the Levant in the Bronze Age. The issue is all about what the Bible says or does not say."[3] Is it possible to find historical truth moving forward? Yes, it is!

- **The Statue of Idrimi, 1500 B.C. (Genesis 10:6)**

This is the earliest certain cuneiform reference in antiquity to the subject of Canaan—as in Canaan land.

- **The Inscription of Balaam/Deir Alla Inscription (Numbers 22–24)**

In Numbers 22–24, Balaam son of Beor is mentioned in the oldest example of western Semitic language. "In an unprecedented discovery, an ancient

---

[3] John H. Walton and J. Harvey Walton, *The Lost World of the Israelite Conquest: Covenant, Retribution, and the Fate of the Canaanites* (Downers Grove, IL: InterVarsity Press, 2017), 7.

text found at Deir Alla, Jordan, in 1967 tells about the activities of a prophet named Balaam. Could this be the Balaam of the Old Testament? The text makes it clear that it is. Three times in the first four lines, he is referred to as "Balaam son of Beor," exactly as in the Bible. This represents the first Old Testament prophet to be dug up in Bible lands—not his tomb or his skeleton, but a text about him. The text also represents the first prophecy of any scope from the ancient West Semitic world to be found outside the Old Testament, and the first extra-biblical example of a prophet proclaiming doom to his own people. . . . It was among the rubble of a building destroyed in an earthquake. It seems to have been one long column with at least 50 lines, displayed on a plastered wall. According to the excavators' dating, the disaster was most likely the severe earthquake which occurred in the time of King Uzziah (Azariah) and the prophet Amos in about 760 B.C. (Amos 1:1; Zechariah 14:5). The lower part of the text shows signs of wear, indicating that it had been on the wall for some time prior to the earthquake."[4]

Joshua's Conquests

- ### The Amarna Letters (Joshua 11:19-23)

These biblical treasures were found by accident when a poor Bedouin woman found broken pieces on the ground in 1887. Later, more than 400 cuneiform tablets were established as being part of the royal archives of Amenhotep III, the Egyptian Pharaoh. These Amarna letters were written to the Egyptian Pharaohs by various kings dwelling in Canaan land and Syria. Written in the time of

---

[4] Bryant G. Wood, "Balaam Son of Beor," *Bible and Spade,* 8, no. 4 (1995): 114.

Moses, these letters give us insight into the conquest of these lands during the time of the Exodus. They appear to be the first evidence of Hebrew tribes entering Canaan. While we cannot connect the events of the Book of Joshua with specific events, "at the very least, the Amarna letters provide a glimpse of the political picture in Palestine at that time. At most, they might give actual Canaanite reaction to Israelite movements."[5]

- **The Walls of Jericho (Joshua 1–6)**

---

[5] Hoerth, *Archaeology and the Old Testament*, 218.

This is just another point in history where critics mocked the biblical account of the walls of Jericho. That was, until German archaeologists Ernst Sellin and Carl Watzinger found them! Multiple excavations have since transpired. John Garstand, Doctor of Science from Oxford University, wrote, "In a word, in all material details and in the date the fall of Jericho took place as described in the biblical narrative . . . The walls fell, shaken apparently by an earthquake, and the city was destroyed by fire, about 1400 B.C. These are the basic facts resulting from our investigations."[6] The walls of Jericho did fall just like the Bible said they fell. Yet, in 1952, Dame Kathleen Kenyon excavated Jericho and concluded, "that there was no walled city for Joshua to conquer."[7] However, others confirmed a walled city.[8] Yet, later, Dr. Wood's research, which was featured in *Time* magazine in 1990, reported Woods' findings, dating the Jericho site at the time the Bible said the events took place (1410 B.C.). "Charcoal found in the debris yielded a Carbon-14 date of 1410 B.C, plus or minus forty years."[9] To learn more, watch the documentary: *Jericho Unearthed*.

- **The Sacrificing of Children to Molech**

In the Book of Leviticus 18:30; Numbers 33:52; Deuteronomy 7:2, 5; 2 Kings 23:10; and Isaiah 57:5-9, we see where God instructed the Israelites to drive out the Canaanites from the land. One of the many detestable practices of these Canaanites was the sacrifice of children to the god Molech. "In spite of the Bible's

---

[6] Lisette Bassett-Brody, *Etched in Stone: Archaeological Discoveries That Prove the Bible* (Washington, DC: WND Books, 2017), 190.

[7] Hoerth, *Archaeology and the Old Testament*, 209.

[8] John Garstang, *Jericho and the Biblical Story, Volume 2* (New York: J. A. Hammerton, 1937), 1222.

[9] Campbell, *Archaeological Evidence*, 63.

numerous references by Greco-Roman historians Kleitarchos, Diodorus, Plutarch, and church fathers like Tertullian,"[10] skeptics refused to concede that this practice ever happened. That was, until Dr. Merrill Unger wrote, "Excavations in Palestine have uncovered piles of ashes and remains of infant skeletons in cemeteries around heathen altars, pointing to the widespread practice of this cruel abomination."[11]

- **The Stela of Baal (Numbers 25:3; Zephaniah 1:4; 1 Kings 18:16)**

The worship of Baal is a rather famous name in the biblical account. In 1932, Claude F.A. Shaeffer discovered a stele depicting Baal, the storm god, with a lightning bolt in his hand. It was found at Ras Shamra (Ugarit).

(**Author's Note:** I came across a website the other day that said, "There is absolutely no historical proof for the Bible." I had to laugh out loud. The Bible even gets minute details correct.)

- **The Concept of a High Place (Jeremiah 32:35)**

The Bible refers multiple times to the worship of other gods in a "high place." These high places were called "bamot" and usually contained an altar. However, they are not always found on top of a mountain, some have been discovered in

---

[10] Ibid., 68.

[11] Unger, *Archaeology and the Old Testament*, 279.

urban areas with man-made mounds. History attests and confirms what the Bible has said about "high places."

Archaeologist, "De Vaux" suggested that Israelite bamot were modeled after the Canaanite ones. The bamah is also known from the Ras Shamra text.[12] In Megiddo, located in the Carmel Ridge overlooking the Jezreel Valley from the west, a bamah was believed to have been found. The structure was a 24 x 30-foot oval platform, which stood six feet tall, was made of large stones and had stairs that led to the top.[13] A wall surrounded the structure. A cultic structure found in Nahariyah, located in Western Galilee, was discovered in 1947 and dates to the Middle Bronze Age, but was used until the Late Bronze Age.[14] It consisted of a circular open-air altar, which compares to the one found in Megiddo, and a rectangular building probably used as a temple workshop. It is also believed that two bamot were found on a hill near Malhah from the seventh and sixth centuries B.C.E. De Vaux says, "There is no need for hesitation: these installations were bamot. Their dates range from the old Canaanite epoch to the end of the monarchy in Judah."[15] Therefore, it seems that the archaeological evidence supports the biblical account in placement of the bamot and the time periods in which they were used."[16]

---

[12] John Gray, *I and II Kings* (Philadelphia: Westminster Press, 1963), 116.

[13] Roland de Vaux, *Ancient Israel: Its Life and Institutions* (Grand Rapids, MI: Eerdmans, 1961), 284.

[14] Othmar Keel and Christopher Uehlinger, *Gods, Goddesses, and Images of God in Ancient Israel* (Minneapolis: Fortress, 1998), 29.

[15] de Vaux, *Ancient Israel*, 285.

[16] Ellen White, "High Places, Altars and the Bamah," *Biblical Archaeology Review* (July 2018), under "T15:54."

- **The Idea of Boundary Stones (Deuteronomy 19:14; Job 24:2; Proverbs 22:28; 23:10; Hosea 5:10)**

The Bible mentions the practice of using an ancient boundary stone to mark certain spaces. It at first seems like a harmless reference; however, it is a statement which suggests a historical fact. So, have archaeologists found ancient boundary stones? Yes, they have. At Tell Gezer they have found an ancient boundary stone. They also have found several others throughout the Middle East.

- **The Concept of Footstools: Tutankhamun; Tiglath-Pileser (Psalms 110:1; Hebrews 10:13)**

It is a common motif that the winning kings would place their foot on the neck of their enemies, for example, the Assyrian King Tiglath-Pileser III (745-727). This concept is mentioned in Joshua 10:24, and referred to in the New Testament in 1 Corinthians 15:25.

- **Queen Jezebel (1 Kings 16: 31-33; 18:19; 2 Kings 9)**

There are few names more famous in the Bible than that of Queen Jezebel. She is known as the symbol for ruthless women who get what they want and when they want it. A seal was discovered by Dr. Morjo Korpel, Old Testament scholar, containing an image of a woman and the designation of a royal female owner. A seal was used to seal documents. "Documents would be tied up with string and a blob of clay placed over the string; a seal would then be impressed into the clay to identify the sender and assure the security of the document. Or a seal would be impressed into the handle of a jar to identify the owner—for example, the so-called l'melekh handles ("[belonging] to the king"), of which there are several thousand. Or a seal could be used to prevent unauthorized entry to a storehouse. Deuteronomy 32:34 speaks of the Lord's attributes "sealed up in My treasuries."[17]

Hezekiah

It was King Hezekiah of Judah who brought the needed reform to Jerusalem. He had the "high places" torn down, and he reestablished the Passover (2 Chronicles 30:26). His name has firmly been established by the archaeological record.

- **The Seal of Hezekiah (2 Chronicles 30:26)**

The bulla seal of Hezekiah was discovered at Ophel excavations by Dr. Eilot Mazar. The seal reads, "Belonging to Hezekiah, (son of) Ahaz, King of Judah."[18]

---

[17] Marjo C.A. Korpel, "Fit for a Queen: Jezebel's Royal Seal," *Biblical Archaeology Review*, May 1, 2008, accessed November 10, 2018, *https://www.biblicalarchaeology.org/daily/biblical-artifacts/inscriptions/fit-for-a-queen-jezebels-royal-seal/*.

[18] Robin Ngo, "King Hezekiah in the Bible: Royal Seal of Hezekiah Comes to Light," *Biblical Archaeology Review*, February 21, 2018, accessed November 1, 2018, https://www.biblicalarchaeology.org/daily/biblical-sites-places/jerusalem/king-hezekiah-in-the-bible-royal-seal-of-hezekiah-comes-to-light/.

- ## The Tunnels of Hezekiah (2 Chronicles 32:2-4; 2 Kings 20:20)

Also, Hezekiah has been contributed the honor of having saved the city of Jerusalem. The Assyrian King, Sennacherib, had decided to invade Jerusalem in 701 B.C. So, Hezekiah fortified the walls of Jerusalem, and had an extensive tunnel system built. A subject that skeptics adamantly denied for years. This tunnel system would ensure that Jerusalem would continue to receive water during the attacks by the Assyrians. The tunnel systems were discovered in 1867 by Sir. Charles Warren. These tunnels are considered the greatest

213

works of water engineering technology in its pre-Classical period with its 1,750 feet of tunnels.

- **The Siloam Inscription**

Discovered about twenty feet from the exit of Hezekiah's tunnel, this inscription tells the process of excavation of the tunnel during the time or Hezekiah. The inscriptions begin with these words: "Behold the excavation. Now this is the history of breaking through..."[19]

- **The Broad Walls of Jerusalem (2 Chronicles 32:5; Nehemiah 2:17; 3:8)**

Hezekiah built up a broad wall in his preparation to protect the city of Jerusalem. Again, skeptics said for years that Jerusalem was an over-embellished story of a much smaller city. That was until archaeologists in 1970 found the broad walls of Hezekiah with its thick 23-foot barrier.[20] Nehemiah 2:17 and 3:8 refer to these walls, as well as Isaiah 22:10. Isaiah said: "You counted the houses of Jerusalem, and you broke down the houses to fortify the wall" (ESV). When the archaeologists were digging, they excavated a cusp of a foundation to an ancient house in Jerusalem right on the edge of the wall, just like Isaiah said. [21]

---

[19] Chrysler Ministry, "Hezekiah's Tunnel," Biblical Archaeology Truth, accessed November 12, 2018, *http://www.biblicalarchaeologytruth.com/hezekiahs-tunnel.html*.

[20] Mike Rogoff, "The Broad Walls of Jerusalem That Fended off the Assyrians," *Haaretz*, April 23, 2013, accessed November 2, 2018, *https://www.haaretz.com/israel-news/travel/.premium-the-jerusalem-wall-and-assyrians-1.5239309*.

[21] Bible Walks, "Broad Wall," Biblewalks.com, January 10, 2016, accessed November 3, 2018, https://biblewalks.com/Sites/BroadWall.html.

- **The Sennacherib Prism/Taylor Prism (2 Kings 19:37)**

This prism—a message of stone—was discovered in the ancient ruins of Nineveh in 1830 by Colonel Taylor. It records the military campaigns of Sennacherib, the Assyrian King. Sennacherib writes, "I have shut up Hezekiah the Judahite...He is trapped like a bird in a cage."[22]

- **King Uzziah (2 Chronicles 26:23; Isaiah 6:1)**

In a Russian Orthodox church, located on the Mount of Olives, holds a discovery that would shock the nation of Israel. An inscription that says, "To this place, the remains of Uzziah, King of Judah were placed. Do not destroy." This ancient inscription was discovered in 1931 by Professor E.L. Sukenik (see this website: *https://www.jewishvirtuallibrary.org/ burial-sites-and-tombs-in-jerusalem-of-the-second-temple-period*).

- **David and Goliath (1 Samuel 17:1-58)**

One might ask: "Do you mean this story has archaeological proof?" Yes, and there seems to be more every day

---

[22] Rusty Russel, "Fallen Empires: Sennacherib's Hexagonal Prism," Bible History, accessed November 12, 2018, *https://www.bible-history.com/empires/prism.html*.

we live.[23] Professor Yosef Garfinkel discovered a tiny piece of pottery in what is considered the ancient city of David. Garfinkel says it may contain evidence supporting the biblical story of David and Goliath. This pottery shard contains what is considered the oldest discovery of the Hebrew language, predating the Dead Sea Scrolls by 850 years.[24]

- **The Stones Like David Used (1 Samuel 17:1-58; Judges 20:15-16; 2 Kings 3:25)**

    We don't have the stones David used to kill Goliath, but we do have proof that such stones were used effectively in war during this time. An insightful article on slings and stones from the late Bronze Age of Britain gives us similar insights.[25] In the ancient site of Israel, ten miles north of Jerusalem lies the ancient province of Benjamin. Archaeologists have discovered hewn stones used for slinging in multiple sites.[26]

- **The City of Gath (1 Samuel 17:1-58; Joshua 13:3)**

    The ancient city of Gath has been excavated by archaeologists who believe they have found the large gates to the city where Goliath lived and fell.[27] They

---

[23] Hank Berrien, "The Story of David and Goliath Gets Archaeological Evidence Backing It Up," *Daily Wire*, October 17, 2018, accessed November 13, 2018, https://www.dailywire.com/news/37279/story-david-and-goliath-gets-archaeological-hank-berrien.

[24] Matthew Kalman, "Proof David Slew Goliath Found as Israeli Archaeologists Unearth Oldest Ever Hebrew Text," *Daily Mail UK*, October 31, 2008, accessed November 2, 2018, *https://www.dailymail.co.uk/news/article-1081850/Proof-David-slew-Goliath-Israeli-archaeologists-unearth-oldest-Hebrew-text.html.*

[25] D. Swan, "Attitudes Toward and Use of the Sling in Late Iron Age Britain," IATL: Reinvention: and International Journal of Undergraduate Research, Volume 7, issue 2, 2014, accessed November 12, 2018, *https://warfarehistorynetwork.com/daily/military-history/ancient-weapons-the-sling/*

[26] Gary Byers, "Slings and Stones," *Rapture Notes*, accessed November 13, 2018, *http://www.rapturenotes.com/slingsandstones.html.*

[27] Michael Tanenbaum, "Archaeologist Finds Goliath's Gate in Biblical City of Gath," *Philly Voice*, August 5, 2015, accessed November 1, 2018, *https://www.*

have found proof of the Philistines diet which consisted of green pea lentils, pigs, and dogs! Many artifacts of the material culture of Philistia have been excavated at the site.[28]

- ## The Goliath Shards/the Qeiyafa Ostracon (1 Samuel 17:1-58)

In the city of Gad, archaeologists have recently found several things confirming the biblical historical narrative of David and Goliath. One such miraculous finding was an ancient piece of pottery shard that held a name similar to "Goliath."[29] While this does not prove the existence of Goliath it does prove the name Goliath was a well-known attested name at the time of the events described in the Bible.

- ## The Armor of Goliath the Philistine (1 Samuel 17:5-11)

The biblical account of what Goliath wore on the day he faced little David is a well-known story. Critics have long accused the Bible for being inaccurate

phillyvoice.com/archaeologists-goliaths-gate-biblical-city-gath/.

[28] Fox News, "Archaeological Excavation: Biblical Giant Goliath's Home Town," Foxnews.com, July 11, 2011, accessed November 14, 2018, https://www. foxnews.com/science/archaeologists-excavate-biblical-giant-goliaths-hometown.

[29] Steven Law, "David Battles Goliath: Is There Evidence?" Patterns of Evidence, October 26, 2018, accessed November 14, 2018, https://patternsofevidence.com/blog/2018/10/26/david-battles-goliath/.

stating that the Bible dressed Goliath in a uniform, much like a hoplite soldier from the 7th or 5th century. In other words, he was written as a Greek soldier! This attack on biblical accuracy has recently been dismantled. Archaeologists, excavating in Gad have confirmed that the biblical description of Goliath's armor fits the weapon discovery of the era in the city of Gad.[30]

- **Goliath as the Front Man for the Philistines (1 Samuel 17:3-4)**

The biblical narrative sets the stage of a fight against the Israelites and the Philistines. Skeptics have long debated the actuality of such an ancient practice at this time. However, recent discoveries have proved that indeed it was common practice to use a single combat soldier to determine the outcome of a war. "Warriors arrayed in this way were called champions; they were at the front of the field and often led the attack. Homer calls them *promachoi,* meaning first-men. We recognize them from the warrior vase found at Mycenae, as well on the Egyptian reliefs at Medinet Habu from 1174 B.C.E. years ago, depicting an invasion by the "Sea People."[31] The concept of a front-man seemed strategically aligned to avoid the loss of an entire army. "War by proxy was a common practice in the Bronze Age, to spare the bloody cost of armies clashing. The peoples assumed their gods would intervene on their behalf (and when they didn't, they assumed the gods were peeved at them). Examples abound."[32]

---

[30] Bohnstrom, *Huge If True.*
[31] Ibid.
[32] Ibid.

- **King David and His Dynasty (1 Samuel 13:14; Acts 13:22)**

The name of David may be well known by the world and the Christian community, but the actuality of his life and the extent of the reach of his "so-called" kingdom have been at the center of furious debates. Once again, the skeptics said that David was a mythical character, or at the very least, a story of tremendous exaggeration among the Israelites, an attempt to appear larger than life in the presence of their enemies. This debate continued until Eliat Mazar took the Bible and started to dig in February 2005, according to the passage of 2 Samuel 5:17 where she found Khirbet Qeiyafa—a site known as the "Palace of King David." She found a steeped stoned structure and realized that this was the ancient city of David. "The ruins are the best example to date of the uncovered fortress city of King David," lead researchers Yossi Garfinkel and Saar Ganor said, according to the *Jerusalem Post*. "This is indisputable proof of the existence of a central authority in Judah during the time of King David."[33] At this site, they found olive seeds that could be carbon-14 dated to the time of David's life.

---

[33] Meredith Bennett-Smith, "King David's Palace Discovered? Archaeologists Find Huge Palace, Storeroom at Khirbet Qeiyafa Site," *Huffington Post*, July 19, 2013, accessed November 1, 2018, *https://www.huffingtonpost.com/2013/07/19/king-david-palace-archaeologists-khirbet-qeiyafa_n_3620053.html*.

- **The Moabite Stone/Mesha Stone (1 Kings 2:11; 2 Kings 3:26, 27; Isaiah 7:13)**

Again, the actual belief that David was a real human being, not a fictious character was at the center of the Davidic debate. In 1868, F.A. Klein, a German missionary, discovered the Moabite Stone/Mesha Stone some 20 miles east of the Dead Sea. The stone contains the words, "Yaweh," and "The House of David." "The skeptics' claim that King David never existed is now hard to defend. Last year, the French scholar Andre Lemaire reported a related "House of David" discovery in the *Biblical Archaeology Review*. His subject was the Mesha Stele (also known as the Moabite Stone), the most extensive inscription ever recovered from ancient Palestine. Found in 1868 at the ruins of biblical Dibon and later fractured, the basalt stone wound up in the Louvre, where Lemaire spent seven years studying it. His conclusion: the phrase "House of David" appears there as well. As with the Tel Dan fragment, this inscription comes from an enemy of Israel boasting of a victory—King Mesha of Moab, who figured in the Bible. Lemaire had to reconstruct a missing letter to decode the wording, but if he's right, there are now two 9th-century references to David's dynasty."[34]

- **The Name of Enshba'al on Pottery (2 Samuel 3-4)**

The name Enshba'al is a name used only, according to archaeologists, during the time that King David reigned. "This name was not used later in the First Temple period," Garfinkel

---

[34] Michael D. Lemonick, "Is the Bible Fact or Fiction?: Archaeologists in the Holy Land Are Shedding New Light on What Did or Did Not Occur in the Greatest Stories Ever Told," "Is the Bible Fact or Fiction?" *Time* magazine, (Volume 146: No 25), December 18, 1995, accessed November 3, 2018, *http://content.time.com/time/magazine/article/0,9171,983854,00.html.*

and Ganor said in a statement. "The correlation between the biblical tradition and the archaeological finds indicates this was a common name only during that period. The name Beda' is unique and does not occur in ancient inscriptions or in the biblical tradition."[35] Discovered at the site of David's palace, in the valley of Elah, a three-thousand- year-old piece of pottery held his name.

- **The Tel Dan Stele**

 This stele was discovered in 1993 by Avraham Biran. This stele was a boast from King Hazael of Aram-Damascus in his defeat of Israel. Why is this so important? It is the first and oldest reference of the biblical King David. "What made the Tel Dan inscription one of the most exciting biblical archaeology discoveries for scholars and the broader public was its unprecedented reference to the "House of David." The stela's fragmented inscription, first read and translated by the renowned epigrapher Joseph Naveh, proved that King David from the Bible was a genuine historical figure and not simply the fantastic literary creation of later biblical writers and editors."[36]

- **Hebron: The City of David (2 Samuel 2:1, 4; 5:4-5; Joshua 10:36)**

You may remember, Abraham came from Hebron, but did you know that when David first became king, his headquarters were in Hebron? Today, it is known as Tel Rumeida, and

---

[35] Jeanna Bryner, "Rare King David-Era Inscription Discovered in Biblical City," *Life Science*, June 16, 2015, accessed October 12, 2018, https://www.live-science.com/51223-king-david-era-inscription-discovered.html.

[36] BAR Soceity Staff, "The Tel Dan Inscription: The First Historical Evidence of King David from the Bible," *Biblical Archaeology Review*, September 10, 2018, accessed October 5, 2018, *https://www.biblicalarchaeology.org/daily/biblical-artifacts/artifacts-and-the-bible/the-tel-dan-inscription-the-first-historical-evidence-of-the-king-david-bible-story/* .

excavations began in the 1960s. Now, archaeologists be-lieve they have found or are at least close to finding David's original palace in Hebron. "A pillar and its attached capital show clear evidence of a royal structure that is believed to be buried in this undisclosed location. "We appear to have a complete castle here," Kfar Etzion Field School Director Yaron Rosental said. "Those who lived here after it did not know of its existence and thus, instead of using its stones to build a new building, as was the usual practice, left it intact."

Once again, our chapter is full of stories furiously de-bated and denied by the skeptics and critics of the con-quest—Joshua, the Walls of Jericho, and the Davidic King-dom. Yet, minute details can be proven from the biblical record along with obscure names and places. The good news is as we move closer toward our own century, there is even more evidence, not less! During the times of the prophets, are there physical proofs of their stories, kings, and person-alities? Well, by now you should know the answer to this question. Yes, of course.

Chapter 10

Kings, Prophets, Personalities, and Enemies of Israel

This would be a great place to remind you that when we started this journey in Chapter 3, we listed 50 people whose lives can be proven outside the Bible. There are numerous kings, prophets, personalities, and enemies mentioned in the Bible which can be proven to have really existed at the time the Bible speaks of their existence.

The Davidic Kingdom grew and expanded into the reign of King Solomon, David's son. Prophets and personalities, along with their enemies mark the Old Testament stories with details which give the stories texture and authentic meaning. These stories are again, reported to have been mythical, or greatly embellished by the people of Israel. One story has been attacked for being inauthentic, yet the archaeological spade, the tools of geologists, and wisdom of anthropologists are confirming something radically different.

The Reign of King Solomon

At the site of Khirbet Summeily in the Negev desert in Israel, Dr. Blakey's team stumbled upon a small village dating

223

from the 10th to the 8th century B.C. The team discovered several small bullas with information which showed the complexity of a political organization previously thought not to exist. The team believes the bullas contain insights into the political depth and level of organization of Kings David and Solomon during the 10th century. These bullas suggest their kingdoms contained a level of organization much larger than the skeptics have long thought.[1] Dr. Hardin said: "We are very positive that these bullae are associated with the Iron Age IIA, which we date to the 10th century B.C., and which lend general support to the historical veracity of David and Solomon as recorded in the Hebrew biblical texts."[2]

---

[1] James W. Hardin, "Iron Age Bullae from Officialdom's Periphery Khirbet Summeily in Broader Context," *Near East Archaeology* 4, no. 77 (2014): 299–301.

[2] News Staff, "New Finds Suggest Both Kings David and Solomon Actually Existed," *Science News*, December 26, 2014, accessed November 15, 2018, *http://www.sci-news.com/archaeology/science-biblical-kings-david-solomon-02371.html.*

- ## The Mines of King Solomon (1 Kings 7:46)

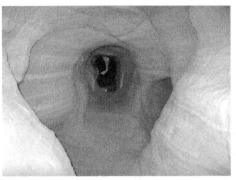

A team led by Dr. Erez Ben-Yosef, discovered that the copper mines, skeptics swore were built by the Egyptians, are dated three centuries later, to the time of King Solomon. "Based on the radiocarbon dating of material unearthed at a new site in Timna Valley in Israel's Aravah Desert, the findings overturn the archaeological consensus of the last several decades. Scholarly work and materials found in the area suggest the mines were operated by the Edomites—a semi-nomadic tribal confederation that, according to the Bible, warred constantly with Israel. "The mines are definitely from the period of King Solomon," says Dr. Ben-Yosef."[3]

- ## First Archaeological Evidence of Solomon's Temple Discovered (1 Kings 5:6; 9:10)

Recently, a new discovery has Israel talking. We have long known about the second Temple, which parts of, are still standing in Israel today. We call this the Temple Mount, the Dome of the Rock. But underneath this Dome of the Rock, Jewish and Christian people believe is the foundation of Abraham's story of Isaac's potential sacrifice, and the foundation of the first Temple which King Solomon built. Nebuchadnezzar II destroyed Solomon's Temple in 587 B.C. Archaeologists believe they have found scientific proof of the

---

[3] American Friends of Tel Aviv University, "Evidence of Solomon's Mines: Archaeologist Date Mines in South of Israel to Days of King Solomon," *Science Daily*, September 3, 2013, accessed September 3, 2018, https://www.sciencedaily.com/releases/2013/09/130903141356.htm.

time of Solomon under the first temple. "It's the first time that we've found artifacts from this period in situ on the Temple Mount," the head of the Israel Antiquities Authority in Jerusalem, Yuval Baruch, said: "It exists."[4]

- **Manure from the Time of King Solomon**

You will probably gasp, "Manure?" Yes. Manure. How does manure prove the existence of King Solomon? Well, the manure came from donkeys dating back to the 10th century, the time of King Solomon. "As *National Geographic* reports, what is remarkable about the find is that the manure suggests significant activity was taking place at the site at a time when King Solomon is believed to have been building the Holy Temple."[5] Now, think about what you have just read. Skeptics say there is no evidence for the Bible's historical narrative. Really? Even ancient manure is pointing toward the realities of these figures!!

- **A Palace-Like Structure at Gezer (2 Samuel 5:25; 1 Chronicles 14:16)**

A 3,000-year-old palace found in biblical Gezer during the time of King Solomon's reign has been discovered. "According to the Old Testament, the city was also associated with the Philistines in David's time: the king broke their power "from Geba as far as Gezer" (2 Samuel 5:25; 1 Chronicles 14:16)"[6] This palace coincides

---

[4] Jamie Seidel, "Israel Heralds First Direct Evidence of King Solomon's Temple," *New.com.au*, October 26, 2016, accessed November 22, 2018, https://www.news.com.au/technology/science/archaeology/israel-claims-first-temple-relic-find/news-story/699428fdc3df06caf04b49a27c6429be.

[5] Stoyan Zaimov, "Archaeological Discovery: 3000-Year-Old Manure in Israel Offers Clues on Bible's King Solomon's Mystery," *Christian Reporter*, accessed November 22, 2018, https://www.christianpost.com/news/archaeological-discovery-3000-year-old-manure-israel-bibles-king-solomon-mystery-180268/.

[6] Philippe Bohstrom, "King Solomon's-Era Palace Found in Biblical Gezer: Mon-

with what the Bible tells us about Solomon's buildings and construction, as well as his wife's gift from her father, the Egyptian Pharaoh (1 Kings 9:16-17).

The newly discovered palace is west of the so-called Solomonic Gate, a six-chambered inner gate, although it is doubtful that a Jerusalemite king actually spent time at Gezer. The excavation team calls the building "Solomon's Palace" because of the biblical tradition of Solomon building grand projects at Hazor, Megiddo, and Gezer. First Kings 9:15 says, "And this is the reason of the levy which King Solomon raised; for to build the house of the Lord, and his own house, and Millo, and the wall of Jerusalem, and Hazor, and Megiddo, and Gezer."[7]

Additional archaeological discoveries are continuing to bring about more clarity to the time of Solomon, stone by stone and broken pottery pieces, olives, dung, and bullas. Professor Dever's illustrated lecture, titled "The Golden Age of Solomon: Fact or Fiction," will show, however, that archaeological findings reflect the description of Solomon's architecture in 1 Kings 9:15-17. While King Solomon's kingdom may have been reasonably modest, Professor Dever says, and not the vast empire portrayed in the Bible, it did exist, and has left archaeological evidence."[8]

As you can clearly see by now in this book, we will find out if Solomon's kingdom was the vast empire portrayed in the Bible; so far, the skeptics' track record has not been that great, when they bet against the Bible as a history book.

---

umental 3000-year-old ruins, Philistine pottery, support biblical tales of Gezer's rise and fall to a jealous Pharaoh," *Haaretz*, August 31, 2016, accessed November 22, 2018, https://www.haaretz.com/archaeology/king-solomon-era-palace-found-in-biblical-gezer-1.5431221.

  [7] Ibid.

  [8] University of New England Media Team, "Visiting Archaeologists to Present Evidence of Solomon's Kingdom," New England University, April 16, 2018, accessed November 22, 2018, https://www.une.edu.au/connect/news/2012/04/visiting-archaeologist-to-present-evidence-of-solomone28099s-kingdom.

- **The Pomegranates of Solomon's Temple (1 Kings 7:18, 20)**

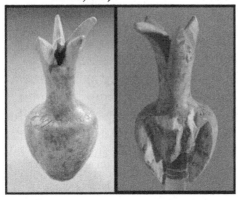

In Exodus 28:31-33, the Bible speaks of pomegranates being used in Temple worship. The Scriptures tell us that King Solomon used "its image to decorate his palace and the Temple of the Lord."[9] In Israel, an ivory pomegranate surfaced as a piece of antiquity. David Briggs, M.A. in religion from Yale Divinity School said, "The pomegranate was discovered in 1979 at the shop of an antiquities dealer and was later sold to the Israeli Museum in 1988 by sellers who remained anonymous. What ties the scepter to Solomon's Temple is an inscription that has been translated as "Holy to the priests, belonging to the House of Yahweh," according to the catalog from the Smithsonian exhibition. . . . The finds provide contrary evidence to . . . a "nihilist" school of biblical scholarship that would claim all events described in the Bible before the Babylonians' exile as fictional."[10]

In 2004, archaeologists declared that this piece was a fake. Dr. Ada Yardeni, a paleographer, however, recanted her interpretation of the Hebrew spellings, working with Hershel Shanks from the Biblical Archaeological Review. She changed her mind based on new evidence.[11]

---

[9] Bassett-Brody, *Etched in Stone*, 164.

[10] David Briggs, "Testaments: Archaeological Discoveries Provide Biblical Evidence," *Stevens Point Journal* (December 1993): 8.

[11] Hershal Shanks, "Ivory Pomegranate under Microscope at Israel Museum," *Biblical Archaeological Review* (March/April 2016).

- ## Megiddo (1 Kings 9:15; 11:6)

This city was mentioned first in the Book of Joshua and now in reference to King Solomon. King Solomon built many buildings and undertook the fortification of this city.

Clearly, when Solomon rebuilt Megiddo, with its large palaces, casemate walls, and massive gates, he also made sure of the town's water supply in times of danger. Thus, the terse biblical statement that Solomon built Megiddo has been greatly amplified by archaeological excavations which have shown his activities to have covered the three essential features of the ancient city: the buildings, the fortifications, and the water supply.[12]

- ## The Queen of Sheba's Gold Mines (1 Kings 10:10)

The Bible says that Solomon was visited by the Queen of Sheba.

British archaeologists exploring the Gheralta plateau in Ethiopia's northern highlands claim to have discovered an enormous goldmine once operated by the ancient kingdom of Saba, home to the legendary Queen of Sheba. The expedition, led by author, lecturer and former British Museum curator Louise Schofield, claims to have found the entrance to the mine, a 20-foot-tall stone stela carved with Sabaean inscriptions

---

[12] Bassett-Brody, *Etched in Stone*, 104.

and symbols, as well as the remnants of a temple dedicated to the chief god of the land of Saba. The discoveries were made as part of Schofield's environmental development work in Ethiopia on behalf of the Tigray Trust.[13]

• Queen of Sheba's Palace (1 Kings 10:10)

Archaeologists have found the palace of the Queen of Sheba. "A team of archaeologists from the University of Hamburg said they discovered the Queen of Sheba's palace and an altar that may have once held the Ark of the Covenant in Axum, Ethiopia."[14] The Smithsonian Institute hosted a seminar showing satellite images of the palace of the Queen of Sheba. [15]

Solomon reigned for forty years (1 Kings 11:42). He died, and his son Rehoboam became the king in his place (1 Kings 11:43).

Kings After Solomon

• Shechem (1 Kings 12:1; Genesis 11:27–12:11)

The Bible says that Rehoboam went to Shechem... "for all of Israel had gone to Shechem to make him king" (1 Kings 12:1). It was at Shechem that God

[13] BAR Staff, "Expedition Claims Evidence of Queen of Sheba Found in Ethiopia," *Biblical Archaeology Review*, January 14, 2012, accessed November 22, 2018, https://www.biblicalarchaeology.org/daily/biblical-sites-places/biblical-archaeology-places/expedition-claims-evidence-of-queen-of-sheba-found-in-ethiopia/.

[14] Don Jade, "Queen of Sheba's Palace Found in Ethiopia," *Rasta Livewire*, November 6, 2010, accessed November 21, 2018, http://www.africaresource.com/rasta/articles/queen-of-shebas-palace-found-in-ethiopia/.

[15] Michael J. Harrower, "Satellite Images and the Queen of Sheba," *Smithsonian's Associates*, September 20, 2011, accessed November 21, 2018, https://smithsonianassociates.org/ticketing/tickets/222938 .

spoke to Abraham about the favor of God upon all his descendants (Genesis 11:27). After Solomon's death, the twelve tribes of Israel split into two kingdoms or tribes. "Shechem was the first capital of the northern tribes of Israel."[16]

- **Rehoboam (1 Kings 14:25-26)**

"Rehoboam is actually the first Judaic king for which scholars have some extrabiblical evidence; he reigned from 931 to 914 BCE. These numbers don't mix perfectly with the recorded reign of Sheshonq I (950–929 BCE)."[17] On a relief stating the victories of Shishak, it lists cities fortified by Rehoboam. "In the center bottom are all the conquered Hebrew city mayors (chieftains) with uplifted hands as a sign of submission to Shishak to whom they paid tribute. Rehoboam fortified 15 cities, four of which were conquered by Shishak and have a corresponding name ring: Gath, Hebron, Adoraim, Aijalon."[18]

---

[16] Bassett-Brody, *Etched in Stone*, 118.

[17] Kmtsesh, "Shesong I and Jerusalem," Ancient Near East: Just the Facts, February 25, 2012, accessed November 21, 2018, https://ancientneareast.org/tag/rehoboam/.

[18] The Bible and Archaeology, "Rehoboam, King of Judah 931-914 BC," Bible Archaeology, accessed November 22, 2018, http://www.bible.ca/archaeology/bible-archaeology-sheshonq-I-shoshenq-shishak-shishaq-bubastite-karnak-conquest-campaign-canaan-battle-relief-topographical-list-187-cities-conquered-name-rings-926bc.htm.

- **King Omri (1 Kings 16:23, 25, 26)**

Omri was a great military leader, administrator, and builder, but a poor godly leader. The Bible says that he sinned much more than Jeroboam! He ruled two years 886–885 B.C. and founded his first capital in the city of Tirzah. It was first excavated by Roland de Vaux. The name Omri is well-attested and confirmed in history.

- **The Mesha Inscription[19]**

This inscription says, "Omri had occupied the land."

- **The Records of Shalmaneser III 841 B.C.[20]**

This inscription says, "Jehu, son of Omri."

---

[19] Bryant G. Wood, "Omri, King of Israel," Association of Biblical Research, October 10, 2005, accessed November 5, 2018, http://www.biblearchaeology.org/post/2005/10/10/Omri-King-of-Israel.aspx.

[20] Ibid.

- **The Annalistic Records of Tiglath-Pileser III**[21]

This inscription says "Omri-Land."

- **The Annalistic Records of Sargon II, 721 B.C.**[22]

This inscription reads, "I conquered... all Omri-Land."

- **King Ahab (1 Kings 16:29)**
  The Name Ahab

Archaeologists have discovered his palace and his name in historical archives. His name is mentioned in the stela of Shalmaneser III when it was discovered in 1861 at Kurkh.

---

[21] Ibid.
[22] Ibid.

- ## Ahab's Palace at Samaria (1 Kings 22:39)

His palace has been discovered in Samaria (1 Kings 22:39). "At Samaria, Ahab expanded the palace and decorated it with ivory (1 Kings 22:39). Excavations revealed many ivory items from Ahab's palace in a building dubbed "the ivory house," where many fragments of carved ivory plaques were found. These are often called the "Samaria Ivories." A group of 64 ostraca inscribed in archaic Hebrew, found in the treasury of Ahab's palace, probably date to the reign of Jeroboam II (ca. 785–753 B.C.), or Menahem (752–742 B.C.)."[23]

- ## Elijah the Prophet: Mount Carmel (1 Kings 18:20; 1 Kings 17:1)

Currently, there is no physical evidence of the prophet Elijah. There are several caves attributing his stay in them; however, we do know that a place called Mount Carmel does exist.

- ## Elisha the Prophet (1 Kings 19:19)

Archaeologists have been digging at Tel Rehov in the Jordan Valley and believe they have found the name of Elisha on a piece of pottery shard, and probably the prophet's home.[24] The prophet Elisha is

---

[23] All About God, "All About Archaeology: Samaria," All About God: Archaeology, 2002, accessed November 22, 2018, *https://www.allaboutarchaeology.org/samaria.htm.*

[24] April Holloway, "Archaeologist May Have Found Name of Bible Prophet Elisha.," *Ancient Origins: Reconstructing the Story of Humanities Past,*

 the one who took the prophet Elijah's place (1Kings 19:19). Archaeologists have dated this site where the pottery shard and house were found to the time of Elisha. During the excavations, archaeologists discovered a special room inside the house with a table and a bench. They also discovered a pottery shard with the name Elisha on it, dated to the 9th century. The discovery has led some to believe this was the room of the prophet Elisha. "We found an ink inscription written in red ink on pottery, but it is broken, unfortunately," Mazar said. "But we reconstructed the name as Elisha." The prophet Elisha was born about seven miles from Tel Rehov in Avel Mehola and went throughout the kingdom of Israel, from Jericho to Samaria to Shunam. "You know, I cannot say for sure this particular Elisha that we found is the biblical Elisha," Mazar said. "You know it's very difficult to say, but it is very tempting, because it is exactly the period when Elisha acted – the second half of the 9th century B.C." Archaeologist Stephen Pfann calls the evidence compelling. "With only six other people by the name of Elisha known in that time for a couple of centuries on either side, we can somehow believe that either there was just the luck that this holy man was also by the name of Elisha, or this was Elisha the prophet himself."[25]

July 28, 2013, accessed November 22, 2018, https://www.ancient-origins.net/news-history-archaeology/archaeologists-may-have-found-home-bible-prophet-elisha-00697 .

[25] Chris Mitchell and Julie Stahl, "Have Archaeologists Found the Prophet Elisha's House?" *Charisma News,* July 23, 2013, accessed November 22, 2018, *https://www.charismanews.com/world/40343-have-archaeologists-found-prophet-elisha-s-house.*

- **The Beehives and Nimshi (1 Kings 19:16; 2 Kings 9:2)**

 One would think that a land which "flows with milk and honey," would be the place to find a trove of beehives. But not until recently has there ever been physical proof of the production of honey from beehives in the Middle East. The beehives were discovered at Tel-Rohv in Beth Shean Valley. But that is not all they found; they found the name Nimshi on three pieces of pottery shards.

A particularly fascinating find at the site is an inscription on a ceramic storage jar found near the beehives that reads "To nmsh." This name was also found inscribed on another storage jar from a slightly later occupation level at Tel Rehov, dated to the time of the Omride Dynasty in the 9th century BCE. Moreover, this same name was found on a contemporary jar from nearby Tel Amal, situated in the Gan HaShelosha National Park (Sachne).[26]

The name "Nimshi" is known in the Bible as the name of the father, and in several verses the grandfather of Israelite King Jehu, the founder of the dynasty that usurped power from the Omrides (2 Kings: 9–12). It is possible that the discovery of three inscriptions bearing this name in the same region and dating to the same period indicates that Jehu's family originated from the Beth Shean Valley and possibly even from the large city located at Tel Rehov. The large apiary discovered at the site might have belonged to this illustrious local clan.[27]

[26] Musa Etetz Israel Museum, "It is the Land of Honey," Musa Etetz Israel Museum Tel-Aviv, 2016, accessed November 22, 2018, *http://eretzmuseum.org. il/e/345/.*

[27] Jonathan Kantrowitz, "First Beehives in Ancient Near East Excavated,"

- ## Jezreel: (1 Kings 18:45-46; 1 Kings 21)

Jezreel was discovered by David Ussishkin and John Woodhead. Jezreel is the place where Elijah ran on ahead of Ahab mentioned in 1 Kings 18:45-46. It has been excavated and confirmed.[28] It is also home to King David's third wife, Michal, as well as part of the tribe of Issachar. "The agricultural installations ranged from small cup marks to large oil and wine presses, including one that may belong to the time of Naboth's orchard, which King Ahab coveted and for which Jezebel had Naboth framed and executed (1 Kings 21). The expedition's survey of archaeology revealed Jezreel to be much larger than previously thought."[29]

- ## The One and Only Jezebel (1 Kings 16:31; 21:25; 2 Kings 10:13; Revelation 2:20)

In 1964, a seal was discovered and brought to the Israel Museum in Jerusalem. The late Nahman Avigad, a paleographer studied this unique seal. It was unique because of its larger size and the fact it was made of opal, the gemstone. Such a fancy seal would strongly

---

Archaeological News, September 4, 2007, accessed November 22, 2018: *http://archaeologynewsreport.blogspot.com/2007/09/first-beehives-in-ancient-near-east.html* .

[28] David Ussishkin and John Woodhead, "Excavations in Tel-Jezreel," Institute of Archaeology of Tel Aviv University, accessed November 22, 2018, *http://archaeology.tau.ac.il/?page_id=2051.*

[29] BAR Staff, "Jezreel Expedition Sheds New Light on Ahab and Jezebel's City," *Biblical Archaeological Review,* May 1, 2016, accessed November 11, 2018, *https://www.biblicalarchaeology.org/daily/archaeology-today/biblical-archaeology-topics/jezreel-expedition-sheds-new-light-on-ahab-and-jezebel%E2%80%99s-city/* .

suggest that it belonged to someone of royalty. Initially, the first letter had been broken off and so the seal set for years. Finally, a Dutch Old Testament scholar by the name of Marjo Korpel, took an interest in the ancient seal. She discovered that the broken off piece, which represented just a few letters said, "belonging to." Although 100 percent certainty cannot be attained, Korpel's assessment of the evidence leads her to conclude, "I believe it is very likely that we have here the seal of the famous Queen Jezebel."[30] This seal, "Belonging to Jezebel," is one of the thousands of biblical treasures throughout the world today.

- **Ben-Hadad (1 Kings 20:1; 2 Kings 13:3)**

In 1903, Assyriologist, Henri Pognon, discovered the Zakkur Stele at Syrai's Tel Afis site. The stele is important for several reasons.

Prominent in the Stele of Zakkur is the name "Bar-Hadad," son of Hazael, king of Damascus. Equivalent to the Aramean name "Bar-Hadad" is the Bible's reference to "Ben-Hadad," who is mentioned several times over a significant period of time. Ben-Hadad appears to be a royal title for the king of Aram whose capital is Damascus.[31]

---

[30] Korpel, *Fit for a Queen.*

[31] S.B. Noegel, *"The Zakkur Inscription," in the Ancient Near East: Historical Sources in Translation, Chavalas, MW Ed* (London: Blackwell, 2006), 307–11.

- **The Pool of Gibeon (2 Samuel 2-4; 1 Kings 3:4; 2 Kings 24:13)**

This ancient city called Gibeon was once a royal city belonging to the Hivites. In 1956, American archaeologist Dr. James B. Pritchard discovered the ancient city of Gibeon and its pool. Dr. Bryant Wood, doctor of Syro-Palestinian archaeology from the University of Toronto said, "This large pool at Gibeon is no doubt the pool where the forces of Israel's second king, David, fought under Joab against the forces of Saul's son Ishbosheth under Abner."[32]

- **Ahab (1 Kings 21:1)**

In the Book of First Kings, it clearly states that Ahab built a palace with inlaid ivory. A specific detail with even more specific information. We know Phoenicians were known for their ivories. Dr. Michael Avi-Yonah, said, "Israel's general prosperity at that time is manifest in the fortifications at Samaria and in the place of the Omride dynasty; fragments of ivory discovered in the palace confirm the tale of the house of ivory which Ahab built."[33]

- **Zechariah, the son of Benaiah (2 Chronicles 20:14; 1 Kings 22:2)**

Zechariah prophesied to King Jehoshaphat in 2 Chronicles. Zechariah's name has been found on a piece of pottery shard. "The partially-preserved ancient

---

[32] Bassett-Brody, *Etched in Stone*, 171.

[33] Michael Avi-Yonah, *A History of Israel and the Holy Land* (New York and London: Continuum, 2005), 88.

Hebrew inscription roughly transliterates into English characters as "ryhu bn bnh." When translated, this name is similar to Zechariah the son of Benaiah, whose name appears in 2 Chronicles 20:14."[34]

- **Jeroboam's Royal Servant: Shema (2 Kings 14:23)**

In 1904, at an excavation in Megiddo, a bronze seal belonging to the "servant of Jeroboam," was discovered. This servant was called, "Shema," and his name was on the seal as well. The seal contained the symbol of a roaring lion— symbol of the Judean kings. [35]

- **Jehu (2 Kings 10:36)**

In 1846, Henry Layard led an excavation in Iraq at the site known as Kalhu, once the ancient capital of the Assyrian Empire. Kalhu was known as Nimrod. Henry discovered

---

[34] Robin Ngo, "First Temple Period Inscription May Preserve Biblical Name," *Bible History Daily: BAR*, August 21, 2103, accessed November 22, 2018, *https://www.biblicalarchaeology.org/daily/biblical-sites-places/jerusalem/first-temple-period-inscription-may-preserve-biblical-name/*.

[35] "Jeroboam II," *New World Encyclopedia*, July 3, 2013, accessed November 22, 2018, *http://www.newworldencyclopedia.org/p/index.php?title=Jeroboam_II*.

a Black Obelisk (think Washington Monument, but black). On this obelisk, there was a picture of King Jehu paying homage and bowing to Shalmaneser III! This is one of the only carved images of a biblical figure in the world! "The second row of pictures on the Obelisk depicts the tribute of one particular king whom we know. When the ancient Assyrian Cuneiform inscription was translated, the biblical world was shocked. The inscription reads, "The tribute of Jehu, son of Omri: I received from him silver, gold, a golden bowl, a golden vase with pointed bottom, golden tumblers, golden buckets, tin, a staff for a king [and] spears."[36]

- **Hezekiah (2 Kings 18-20)**

A bulla with the name of Hezekiah, from the 8th century was discovered at the excavation of Ophel. It made history, because it was the first time a bulla of an Israeli or Judean king had been found. "The seal of the king was so important. It could have been a matter of life or death, so it's hard to believe that anyone else had the permission to use the seal."[37]

- **The Prophet Isaiah (2 Kings 19:1-2)**

A 2,700-year-old bulla was discovered by Dr. Mazar, found in the untouched remains of the Iron Age, outside a royal bakery. The name on the bulla has caused quite a stir in the archaeological community,

[36] Tim Kimberely, "Top Ten Discovered in Archaeology #10: Jehu's Tribute to Shalamaneser III," *Credo House*, July 8, 2010, accessed November 22, 2018, *https://credohouse.org/blog/top-ten-biblical-discoveries-in-archaeology-9-jehus-tribute-to-shalmaneser-iii.*

[37] William Heilpern, "Biblical King Seal Discovered In Dump Site," CNN, December 4, 2015, accessed November 22, 2018, *https://www.cnn.com/2015/12/03/middleeast/king-hezekiah-royal-seal/index.html.*

for the bulla is reported to say, "Isaiah, the Prophet." "We found the eighth-century B.C.E. seal mark that may have been made by the prophet Isaiah himself only 10 feet away from where we earlier discovered the highly-publicized bulla of King Hezekiah of Judah," said Dr. Eilat Mazar of the Hebrew University in Jerusalem, in a statement."[38]

- **King Cyrus (Isaiah 44:28–45)**

Isaiah prophesied the coming kingdom of King Cyrus by name 150 years before his events. "During excavations at Babylon (1879–1882), archaeologist Hormuzd Rassam discovered a small (ten inches), clay, barrel-shaped cylinder that contained an inscription from Cyrus. Now housed in the British Museum, the cylinder reported the king's policy regarding captives: "I [Cyrus] gathered all their [former] inhabitants and returned [to them] their habitations" (Pritchard, 1958, 1:208). As noted, scholar Jack Finegan observed: "The spirit of Cyrus's decree of release which is quoted in the Old Testament (2 Chronicles 36:23; Ezra 1:2-4) is confirmed by the Cyrus cylinder."[39]

- **King Jehoichin's Ration Records (2 Kings 24:2-30)**

In 2 Kings 24 it tells us the amazing story of how King Jehoiachin rationed out food to his people during a time of lack.

Several administrative documents have been found in ancient

---

[38] James Rogers, "Archaeologists May Have Found the Prophet Isaiah's 'Signature,"FoxNews,February22,2018,accessedNovember22,2018,*https://www.foxnews.com/science/major-biblical-discovery-archaeologists-may-have-found-the-prophet-isaiahs-signature.*

[39] Jack Finegan, *Light from the Ancient Past* (NJ: Princeton University Press, 1948), 191.

Babylon that record events and transactions that took place during the reign of Evil-Merodach. These documents were preserved on clay cuneiform tablets, of which many have been found broken into several pieces. Jehoiachin's name, however, is clearly legible on the tablets. Not only is he mentioned, but documentation for an allotment of grain, oil, and foodstuffs is also provided.[40]

- **The King Josiah (2 Chronicles 34:3)**

    The prophet Jeremiah was born the same year as King Josiah. Josiah was only twenty when he became king, and he brought many reforms to the backslidden Israelites. According to 2 Kings 22:8, as he was cleaning Solomon's Temple, dedicated to bringing back the Israelites to the fear of God, the Book of the Law, given by Moses was discovered. Is there any archaeological evidence for the time of Josiah? Yes, there is!

- **Ostracon Found at Mesad Hashavyahu (Jeremiah 1:2)**

A piece of ostracon, almost eight inches in height was found at Mesad Hashavyahu, a fort on the Mediterranean coast. This ostracon was dated to the last half of Josiah's reign, discovered in the guardroom of the fortress gate. "Jewish names, reference to the Sabbath, and allusions to Jewish law, this potsherd leads to the conclusion that the fort was under Jewish control and that Josiah laid claim to the coastal region and the important highway that ran through it."[41]

---

[40] Hoerth, *Archaeology and the Old Testament*, 378–79.

[41] Ibid., 360.

- **Darius the Great's Tomb (Ezra 6:1-3)**

We know where his tomb is located. (Try googling it for fun!) However, recently archaeologists have discovered an ancient stele with his name on it...in Russia! Discovered in the town of Phanagoria in Russia, this stele records his victory. "Archaeologists suggest the king erected a marble stele in the city after his victory over the Greeks. The monument featured an inscribed text proclaiming the king's triumph. Later, suggests the archaeologists, a fragment of the overturned and broken stele reached Phanagoria, quite possibly as ballast on a ship that called into the Phanagoria port, as there is no natural stone of the kind on the Taman peninsula. "The inscription on the stele made in the name of King Darius I is evidently devoted to the crushing of the Ionian revolt," says Vladimir Kuznetsov, director of the Phanagorian expedition."[42]

- **The Susa Palace (Esther 1:2, 5; 9:12-13; Nehemiah 1:1)**

This is the palace Queen Esther would have walked in, lived in, and represented the Jewish people in Susa. Susa is an ancient city and has been excavated. "The biblical city of Shushan, now the modern Iranian city of Shush, has been added to the United Nations Educational, Scientific, and Cultural Organization (UNESCO) World Heritage."[43] "In the Bible, the city is known

---

[42] Popular Archaeology, "Darius Stele Found in Ancient Town of Phanagoria in Russia," Popular Archaeology, August 9, 2016, accessed November 22, 2018, *https://popular-archaeology.com/article/darius-i-stele-found-in-ancient-town-of-phanagoria-in-russia/.*

[43] Robin Whitlock, "The Ancient City of Susa in Iran Is a Worldwide Treasure," Ancient Origins: Reconstructing the Story of Humanities Past, July 11, 2015, accessed November 22, 2018, *https://www.ancient-origins.net/news-general/*

primarily from the story of Esther in which Haman the Agagite planned to annihilate the Jews of Persia. According to the story, Esther outwitted him by persuading her husband, King Ahasuerus of Persia, to sabotage Haman's plan."[44]

- **Esther and King Xerxes (Ahasuerus), the Winged Lion Drinking Cup (Esther 1:7)**

The Bible tells us in Esther 1:2-10, that King Ahasuerus reclined in his palace and he and his guests drank from golden goblets, each with a different sign. Archaeologists have found these goblets!

- **A Stone Relief With Darius the Great and His Son Xerxes (Esther 4:11)**

A stone relief (stele) was found with Darius the Great and his son Xerxes. Darius and Xerxes were great builders, especially Darius.

Darius was the greatest royal architect of his dynasty, and during his reign, Persian architecture assumed a style that remained unchanged until the end of the empire. In 521 B.C. he made Susa his administrative capital, where he restored the fortifications and built an audience hall (apadana)

---

ancient-city-susa-iran-worldwide-treasure-003399.
[44] Ibid.

and a residential palace. The foundation inscriptions of his palace describe how he brought materials and craftsmen for the work from all quarters of the empire. At Persepolis, in his native country of Fars (Persis), he founded a new royal residence to replace the earlier capital at Pasargadae. The fortifications, apadana, council hall, treasury, and a residential palace are to be attributed to him, although not completed in his lifetime. He also built at Ecbana and Babylon."[45]

- **Israel Needs a Prophet**

The Israelites were in deep trouble, Josiah's death brought his son, Jehoahaz to the throne of Judah. The Pharaoh Neco tried him and placed him into chains. The prophet Jeremiah tells Judah that their king would never return (Jeremiah 22:11-12). The prophet Jeremiah found himself "without godly political support . . . and he was forced to communicate through Baruch, his secretary."[46]

- **The Lavishness of Jehoiakim (Jeremiah 22:13; 36; 2 Kings 23:36; 24;1; 2 Chronicles 36:6)**

Jehoiakim was a stubborn king who had been bravely rebuked by the prophet Jeremiah. This arrogant king even tore up the Word of God and mocked the messenger of God. Jeremiah the prophet had rebuked him for using unpaid labor to build his "spacious upper rooms"

---

[45] J.H. Munn-Rankin, "Darius the Great I of Persia," *Britannica Encyclopedia*, 2018, accessed November 22, 2018, *https://www.britannica.com/biography/Darius-I*.

[46] Hoerth, *Archaeology and the Old Testament, 360*, 362.

(Jeremiah 22:13). "Carved proto-Aeolic capital found at Ramat Rahel, just south of Jerusalem. The finely constructed and decorated palace/fortress found at the site has been attributed to Jehoiakim."[47] "In the debris that covered the citadel after its destruction by the Babylonians, many luxury objects, such as imported Assyrian palace ware were found. A unique find is a seal impression with the inscription to Eliaqim, steward of Yochin is ascribed to an official of King Jehoiachin, king of Judah, who was the son of King Jehoiakim."[48]

- **The Sarsekim Tablet (Jeremiah 39:3)**

The British Museum acquired a small stone tablet in 1920. It was the name on this small stone tablet that had the archaeological world talking. The "small stone tablet" mentions a Babylonian official alive in 595 B.C. and less than 10 years later Jeremiah mentioned an official by the same name. One member of the British Museum's staff, Dr. Irving Finkel, who works in the Department of the Middle East, said: "A mundane commercial transaction takes its place as a primary witness to one of the turning points in Old Testament history. This is a tablet that deserves to be famous."[49] Yet, concerning the significance of the find, Dr. Finkel stated: "If Nebo-Sarsekim existed, which other lesser figures in the Old Testament existed? A throwaway

---

[47] Ibid., 363.

[48] "Ramat Rahel, "A Royal Citadel and a Palace of the Last Kings of Judah: Archaeological Site #7," Israeli Minister of Foreign Affairs, June 24, 2001, accessed November 22, 2018, *http://www.mfa.gov.il/mfa/israelexperience/history/pages/ramat%20rahel%20-%20a%20royal%20citadel%20and%20a%20palace%20of%20the.aspx.*

[49] Dalya Alberge, "Museum Tablet Lends New Weight to Biblical Truth," *Times*, July 11, 2007, accessed November 22, 2018, *http://www.timesonline.co.uk/tol/comment/faith/article2056362.ece.*

detail in the Old Testament turns out to be accurate and true. I think that it means that the whole of the narrative [of Jeremiah] takes on a new kind of power."[50]

- **The Temple of Ishtar/the Queen of Heaven (Jeremiah 7:18)**

Ishtar is referred to by Jeremiah as the "queen of heaven." The kingdom of Babylon was decorated with an entrance dedicated in her honor as you entered the royal court of Nebuchadnezzar II. These gates have been discovered as previously mentioned, as well as her deity. Here is a physical representation of her.

- **Gedaliah (Jeremiah 40:5)**

The Bible not only gets the big names correct like Ahab, but even the small, seemingly insignificant names like Gedaliah mentioned in Jeremiah 40:5. Gedaliah lived during the time period of Jeremiah the prophet. Nebuchadnezzar, after destroying Jerusalem, placed Gedaliah over the poor who lived to tell another day. "According to Ernest Wright, doctor of ancient Near East Studies from John Hopkins University, and inscription found on a clay seal says, "Belonging to Gedaliah, the one who was over the house."[51]

---

[50] Nigel Reynolds, "Tiny Tablets Provide Proof of Old Testament," *Telegraph,* July 13, 2007, accessed November 22, 2018, *www.telegraph.co.uk/news/main.jhtml?xml=/news/2007/07/11/ ntablet111.xml.*

[51] Ernest G. Wright, "Some Personal Seals of Judea Royal Officials," *Biblical Archaeologist* 1 (1938): 2.

- **Gemariah (Jeremiah 36: 11-12)**

The Bible simply says to us that Gemariah was the son of Shaphan. It's amazing that such a brief encounter with a name can reach forward into our hearts and confirm, yet another biblical reality of a real person who lived during the exact time where the Bible places them! In 1982, archaeologists were digging through debris of a two-thousand-year-old building leveled by Nebuchadnezzar II in 586 B.C. A volunteer stumbled upon another ancient bulla with the wording, "Belonging to Gemariah son of Shapan."

- **Nebuchadnezzar II**

No king in the Bible is mentioned as much as Nebuchadnezzar II. He was feared, revered, and the central character to many of the Bible stories heard as a child. He, however, is more than a flannelgraph character made up to be the central villain in a story; he is real. For years, the skeptics attacked and attacked the Bible using the previous fact that nowhere in history, outside the Bible, is Nebuchadnezzar's name found. The skeptics cried that a man who supposedly built as many buildings as the Bible refers to his having built should be found somewhere in ancient history. Yet, the stones remained silent for many thousands of years, until the day they found a brick with his name on it. It appears that Nebuchadnezzar II had his name implanted on fired bricks and placed as a decorative item on most every building he had constructed.

Archaeologists have also found a ceramic cylinder inscribed in cuneiform script with the name of the Babylonian King Nebuchadnezzar II, who is referred to in the Bible more than any other foreign king (see 2 Kings 24:1). The cylinder enumerates his building activities and was made in ca. 604–562 B.C. The artifact is 8.38 inches long. It is currently (2011) located in The Metropolitan Museum of Art in New York on loan from the Yale Babylonian Collection.[52]

- **Jeremiah's Personal Secretarial Scribe/Baruch (Jeremiah 36:29, 32)**

This is important because there are two bullas attributed to this scribe, one found in 1975 in a burnt house by Yigul Shiloh and another one with a fingerprint impression of possibly, Baruch himself. The later has been under great scrutiny for having been a forgery, the first one has not. This bulla is attributed to the personal scribe of Jeremiah the prophet as recorded in Jeremiah 36:32 by saying, "Baruch, son of Neriah, the scribe" (NASB).[53]

- **The Ophel Treasure (2 Chronicles 27:3)**

There are three holy symbols in Judaism—the shofar, the Menorah, and the Torah Scroll—and all three showed up on gold at the same time! This seventh century find was discovered at the foot of the Temple in Jerusalem, at the Ophel site. "We have been making significant finds from the First Temple Period in this area, a much earlier time in Jerusalem's history, so discovering a golden seven-branched Menorah from the seventh century C.E. at the foot of the Temple Mount was a complete surprise."[54]

---

[52] Holden and Geisler, *The Popular Handbook*, 269–272.

[53] Ibid., 75.

[54] *Noah Wiener, "The Ophel Treasure," BAR: Biblical History, August 1,*

- ## The Book of Daniel

This is another story and book in the Bible that has undergone immense scrutiny for years as there was no evidence that any of its stories could be confirmed by the archaeological record. Again, skeptics said, these stories are not true; they are make-believe myths that tell moral stories of courage and loyalty to God. However, this is no longer the case. As you know, Nebuchadnezzar has been firmly established as a real human being, not a fictious character like previously assumed.

- ## The Babylonian Chronicles: Nebuchadnezzar (Daniel 3:6)

The *Babylonian Chronicle* records events in ancient Babylon which date from about 750 B.C. to 280 B.C. The Chronicles are part of that chronicle and records events from 605–594 B.C. including Nebuchadnezzar II's campaigns in the west, where Jerusalem was located. These Chronicles also record the defeat of the Assyrians and the fall of the Assyrian Empire and the rising threat of Egypt. They record the Battle of Carchemish where Nebuchadnezzar II of Babylon defeated Pharaoh Necho of Egypt in 605 B.C., the power of Egypt. They also record Nebuchadnezzar's rise to power and the power he exhibited.

2015, accessed November 12, 2018, https://www.biblicalarchaeology.org/daily/biblical-sites-places/jerusalem/the-ophel-treasure/.

- ## Shadrach, Meshach, and Abednego (Daniel 3: 8-28)

The story of the three Hebrew men is a children's story, or at least that is what some think. During the first excavation of the ancient city of Babylon, a strange building was discovered. Originally, archaeologists assumed that it was a fire building used to glaze and fire pottery, because it appeared to be a kiln—the kind of firing kiln used to make bricks in the ancient world. However, a cuneiform inscription revealed the purpose of the structure. The inscription said, "This is the place of burning where men who blasphemed the gods of Chaldea died by fire."[55] How was that for a little history?

- ## Daniel and Belshazzar (Daniel 5:5-12)

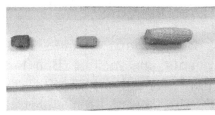

I am sure you remember the story of Belshazzar—the story where the king was drinking, and a hand wrote on the wall during his party festivities. Archaeologists have confirmed the name Belshazzar in history as a real live human being.

Cuneiform texts dated in the twelfth year of Nabonidus record oath formulas which are unusual in that Belshazzar is associated with his father on terms of approximate equality. . . . Two texts in the Yale Babylonian Collection, also dated in the twelfth year of Nabonidus' reign, contain similar oaths. . . . These three passages show conclusively that the Babylonian oath formula in the twelfth year of the reign of Nabonidus placed Belshazzar on an equality with his father.[56]

These Babylonian administrative documents have confirmed the name. Belshazzar was more than a mythical character; he was real.

[55] Henry Rimmer, *Dead Men Tell Tales* (Grand Rapids, MI: Eerdmans, 1939), 325.

[56] Raymond Philip Doughtery and William M. Laff, *Nabonidus and Belshazzar* (Cambridge, MA: Yale University Press, 1929), 216.

- ## Daniel and the Lions' Den (Daniel 6: 1-25)

If you thought the story of the three Hebrew children was a stretch for the archaeological spade, then wait until you read this account of Daniel and the lions' den. No, archaeologists don't have the lion who refused to eat Daniel, nor do they have Darius's writing, explaining the story in his own words. However, archaeologists do have an interesting story from the city of Babylon. In 538 B.C., Daniel was tricked by his enemies and regrettably thrown into the lions' den by Darius who really liked Daniel. When they were excavating the city of ancient Babylon, the excavator, Dieulafoy, fell into what looked like a well, but upon examination found an inscription: "The place of execution where men who angered the king died torn by wild animals." At the palace in Shushan (Babylon) (Suza), a record list was found of 484 men of high rank who had died in a lion's den. (While, I cannot find the source of this quote, it is listed many times on the Internet and attributed to Marcel and Jane Dieulafoy, French archaeologists who wrote of their expedition in the book, *A Susa Journal of Excavations,* in 1888.) It is a certainty that ancient Susa was known for their use and symbolism of the lion.

- ## The Horns of the Altar (Amos 5:5; 8:14)

Most people have heard a man or woman of God refer to the "horns of the altar." In 1973, the American Schools of Oriental Research discovered the ruins of a "four-horned altar found in Beersheba, embedded in a restored storehouse wall, dated to the eighth century B.C."

Closing

I know of no better place to end than to describe the archaeological find of the horns of the altar. While, we have sifted through steles, ostraca, obelisks, bullas, papyrus, cuneiform, and a host of other material, none can tell the point of the story. The real point of all this is that your faith must become "lethal"—dangerous. It too must be deadly or fatal to the Enemy of your soul. Logical, rational thinking will bring you a long way in a world where God's Word is logos (John 1:1; rational and logical). But your faith will always require a certain sense of ambiguity, wonder, and mystery. Now, don't get me wrong, I am not trying to undue the pages of this book. I must admit my bias at the closing of this first volume—I am not Saint John; I am not even like Saint Peter; I am doubting Thomas. Thomas said he wouldn't believe Jesus had risen from the dead unless he saw the nail prints in His hands. The amazing thing about that New Testament story is Jesus showed him His hands! You have seen proof that the people, places, and things in the Bible are not mythical, imaginary individuals, woven together by a master storyteller to explain moral lessons of courage and character. No, they were real people, and the Bible is the greatest history book of all time, so say the archaeologists who train archaeologists! Yes, there are problems with some stories. There are still people to find, and artifacts yet to be dug up, mysteries still to solve, and chronological timelines to be solved, but that changes nothing compared to the mountain of evidence. The mathematical probability is on our side, not that of the skeptics, and they know it . . . even if they refuse to admit it. Yet, all the knowledge in the world cannot and will not lead you to the cross of Christ without faith, and that is the real story of *Lethal Faith*!

Bibliography

Bibliography

Alberge, Dalya. "Museum Tablet Lends New Weight to Biblical Truth." *Times* (July 11, 2007). Accessed November 22, 2018: *http://www.timesonline.co.uk/tol/comment/faith/article2056362.ece*.

Albright, William F. *The Archaeology of Palestine*. Middlesex: Harmondswoth, 1960.

All About God. "All About Archaeology: Samaria." All About God: Archaeology, 2002. Accessed November 22, 2018: *https://www.allaboutarchaeology.org/samaria.htm*.

Amanpour, Christiane. "Joseph of Biblical Times: Archaeologists Seek Ancient Famine Evidence." ABC News. December 21, 2012, accessed November 12, 2018. *https://abcnews.go.com/2020/video/joseph-biblical-times-archeologists-seek-ancient-famine-evidence-18042343*.

American Friends of Tel Aviv University. "Evidence of Solomon's Mines: Archaeologist Date Mines in South of Israel to Days of King Solomon." *Science Daily* (September 3, 2013). Accessed September 3, 2018: *https://www.sciencedaily.com/releases/2013/09/130903141356.htm*.

Anderson, Clive and Brian Edwards. *Evidence for the Bible*. Leominister, England: Day One, 2014.

Archer, Gleason. "Old Testament History and Recent Archaeology From Abraham to Moses." *Biblotheca Sacre,* 127, no. 505 (1970).

Ashton, John and David Down. *Unwrapping the Pharaohs: How Egyptian Archaeology Confirms the Biblical Timeline.* Green Forest, AR: Master Books, 2006.

Ayali-Darshan, Noga. "Baal, Son of Dagon: In Search of Baal's Double Paternity." *The Journal of Oriental Studies* 133, no. 4 (Oct.–Dec. 2013).

BAR Staff. "Expedition Claims Evidence of Queen of Sheba Found in Ethiopia." *Biblical Archaeological Review* (January 14, 2012). Accessed November 22, 2018: *https://www.biblicalarchaeology.org/daily/biblical-sites-places/biblical-archaeology-places/expedition-claims-evidence-of-queen-of-sheba-found-inethiopia/.*

BAR Staff. "Jezreel Expedition Sheds New Light on Ahab and Jezebel's City." *Biblical Archaeological Review* (May 1, 2016). Accessed November 11, 2018: *https://www.biblicalarchaeology.org/daily/archaeology-today/biblical-archaeology-topics/jezreel-expedition-sheds-new-light-on-ahab-and-jezebel%E2%80%99s-city/.*

Bassett-Brody, Lisette. *Etched in Stone: Archaeological Discoveries That Prove the Bible.* Washington, D.C.: WND Books, 2017.

Bennett-Smith, Meredith. "King David's Palace Discovered? Archaeologists Find Huge Palace, Storeroom at Khirbet Qeiyafa Site." *Huffington Post* (July 19, 2013). Accessed November 1, 2018: *https://www.huffington-post.com/2013/07/19/king-david-palace-archaeologists-khirbet-queiyafa_n_3620053.html.*

Berrien, Hank. "The Story of David and Goliath Gets Archaeological Evidence Backing It Up." *Daily Wire* (October 17, 2018). Accessed November 13, 2018. *https://www.dailywire.com/news/37279/story-david-and-goliath-gets-archaeological-hank-berrien.*

Bible Walks. "Broad Wall." *Biblewalks.com* (January 10, 2016). Accessed November 3, 2018. *https://biblewalks.com/Sites/BroadWall.html.*

Bietak, M. *Avaris and Piramesse: Archaeology Exploration in the Eastern Nile Delta.* London: British Academy, 1986.

Bietak, Manfred. *Egypt and the Levant: The Egyptian World.* New York: Routledge, 2002.

Biran, A. "City of the Golden Calf." *Bible and Spade.* 5 (1976).

Bohnstrom, Philippe. "Huge If True." *Haartetz.* Accessed October 17, 2018: *https://www.haaretz.com/archaeology/.premium-huge-if-true-the-archaeological-case-for-goliath-1.6568421.*

Bohstrom, Philippe. *"King Solomon's-Era Palace Found in* Biblical Gezer: Monumental 3000-year-old ruins, Philistine pottery, support biblical tales of Gezer's rise and fall to a jealous Pharaoh." *Haaretz* (August 31, 2016). Accessed November 22, 2018: *https://www.haaretz.com/archaeology/king-solomon-era-palace-found-in-biblical-gezer-1.5431221.*

Briggs, David. "Testaments: Archaeological Discoveries Provide Biblical Evidence." *Stevens Point Journal* (Decembedr 1993), 8.

Brown, Robert McAffee. *The Bible Speaks to You.* Philadelphia: Westminister Press, n.d.

Bryant, Dewayne. "Abraham's Camel." Apologetics Press, 2014, accessed November 2, 2018. *http://www.apologeticspress.org/APContent.aspx?category=9&article=4800.*

Bryner, Jeanna. "Rare King David-Era Inscription: The First Historical Evidence of King David from the Bible." *Biblical Archaeology Review* (September 10, 2018). Accessed October 5, 2018: *https://www.biblicalarchaeology.org/daily/biblical-artifacts/artifacts-and-the-bible/the-tel-dan-inscription-the-first-historical-evidence-of-the-king-david-bible-story/.*

Byers, Gary. "Slings and Stones." *Rapture Notes.* Accessed November 13, 2018: *http://www.rapturenotes.com/slingsandstones.html.*

Camp, Ashby. "Israel, Egypt, and the Exodus." *Outlet,* 2016, accessed November 5, 2018. *http://www.theoutlet.us/Israel.Egypt.andtheExodus.pdf.*

Campbell, Charlie. *Archaeological Evidence for the Bible.* Carlsbad, CA: The Always Be Ready Apologetics Ministries, 2012.

Chrysler Ministry. "Hezekiah's Tunnel." Biblical Archaeology Truth. Accessed November 12, 2018: *http://www.biblical archaeologytruth.com/hezekiahs-tunnel.html.*

Clayton, Peter A. *Chronicles of the Pharaohs: The Reign-by-Reign of the Rulers and Dynasties of Ancient Egypt.* London: Thames and Hudson, 1994.

Climer, Phillip. Archaeology and the Bible. Accessed November 16, 2017. *http://www.answersingenesis.org.*

Cline, Eric H. *Biblical Archaeology: Very Short Introduction.* New York: Oxford, 2009.

Collins, Steven and Latayne C. Scott. *Discovering the City of Sodom: The Fascinating, True Account of the Discovery of the Old Testament's Most Infamous City.* New York: Howard Books, 2013.

Connelly, Douglas. *"The Ultimate Guide to Bible Prophecy and End Times."* Guideposts. New York: Guideposts, 2013.

David, Ann Rosalie. *The Pyramid builders of Ancient Egypt: A Modern Investigation of Pharaoh's Workforce.* London: Guild Publishers, 1996.

de Vaux, Roland. *Ancient Israel: Its Life and Institutions.* Grand Rapi9ds, MI: Eerdmans, 1961.

Doughtery, Raymond Philip and William M. Laff. *Nabonidus and Belshazzar.* Cambridge, MA: Yale University Press, 1929.

Ebling, Jennie, et.al. *The Old Testament in Archaeology and History.* Waco, TX: Baylor University Press, 2017.

Edwards, I.E.S., et.al. *The Cambridge Ancient History, Volume II, Part One.* Cambridge, UK: Cambridge University Press, 1980.

Encyclopedia Britannica of World Religions. Edited by Jacob E. Safra. London: Britannica Encyclopedia, 2006.

Eusebius. *Ecclesiastical History*, 26.

Fagan, Brian. *Egypt of the Pharaohs.* Washington, DC: National Geographic, 2001.

Fagan, Brian M. *The Oxford Companion to Archaeology.* New York: Oxford University Press, 1996.

Fox News. "Archaeological Excavation: Biblical Giant Goliath's Home Town." Foxnews.com (July 11, 2011). Accessed November 14, 2018: *https://www.foxnews.com/science/archaeologists-excavate-biblical-giant-goliaths-hometown.*

Gaille, Brandon. 29 Good Bible Sales Statistics. Accessed April 23, 2018. *http://www.brondongaille.com/27-good-bible-sales-statistics/.*

Garstang, John. *Jericho and the Biblical Story*, Volume 2. New York: J.A. Hammerton, 1937.

Gaster, T. "Ras Shamra 1929–39." *Antiquity* 13 (January 1939): 304.

Geisler, Norman L., and Ronald M. Brooks. *When Skeptics Ask: A Handbook on Christian Evidences: Revised and Updated.* Grand Rapids, Michigan: Baker Books, 2013.

Glueck, Nelson. *Rivers in the Desert.* New York: Grove Press, 1959.

Gray, John. *I and II Kings.* Philadelphia: Westminster Press, 1963.

Green, Alberto R.W. "Syria: The Upper Country." In *The Storm-God in the Ancient Near East*. Vol. 8, *Biblical and Judaic Studies Volume*, 164–65. Winona Lake, Indiana: Eisenbrauns, 2003.

Hadley, Judith M. *The Cult of Asherah in Ancient Israel and Judah: Evidence for a Hebrew Goddess*. Cambridge, UK: University of Cambridge, 2000.

Hamblin, Dora Jane. Has the Garden of Eden Been Located at Last?" *The Smithsonian*. 18, No. 2 (May 1987).

Hannay, James Ballanytne. *Sex Symbolism in Religion*. Amsterdam, The Netherlands: Fredonia Books, 1922.

Hardin, James W. "Iron Age Bullae from Officialdom's Periphery Khirbet Summeily in Broader Context." *Near East Archaeology* Vol. 4, No. 77 (2014), 299-301.

Harrower, Michael J. "Satellite Images and the Queen of Sheba." *Smithsonian's Associates* (September 20, 2011). Accessed November 21, 2018: *https://smithsonianassociates.org/ticketing/tickets/222938*.

Heilpern. William. "Biblical King Seal Discovered in Dump Site." CNN (December 4, 2015). Accessed November 22, 2018: *https://www.cnn.com/2015/12/03/middleeast/king-hezekiah-royal-seal/index.html*.

Henry, David. "Explanation of Gad and Meni, Mentioned by Isaiah." *The Gentlemen's Magazine: and Historical Chronicle*, 41 (January 1771).

Hoerth, Alfred J. *Archaeology and the Old Testament*. Grand Rapids, Michigan: Baker Academics, 1998.

Hoffmeier, James K. ed. and Alan Millard. *Future Biblical Archaeology: Reassessing Methodologies and Assumptions*. Grand Rapids, Michigan: Eerdmans Publishing, 2004.

Holden, Joseph M. and Norman Geisler. *The Popular Handbook of Archaeology and the Bible: Discoveries That Confirm the Reliability of Scripture.* Eugene, Oregon: Harvest House Publishing, 2013.

Hollis, Susan Tower. *The Ancient Egyptian.* "Tale of Two Brothers": A Mythological, Religious, Literary, and Historico-Political Study. London: Bannerston, 2008.

Holloway, April. "Archaeologist May Have Found Name of Bible Prophet Elisha." *Ancient Origins: Reconstructing the Story of Humanities Past* (July 28, 2013). Accessed November 22, 2018: *https://www.ancient-origins.net/news-history-archaeology/archaeologists-may-have-found-home-bible-prophet-elisha-00697.*

Hrusa, Ivan. "Prinicples of Mesopotamanian Divinities," in *Ancient Mesopotamian Religion,* translated by Michael Tait. Buch-und Medienhandel GmbH, Munster: Ugarit-Verlag, 2015.

Hutton, Ronald. *Blood and Mistletoe: The History of the Druids in Britain.* New Haven: Yale University Press, 2009.

Irenaeus. *Against Heresies.*

Jade, Don. "Queen of Sheba's Palace Found in Ethiopia." *Rasta Livewire* (November 6, 2010). Accessed November 21, 2018: *http://www.africaresource.com/rasta/articles/queen-of-shebas-palace-found-in-ethiopia/.*

James, E.O. *The Ancient Gods: The History and Diffusion of Religion in the Ancient Near East and the Eastern Mediterranean.* New York: G.P. Putnam's Sons, 1960.

Jordan, Michael. *Encyclopedia of Gods: Over 2,500 Deities of the World.* New York: Facts On File, 1993.

Kalman, Matthew. "Proof David Slew Goliath Found as Israeli Archaeologists Unearth Oldest Ever Hebrew Text." *Daily*

Mail UK (October 31, 2008). Accessed November 2, 2018. *https://www.dailymail.co.uk/news/article-1081850/ Proof-David-slew-Goliath-Israeli-archaeologists-unearth-oldest-Hebrew-text.html.*

Kantrowitz, Jonathan. "First Beehives in Ancient Near East Excavated." *Archaeological News* (September 4, 2007). Accessed November 22, 2018: *http://archaeologynews-report.blogspot.com/2007/09/first-beehives-in-ancient-near-east.html.*

Kearns, Emily. *Ancient Greek Religion.* Chichester, West Sussex: Wiley-Blackwell, 2010.

Keel, Othmar and Christopher Uehlinger. *Gods, Goddesses, and Images of God in Ancient Israel.* Minneapolis: Fortress Press, 1998.

Kimberely, Tim. "Top Ten Discovered in Archaeology #10: Jehu's Tribute to Shalamaneser III." *Credo House* (July 8, 2010). Accessed November 22, 2018: *https://credohouse. org/blog/top-ten-biblical-discoveries-in-archaeology-9-jehus-tribute-to-shalmaneser-iii.*

Kitchen, K.A. *Ancient Orient and Old Testament.* Downers Grove, IL: InterVarsity Press, 1993. Inside Inscription.

Kitchen, Kenneth A. *On the Reliability of the Old Testament.* Grand Rapids, MI: Eerdmans, 2003.

Kmtsesh. "Shesong I and Jerusalem." Ancient Near East: Just the Facts (February 25, 2012). Accessed November 21, 2018: *https://ancientneareast.org/tag/rehoboam/.*

Korpel, Marjo C.A. "Fit for a Queen: Jezebel's Royal Seal." *Biblical Archaeology Review* (May 1, 2008). Accessed November 10, 2018: *https://www.biblicalarchaeology.org/ daily/biblical-artifacts/inscriptions/fit-for-a-queen-jezebels-royal-seal/.*

Korzhumbayeva, Algerim. "Haran." *Electrum Magazine.* "Why the Past Matters." (March 2, 2013), accessed November 1, 2018. *http://www.electrummagazine.com/2013/03/harran-ancient-crossroads-city-of-mesopotamia/.*

Lambert, W.G. *Babylonian Creation Myths.* Winona Lake, Indiana: Eisenbrauns, 2013.

Langdon, S. *Tammuz and Ishtar: A Monograph Upon Babylonian Religion and Theology: Containing Extensive Extracts from the Tammuz Liturgies and All of the Arbela Oracles.* London: Oxford University, 1914.

Law, Steven. "Part 1-Ancient Graveyard of Slaves Discovered in Egypt—Could-They Be Hebrews?" Evidence: Patterns of Evidence (July 14, 2017), accessed November 12, 2018, *http://www.patternsofevidence.com/blog/2017/07/14/ancient-graveyard-of-slaves-discovered-in-egypt-could-they-be-hebrews/.*

Law, Steven. "Part 2-Ancient Graveyard of Slaves Discovered in Egypt—Could They Be Hebrews?" Evidence: Patterns of Evidence (July 21, 2017), accessed November 12, 2108, *http://www.patternsofevidence.com/blog/2017/07/21/part2-ancient-graveyard-of-slaves-discovered-in-egypt-could-they-be-hebrews/.*

Law, Steven. "David Battles Goliath: Is There Evidence?" *Patterns of Evidence* (October 26, 2018). Accessed November 14, 2018: *https://patternsofevidence.com/blog/2018/10/26/david-battles-goliath/.*

Lemonick, Michael D. "Is the Bible Fact or Fiction?: Archaeologists in the Holy Land Are Shedding New Light on What Did or Did Not Occur in the Greatest Stories Ever Told." "Is the Bible Fact or Fiction?" *Time magazine* (Volume 146: No. 25, December 18, 1995). Accessed November 3, 2018: *http://content.time.com/time/magazine/article/0,9171,983854,00.html.*

Leston, Stephen. *The Bible in World History: Putting Scripture Into a Global Context.* Uhrichsville, Ohio: Barbour Books, 2011.

Lightfoot, Neil R. *How We Got the Bible, Third Edition.* Grand Rapids, Michigan: Baker Books, 2003.

Livingston, David. "Ancient Days: Comparison of Genesis With Creation Stories of the Ancient Near East." *Ancient Days.* Accessed September 1, 2018, *http://www.davelivingston.com/creationstories.htm.*

Ludwig, Charles. *Ludwig's Handbook of Old Testament Rulers and Cities.* Denver, Colorado: Ancient Books, 1984.

Machine, WayBack. "Adriaan Reland (1676–1718)." The Wayback Machine. Accessed November 16, 2017. *http://www.web.archive.org.*

Mackey, D. "Sothic Star Dating: The Sothic Star Theory of the Egyptian Calendar." Abridged thesis, Sydney, Australia, 1995. Accessed November 10, 2018, *http://www.specialityinterest.net/.*

Mahoney, Timothy P. *Patterns of Evidence: A Filmmaker's Journey: You Never Know Where a Crisis of Faith Will Lead You.* St. Louis Park, MN: thinking Man Media, 2015.

Mariottini, Claude. "Abraham and Archaeology." Claude Mariottini: Professor of Old Testament. March 1, 2006, accessed November 1, 2018. *https://claudemariottini.com/2006/03/01/abraham-and-archaeology/.*

Marks, Joshua J. "Eridu." *Encyclopedia of Ancient History, July 20, 2010,* accessed November 2, 2018. *https://www.ancient.eu/eridu/.*

McClellan, Matt. "Abraham and the Chronology of Ancient Mesopotamia." *Answers Research Journal,* No. 5, 2012.

McDowell, Josh. "The Historical Reliability of the New Testament." *Bible and Spade* 27.2 (Spring 2014).

Mitchell, Chris and Julie Stahl. "Have Archaeologists Found the Prophet Elisha's House?" *Charisma News* (July 23, 2013). Accessed November 22, 2018: *https://www.charismanews.com/world/40343-have-archaeologists-found-prophet-elisha-s-house.*

Munn-Rankin, J.H. "Darius the Great I of Persia." *Britannica Encyclopedia* (2018). Accessed November 22, 2018: *https://www.britannica.com/biography/Darius-I.*

Musa Etetz Israel Museum. "It is the Land of Homey." Musa Etetz Israel Museum Tel-Aviv, 2016. Accessed November 22, 2018: *http://eretzmuseum.org.il/e/345/.*

News Staff. "New Finds Suggest Both Kings David and Solomon Actually Existed." *Science News* (December 26, 2014). Accessed November 15, 2018: *http://www.sci-news.com/archaeology/science-biblical-kings-david-solomon-02371.html.*

Newsweek. "Yes, Virginia, There Was a Golden Calf." *Newsweek* 116, no. 6 (8/6/1990).

Ngo, Robin. "King Hezekiah in the Bible: Royal Seal of Hezekiah Comes to Light." *Biblical Archaeology Review* (February 21, 2018). Accessed November 1, 2018: *https://www.biblicalarchaeology.org/daily/biblical-sites-places/jerusalem/king-hezekiah-in-the-bible-royal-seal-of-hezekiah-comes-to-light/.*

Norman, Jeremy. "Construction of the Etemenanaki Ziggurat: Later Known as the Tower of Babel." History of Information, accessed November 11, 2018. *http://www.historyofinformation.com/expanded.php?id_154.*

Oswalt, John N. *The Bible Among Myths: Unique Revelation or Just Ancient Literature?* Grand Rapids, Michigan: Zondervan, 2009.

Patterns of Evidence. Researcher Uses Evidence to Confirm Existence of 53 People in Bible. September 8, 2017. Accessed July 17, 2018. *http://www.patternsofevidence. com/blog/2017/09/08/researcher-uses-evidence-of-53-people-in-the-bible/*.

Perkins, Sid. *Science Magazine.* Science, accessed October 2, 2018. *http://www.sciencemag.org/news/2015/07/four-legged-snake-fossil-stuns-scientist-and-ignites-controversy.*

Popular Archaeology. "Darius Stele Found in Ancient Town of Phanagoria in Russia." *Popular Archaeology* (August 9, 2016). Accessed November 22, 2018: *https://popular-archaeology.com/article/darius-i-stele-found-in-ancient-town-of-phanagoria-in-russia/.*

Potts, D.T. *The Archaeology of Elam: Formation and Transformation of the Ancient Iranian State.* Cambridge, UK: Cambridge University, 2016.

Price, Randall. *The Stones Cry Out: What Archaeology Reveals about the Truth of the Bible.* Eugene, Oregon: Harvest House, 1997.

Price, Simon. *Religions of the Ancient Greeks: Key Themes in Ancient History.* Cambridge, England: Cambridge University, 1999.

Prigg, Mark. "Was Noah's Ark Round? 3,700-year-old clay tablet reveals giant boat was made out of reeds and bitumen." Daily Mail, accessed October 10, 2018. *http://www.daily-mail.co.uk/scienetech/article-2545941/Was-Noahs-Ark-ROUND-3-700-year-old-clay-tablet-reveals-boat-coracle-reeds-bitumen.html.*

Rahel, Ramat. "A Royal citadel and a Palace of the Last Kings of Judah: Archaeological Site #7." Israeli Minister of Foreign Affairs (June 24, 2001). Accessed November 22, 2018: *http://www.mfa.gov.il/mfa/israelexperience/history/pages/ramat%20rahel%20-R20a%20royal%citadel%20 and%20a%20palace%20of%20the.aspx.*

Ramsay, William, Sir. *St. Paul the Traveler and the Roman Citizen.* Grand Rapids, Michigan: Hodder and Stoughton/Reproduction: Baker Books, 1960.

Reynolds, Nigel. "Tiny Tablets Provide Proof of Old Testament." *Telegraph* (July 13, 2007). Accessed November 22, 2018: *www.telegraph.co.uk/news/main.jhtml?xml=/news/2007/07/11/ntablet111.xml.*

Rimmer, Henry. *Dead Men Tell Tales.* Grand Rapids, MI: Eerdmans, 1939.

Ripinsky, Michael. "The Camel in Dynastic Egypt." *The Journal of Egyptian Archaeology*, 71 (1985).

Rogers, James. "Archaeologists May Have Found the Prophet Isaiah's Signature." Fox News (February 22, 2018). Accessed November 22, 2018: *https://www.foxnews.com/science/major-biblical-discovery-archaeologists-may-have-found-the-prophet-isaiahs-signature.*

Rogoff, Mike. "The Broad Walls of Jerusalem That Fended off the Assyrians." *Haaretz* (April 23, 2013). Accessed November 2, 2018: *https://www.haaretz.com/israel-news-travel-.premiium-the-jerusalem-wall-and-assyrians-1.5239309.*

Rohl, David. *Pharaohs and Kings.* New York: Crown Publishing Group, 1996.

Russell, Rusty. "Fallen Empires: Sennacherib's Hexagonal Prism." Bible History. Accessed November 12, 2018: *https://www.bible-history.com/empires/prism.html.*

Search for Noah's Ark. Berossus: Babyloniaca, accessed October 14, 2018. *http://www.noahs-ark.tv/noah-ark-flood-creation-stories-myths-berossus-xisuthrus-babylonica-history-of-babylonia-abydenus-apollodorus-alexander-polyhistor-josephus-eusebius-georgius-syncellus-oannes-280bc.htm.*

Seidel, Jamie. "Israel Heralds First Direct Evidence of King Solomon's Temple." *New.com.au.* (October 26, 2016). Accessed November 22, 2018: *https://www.news.com.au/technology/science/archaeology/israel-claims-first-temple-relic-find/news-story/699428fdc3df06caf04b49a27c-6429be.*

Shafer, Jeff. "We Hate You. Now Give Us Your Kids So That We Can Turn Them Against You." March 22, 2011. Accessed April 9, 2018. *http://www.blogs.christianpost.com/liberty/we-hate-you-now-give-us-your-kids-so-that-we-can-turn-them-against-you-5301/.*

Shanks, Hershal. "Ivory Pomegranate under Microscope at Israel Museum." *Biblical Archaeological Review* (March/April 2016).

Shanks, H. "Strata." *Biblical Archaeology.* 23, No. 2 (March/April 1997).

Shiestl, Robert. "The Statue of an Asiatic Man From Tell El-Dab'a, Egypt." *Egypt and the Levant,* no. 16 (2006).

Silverberg, Robert. *Great Adventures: Archaeology: Edited and with an Introduction by Robert Silverberg.* New York: Dial Press, 1964.

Silverman, David P. *Ancient Egypt.* New York: Oxford University Press, 1997.

Snaith, N.H. "The Cult of Molech." *Vetus Testamentum* 16, no. 1 (1966).

Society of Biblical Archaeology. *Proceedings of the Society of Biblical Archaeology: November 1882–June 1883.* London: Harrison and Sons, 1883.

Sparks, Brad C. "Egypt Text Parallels to the Exodus: The Egyptology Literature" at the recent Out of Egypt: Israel's Exodus Between Text and Memory, History and Imagination Conference. Host, Thomas E. Levy (San Diego, CA. 2013).

Swan, D. "Attitudes Toward and Use of the Sling in Late Iron Age Britain." *IATL:Reinvention: and International Journal of Undergraduate Research,* Vol. 7, Issue 2, 2014. Accessed November 12, 2018: *https://warfarehistorynetwork.com/daily/military-history/ancient-weapons-the-sling/*.

Tannenbaum, Michael. "Archaeologist Finds Goliath's Gate in Biblical City of Gath." *Philly Voice* (August 5, 2015). Accessed November 1, 2018: *https://www.phillyvoice.com/archaeologists-goliaths-gate-biblical-city-gath/*.

The Bible and Archaeology. "Rehobaom, King of Judah 931–914 B.C." *Bible Archaeology.* Accessed November 22, 2018: *http://www.bible.ca/archaeology/bible-archaeology-sheshonq-I-shosheng-shishak-shishaq-bubastite-karnak-conquest-campaign-canaan-battle-relief-topographical-list-187-cities-conquered-name-rings-926bc.htm*.

The Electronic Text Corpus of Sumerian Literature. The Sumerian King List: Translation, accessed September 14, 2018. *http://www.etcsl.orinst.ox.ac.uk/section2/tr211.htm*.

Think About It. "Why the Bible Is the True Best Seller." Accessed April 23, 2018. *http://www.nowthinkgaboutit.com/2012/06/why-the-bible-is-the-true-best-seller/*.

Thompson, J. A. *The Bible and Archaeology.* Grand Rapids, Michigan: Eerdmans, 1975.

Turner, Ryan. "What Is Apologetics?" An Outline. Accessed November 16, 2017. *http://www.carm.org*.

"The Queen Mother of the Cult in the Ancient Near East." in *Women and Goddess Traditions in Antiquity and Today,* edited by Karen L. King. Minneapolis: Fortress Press, 1997.

"Understanding Haplogroups: How are the haplogroups named?" Family Tree DNA, accessed November 4, 2018. *http://www.familytreedna.com/understanding-haplogroups.aspx*.

271

Unger, Merrill F. *Archaeology and the Old Testament.* Grand Rapids, MI: Zondervan Publishing House, 1954.

University of New England Media Team. "Visiting Archaeologists to Present Evidence of Solomon's Kingdom." New England University (April 16, 2018). Accessed November 22, 2018: *https://www.une.edu.au/connect/news/2012/04visiting-archaeologist-to-present-evidence-of-solomone280992-kingdom.*

Ussishkin, David and John Woodhead. "Excavations in Tel-Jezreel." Institute of Archaeology of Tel Aviv University. Accessed November 22, 2018: *http://archaeology.tau.ac.il/?page_id=2051.*

van der Veen, Peter, Christopher Theis, and Manford Gorg. "Israel in Canaan (Long) Before Pharaoh Merneptah?" *Journal of Ancient Egyptian Interconnections.*

Waddell, W.G. *History of Egypt and Other Works by Manetho.* Boston, MA: Harvard University Press, 1940.

Walton, John H. and J. Harvey Walton. *The Lost World of the Israelite Conquest: Covenant, Retribution, and the Fate of the Canaanites.* Downers Grove, IL: InterVarsity Press, 2017.

White, Ellen. "High Places, Altars, and the Bamah." *Biblical Archaeology Review* (July 2018).

Whitlock, Robin. "The Ancient city of Susa in Iran Is a Worldwide Treasure." *Ancient Origins: Reconstructing the Story of Humanities Past* (July 11, 2015). Accessed November 22, 2018: *https://www.ancient-origins-net/news-general-ancient-city-susa-iran-worldwide-treasure-003399.*

Wiener, Noah. "The Ophel Treasure." *BAR: Biblical History* (August 1, 2015). Accessed November 12, 2018: *https://www.biblicalarchaeology.org/daily/biblical-sites-places-jerusalem/the-ophel-treasure/.*

Wight, Fred H. "Highlights of Archaeology in Bible Lands." No name. Chapter Six: 1955. *http://baptistbiblebelievers. com/LinkClick.aspx?fileticket=uz3E9va3Kgs%3d&tabid= 456&mid=1433.*

Wilson, Clifford. "Ebla: It's Impact on Bible Records." Institute for Creation Research. April 1, 1977, accessed November 1, 2018. *https://www.icr.org/article/ebla-its-impact-bible-records/.*

Wood, Bryant G. "Balaam Son of Beor." *Bible and Spade* (Vol. 8, No. 4, 1995), p. 114.

Wood, Bryant G. "Is There Archaeological Evidence of the Sons of Jacob, the Tribal Leaders of Israel?" *Christian Answers,* 1998, accessed November 2, 2018. *www.christiananswers. net/q-abr-a028.html.*

Wood, Bryant G. "Omri, King of Israel." Association of Biblical Research (October 10, 2005). Accessed November 5, 2018: *http:// www.biblearchaeology-org/post/2005/10/10/Omri-King-of-Israel.aspx.*

Wood, Bryant G. "The Sons of Jacob: New Evidence for the Presence of the Israelites in Egypt." *Biblical Archaeology* (January 28, 2016), accessed November 5, 2018, *http:// www.biblearchaeology.org/post/2016/01/28/The-Sons-of-Jacob-New-Evidence-for-the-Presence-of-the-Israelites-in-Egypt.aspx.*

Wright, Ernest G. "Some Personal Seals of Judea Royal Officials." *Biblical Archaeologist* 1 (1938): 2.

Wright, G.R.H. "Temple at Schechem." *Zeitschrift fur die Alttestamentliche Wissenschaft,* 80 (January 1968).

Yonker, Randall W. "Late Bronze Age Camel Petroglyphs in the Wadi Nasib Sinai." *Near East Archaeological Society Bulletin,* 42 (1997).

Zaimov, Stoyan. "Archaeological Discovery:3000-Year-Old Manure in Israel Offers Clues on Bible's King Solomon's Mystery." *Christian Reporter.* Accessed November 22, 2018: *https://www.christianpost.com/news/archaeological-discovery-3000-year-old-manure-israel-bibles-king-solomon-mystery-180268/.*

Zondervan. *Resource Reference Library.* Grand Rapids, Michigan: Zondervan, 1983.

*Please go to *www.neverbefore.tv* for a list of gratitutde for our contributors and special thanks to the spectorial library of the Bible lands from Dr. Todd Bolen.

Glossary

GLOSSARY

A

Anathema—A ban or curse solemnly pronounced by ecclesiastical authority.

Annals—A record of events arranged in yearly sequence; historical records; chronicles.

Antiquarian—Of or relating to antiquities.

Apocrypha—Early Christian writings not included in the Bible; statements of dubious authenticity.

Apologetics—A systematic, argumentative discourse of a doctrine; a branch of theology devoted to the defense of the divine origin and authority of Christianity.

Archaeology—The scientific study of material remains (such as tools, pottery, jewelry, stone walls, and monuments) of past human life and activities.

B

Bamah—singular) High places.

Bamot—(plural) High places.

Bulla—An edict or decree; also, a solemn papal letter sealed with a "bulla" or red-ink imprint.

Bull—A term used to refer to inscribed pieces of clay; a red-ink imprint.

C

Canon—A regulation or dogma decreed by a church council.

Canonization—To sanction by ecclesiastical authority.

Casemate—A vaulted chamber, usually constructed underneath the rampart. It was intended to be impenetrable and could be used for sheltering troops or stores.

Codex—A bound book, a manuscript book, especially of Scripture, classics, or ancient annals.

Covenant—A usually formal, solemn, and binding agreement; a written agreement or promise usually under seal between two or more parties, especially for the performance of some action.

Cuneiform—Composed of or written in wedge-shaped characters.

D

Diorite (n); Dioritic (adj)—A granular crystalline igneous rock.

Dynasty—A succession of rulers of the same line of descent; born into a powerful group or family that maintains its position for a considerable time.

E

Excavation—A cavity formed by cutting, digging, or scooping.

Exegesis—An explanation or critical interpretation of a text.

F

Fayum—"Waterway of Joseph." A canal in Egypt connecting to the Nile River as a tributary.

G

German Higher Criticism—Higher criticism is a branch of criticism that investigates the origins of ancient texts in order to understand "the world behind the text." In 1899, a new way of looking at Scripture was beginning to appear on the scene—a view called German higher criticism, or German rationalistic criticism. Take note of the descriptive words, "higher" and "rationalistic." These words lent a kind of lofty and sophisticated aura to these critics. After all, they claimed to take a rational approach to the study of the Bible. No longer did they approach the Bible from a believer's standpoint, one of trusting the authority of Scripture, but rather they put the Bible under the microscope of a rational or skeptical point of view. Probably no other set of teachings (other than Darwin's theory) did more to set the stage for Stalin, Hitler, and Marx, than higher "rational" criticism.

H

Heresy—An opinion or doctrine contrary to church dogma.

Hermeneutics—The study of the methodological principles of interpretation (as of the Bible).

Hoplite—Untrained citizen soldiers who helped fill out the army when needed.

I

In Situ—The item remains where it is while something is being done to it.

L

Lapis Lazuli—A semiprecious stone that is usually rich azure blue.

Lethal—Very potent or effective; capable of causing death. (The author of this book is using the term in the sense of "very potent or effective" in connection with *faith.* Example: Believers need a potent, effective faith to help them stand the tests and trials of life; thus, they need a "lethal faith.")

Levant—A geographical term referring to a large area in the Eastern Mediterranean region. Today, it includes the countries of Israel, Jordan, Lebanon, Palestine, and Syria.

M

Millo—A rampart fortress for protection from attacking forces.

O

Obelisk—An upright, four-sided usually monolithic pillar that gradually tapers as it rises and terminates in a pyramid.

Osmosis—In biology, the process that causes a liquid (especially water) to pass through the wall of a living cell.

Also, an ability to learn and understand things gradually without much effort.

Ostracon—A potsherd used as a writing surface.

P

Papyrus—A tall perennial marsh plant of the Nile valley made into writing paper.

Parchment—The skin of a sheep or goat prepared for writing on.

Pentateuch—Five books. The Jews call the first five books of the Bible the Torah. These books contain some of the oldest and most famous stories in the Bible, including those of Adam and Eve, Joseph and his brothers, and Moses and the Ten Commandments.

Pharaoh—A ruler of ancient Egypt, both political and religious.

Platonic—Feelings or a relationship that are characterized by an absence of romance (a *platonic* relationship in this sense might simply be called a friendship).

Post-Christian—Following the decline of Christianity as a majority religion; post Christian values.

Postmodern—Of, relating to, or being an era after a modern one.

Potsherd—A broken piece of ceramic material, especially one found on an archaeological site.

R

Rickets—A deficiency disease that affects the young during the period of skeletal growth, and is characterized especially by soft and deformed bones, and is caused by failure to assimilate and use calcium and phosphorus normally due to inadequate sunlight or vitamin D.

S

Sarcophagus—An above-ground stone container for a coffin of dead body that often is decorated with art, inscriptions, and carvings.

Serendipity—The phenomenon of finding valuable or agreeable things not sought for.

Shekel—An ancient unit of weight; a unit of value based on a shekel weight of gold or silver; a coin weighing one shekel; the basic monetary unit of Israel.

Shema—The Jewish confession of faith.

Stela—Usually a carved or inscribed stone slab or pillar used for commemorative purposes.

Stele—An upright stone slab or pillar bearing an inscription or design and serving as a monument, marker, or the like. Also, it is referred to as a stela.

Styli—The plural form of stylus (an instrument for writing or marking).

Sulfur balls—a bubble of hot volcanic gas encased in a sulfurous mud skin that solidified on contact with air.

T

Theology—The study of religious faith, practice, and experience; the study of God and of God's relation to the world.

Trinitite—A glassy residue left on the desert floor after an atomic blast; color is usually greenish.

W

Wadi—The bed or valley of a stream in regions of northern Africa where it is usually dry except during the rainy season, which often forms an oasis or gully.

Y

Yahweh—Jehovah; God; used especially by the ancient Hebrews.

Index

Index

The Lethal Faith Series

- **Volume One:** *Lethal Faith: Old Testament*

- **Volume Two:** *Lethal Faith: New Testament*

- **Volume Three:** *Lethal Faith: Cosmology*

- **Volume Four:** *Lethal Faith: Naturalism*

- **Volume Five:** *Lethal Faith: The Wonder and Miracle Design of the Human Body*

- **Volume Six: Lethal Faith:** *Why Is There Evil in the World?*

- **Volume Seven:** *Lethal Faith: Prophecies and the Bible*

- **Volume Eight:** *Lethal Faith: Human Sexuality and Why Gender Matters.*

- **Volume Nine:** *Evolution and Creation: Doubts, Challenges, and Facts*

You can order bulk orders for your classroom, church or group by contacting us:

The Never Before Project

1055 North Main Street
Madisonville, KY, 42431
270-825-3513
www.neverbefore.tv
www.neverbeforeco@gmail.com

Made in the USA
Columbia, SC
27 February 2020

88424536R00163